MARTIN LUTHER AND HIS LEGACY
A PERSPECTIVE ON 500 YEARS OF REFORMATION

ROY LONG

MARTIN LUTHER AND HIS LEGACY
A PERSPECTIVE ON 500 YEARS OF REFORMATION

Roy Long

LONDON **2017**
COUNCIL OF LUTHERAN CHURCHES
(THE LUTHERAN COUNCIL OF GREAT BRITAIN)

First published in 2017

By Council of Lutheran Churches
30 Thanet Street
London WC1H 9QH

The Lutheran Council of Great Britain is a registered charity (No. 232042) and a company limited by guarantee (No. 557552), incorporated in England and Wales. The registered address is 30 Thanet Street, London WC1H 9QH, UK.

Copyright © Roy Long, 2017

All rights reserved. No part of this publication may be reproduced or transmitted in any form or by any means, electronic or mechanical, including photocopying, recording or any information storage and retrieval system, without either prior permission in writing from the publisher or a licence permitting restricted copying.

ISBN 978 0 244 93000 4

Designed by Robin and Sarah Farrow

Images from various churches kindly supplied by members of the Council of Lutheran Churches, used with their permission.

Maps produced by Sarah Weigold.

Cover image: Great Trinity Lane, copyright of and reproduced by kind permission of the London Metropolitan Archives, City of London (Collage database record number 2995).

Contents

Foreword		page vii
Introduction		ix
Part 1	Martin Luther	
	Martin Luther: An Introduction	3
	Martin Luther: The Years of Obscurity (1483-1517)	7
	The Trials of Martin Luther (1517-1522)	12
	Reform, Reconstruction, and Controversy (1522-1530)	18
	Luther's Later Years (1530-1546)	22
Part 2	Luther and His Legacy	
	Luther and Lutherans	27
	Luther's Legacy	30
	The Word of God	33
	The Sacraments	42
	The Christian Church	47
	Vocation, Priesthood and Ministry	55
	Luther and Education	61
	Worship, Music and Prayer	68
	Luther and Other Faiths	78
	Author's Postscript to Part Two	85
Part 3	Luther's Legacy in Britain and Ireland	
	The Reformation	89
	The Hidden Years (1575-1669)	105
	The First Lutheran Congregations in Britain and Ireland	109
	From the 19th Century to the Outbreak of the First World War	118
	From the Beginning of the First World War to the Present Day	123
	Theological Education	136
	Lutherans in Scotland and Wales	140

	The Lutheran Church in Ireland	148
	Author's Postscript to Part Three	150
Part 4	Lutherans in Britain Today	
	Nordic and Baltic Lutherans	155
	German-speaking Lutherans in Britain	183
	Lutherans from Central Europe	189
	Lutherans from Africa and Asia	195
	Lutheran Ministries in English	200
Appendices		
	Relations with the Roman Catholic Church	207
	The Anglican-Lutheran Society	210
	Useful Addresses	212
	Maps	214
Acknowledgements		219
About the Author		220

Foreword

Roy Long's book marks and celebrates the presence of Lutherans here in the United Kingdom. The story of Lutherans in the UK is in many ways both an unknown and untold story for most people of these islands. The Anglican churches of Britain and Ireland and the Lutheran churches of the Continent and Scandinavia are parallel results of the same turbulent and momentous period of history called the Reformation. Anglicans and Lutherans in Europe therefore rarely coexist in large numbers.

Theologically the two traditions are close. Globally the two communions are of comparable size. They have never excommunicated one another. Both communions actively seek greater unity among the churches. Through the Porvoo Agreement, most but not all Lutherans in the UK are in communion with the Anglican churches of these islands. The Lutheran presence in the UK is very diverse. Nominally Lutherans number about 200,000. Most of the member churches and congregations belonging to the Council of Lutheran Churches have cultural and ecclesiastical links elsewhere. Many different languages are spoken in our services. Many different cultural traditions give colour to our communities. Our presence here spans several centuries.

In the Council of Lutheran Churches the churches don't see themselves as guardians of the borders of Lutheranism, but as believers who joyfully affirm the centre of the Christian faith, being justified by God's grace. Lutherans are marked by serious theological studies, joyful hymnody, rich and varied liturgies, a strong ecumenical attitude and an obligation towards tolerance. We see and welcome growing interchange with other churches in spite of old and new theological challenges.

With the 500 year commemoration of the Reformation, we welcome the Rev'd Dr Roy Long's new book about the Lutheran presence in the UK. There is some of this story that remains to be told, and we hope that others may pick up the baton, or convene a group, to study and document the fascinating histories of Lutherans in these lands, and meanwhile we hope this book will receive a wide readership.

The Rev'd Torbjørn Holt
Rector and Senior Chaplain of the Norwegian Church
Chair of Trustees, Council of Lutheran Churches
London, 17 July 2017

Introduction

This book is being completed in the summer of 2017, the year in which Christians throughout the world are joining together to commemorate the symbolic start of the 16th century Reformation, when Martin Luther fixed his 95 Theses onto the door of the Castle Church in Wittenberg. Whether or not he did actually nail them to the church door is a matter of debate, but what is beyond doubt is that the Theses *were* published, that they were intended for debate with other theologians, and for that reason were published in Latin. However, they were soon translated into German, and, thanks to the new miracle of printing, quickly became public property. Thus began the Reformation, a movement which spread across Germany and into many other parts of Europe, triggered many forms of church doctrine and organisation – some of which differed significantly from Luther's own ideas – and eventually became a world-wide phenomenon.

This book has been commissioned by the Council of Lutheran Churches (otherwise known as the Lutheran Council of Great Britain – the name which it has used for most of the years that it has existed, and which is employed in the pages that follow) as part of its contribution to the 500th anniversary commemorations. It was originally intended that there should be three booklets, dealing with Luther and his Legacy, Lutherans in Great Britain and Ireland, and Lutherans and Ecumenism, but it was felt that it would be better to combine these three elements into one, and, as it now stands, the book has four parts covering these topics. The component parts of the book were originally written as three separate documents, and, while every effort has been made to weld them together as seamlessly as possible, some unintentional repetitions may occur.

The first Part sets the scene and presents readers with a brief summary of Luther's life, but it is emphatically *not* a biography (there are enough of those already!) It presents a simple outline of the reformer's life, setting pointers to important themes which will be developed in Part Two.

That second Part deals with what Luther actually taught and what he bequeathed to successive generations of believers. It has not been easy to decide what to include and what to leave out, and inevitably there will be readers who think that the wrong choices have been made.

Part Three brings this home to Great Britain and Ireland and gives an outline of the history of Lutherans in these islands up to the end of the first decade of the 21st century. It might seem strange to include Lutherans in Ireland in such an outline, but the justification for this is that until 1922 the whole of Ireland was part of the United Kingdom and, although Éire is now an independent republic and has its own Lutheran Church, there were two-and-a-half centuries of common Lutheran history.

The fourth Part looks at Lutherans in Britain and Ireland today and, in the case of those churches whose roots lie elsewhere, sketches in the background of their home churches. It also outlines the agreements that have been made, such as "Meissen" and "Porvoo".

This is not the first publication in Great Britain about Lutherans and Lutheranism. As early as 1951, only three years after it was established, the Lutheran Council produced *The Manual of Lutheran Activity in Great Britain*, which gave a brief introduction to Lutheranism after the massive influx of Lutherans into the country during and after the Second World War and which provided some fascinating statistics. The *Manual* was edited by Rev'd E. George Pearce, who at that time was pastor of two English-speaking Lutheran congregations in north London and Chairman of the Lutheran Council. Dr Pearce later produced a booklet in connection with the celebrations marking the 400th anniversary of the first Lutheran congregation in Britain in 1669. This was entitled *The Story of the Lutheran Church in Britain through Four Centuries of History* (1969), and was published by the Evangelical Lutheran Church of England, so, inevitably, it tended to focus on the history of that body.

A more substantial book from the Lutheran Council appeared in 1975. Simply entitled *The Lutheran Council of Great Britain*, this was edited by George Cienciała, a member of St John's Lutheran Church in London, and it combined a history of Lutherans in Britain up to the mid-1970s with anecdotes from many different pastors and lay people. Finally, the Lutheran Council produced a very slim booklet in 2004 called *Lutheran Churches in Great Britain*. Edited by Rev'd Thomas Bruch, who was then the General Secretary of the Lutheran Council, this booklet gave the briefest of histories of Lutherans in Britain, and then answered questions that it was thought other Christians might ask. Roy Long's *The Lutheran Church* (1984), published around the time when Christians were remembering the 500th anniversary of Martin Luther's birth, has chapters on Martin Luther, Lutherans in Britain, and what Lutherans believe. In some respects this present work is an expanded and updated version of that book.

In conclusion to this introduction two things need to be noted. The first has to do with terminology, and, in particular, how Lutherans refer to their ordained clergy. In English, Lutheran ministers have traditionally been known by the title of *pastor*, and this is the word that Luther himself often used. This has remained the normal usage in Germany, although in some places the word *Pfarrer* can be found. In the Nordic countries – though not in Finland – the term that is usually used is derived from the Old Norse *prestur* (for example, in Danish the word is *præst*), and this would normally be translated into English as "priest". Lutheran churches in other countries have their own distinctive words for their ordained clergy. After careful consideration, and despite the sensitivities about the use of the word "pastor" it has been decided by the author to use that word, though other terms may be used from time to time.

The second thing is about how the book is set out. Readers will notice that there is no bibliography at the end; instead, suggestions for further reading are given throughout the text. It must be remembered, however, that any recommendations represent only a tiny fraction of the immense amount of reading matter available. There has been a recent explosion in the publication of books on Martin Luther and the Reformation and it has been felt wise to limit the inclusion of titles to those published before 30 June 2017.

A note from the author ...

I am a retired pastor in the Lutheran Church in Great Britain and I have written this book as a way of expressing my thanks for almost sixty years of fellowship with Lutherans of many different national and cultural backgrounds, both here and throughout the world. I am grateful to the members of the Council of Lutheran

Churches for entrusting me with this responsibility. However, much of my career has been in education and I make no claims to be either an historian or a theologian. This means that, with the best will in the world, there may be unintended errors, but I am grateful to those colleagues who read various parts of the book during the process of writing it, and whose contributions I have acknowledged at the end. Even so, I take full responsibility for any mistakes that do occur and would appreciate being told about them. More than anything else, this is intended as a book to set people thinking and encourage them to explore ideas for themselves.

Roy Long
1 July 2017

Part 1 | Martin Luther

Deutsche Kirche (German Church) in Liverpool

Chapter 1 | Martin Luther: An Introduction

As we said in the Introduction, this first Part of our book is definitely *not* a biography of Martin Luther. Its aim, however, is to present the reader with a brief outline of the salient features of his life and to highlight a number of topics that we shall return to in Part Two.

There are countless biographies of Luther, written in dozens of languages, but since this booklet is being written in Great Britain, the biographies referred to are, for the most part, ones that have been written in English, or ones that have been translated from other languages.

The first biography of Luther in English appeared as part of the famous *Book of Martyrs,* first published in 1563 and subsequently revised and re-published no less than three times during the reign of Queen Elizabeth I (reigned 1558-1603). This collection of narratives is our primary source of information about the martyrs who died in Britain during the middle decades of the 16th century, but its author, John Foxe (1516-1587), also included accounts of the exploits of people from other countries. In the case of Luther, his story is based on second hand evidence in the form of an English translation of the brief biographical pen-portrait by the reformer's younger colleague, Philip Melanchthon (1497-1560). Melanchthon had written this in Latin in Heidelberg in 1548, but the man who translated it into English (1561), a certain Henry Bennet, made several errors in translation. For instance, he mistakenly suggests that Luther nailed the 95 Theses to the door of the Castle Church on 2 November, rather than 31 October, and Foxe simply included such errors as they stood. Fortunately, a new and corrected translation of Melanchthon's narrative is now available, together with the much longer work of Luther's great opponent, Johannes Cochlaeus (1479-

1552). Reading both texts demonstrates vividly how biographers can take the same facts but interpret them in quite different ways.

There are also hundreds of books which try to interpret Luther's legacy and these, too, are written from a variety of viewpoints and present his thinking in many different lights: great re-discoverer of true Christianity; destroyer of the unity of the church; creator of the modern German language; spiritual forerunner of Adolf Hitler and National Socialism – readers can take their pick from these and many other interpretations.

FURTHER READING

One of the best ways to approach Luther is to read what he himself wrote, but this was either in Latin or German. The standard German edition of his works, the ***Weimarer Ausgabe***, which began publication in 1883, the year of the celebrations of the 400th anniversary of his birth, now runs to over two hundred volumes. For a long time very few of Luther's works were translated into English, and what there was consisted mostly of selections from his major works. A typical example of this is that of John Dillenberger, **Martin Luther: Selections from his writings, edited and with an introduction (New York, Doubleday & Company, Inc., 1961. No ISBN)**. There are several selections intended for students, such as *Luther*, by Ian Siggins **(Edinburgh, Oliver and Boyd, 1972. ISBN: 0-05-002538-4)** or the book in the Open University's *Documents of Modern History* series, **Martin Luther**, which was edited by the distinguished Luther scholar, E. Gordon Rupp, and his colleague, Benjamin Drewery, of the University of Manchester **(London, Edward Arnold, 1970. ISBN: 0-7131-5498-5)**.

Some of Luther's works had been translated into English in their entirety – most notably his ***Commentary on Galatians*** in 1575, and his ***Table Talk*** in the mid-17th century – but the great breakthrough came in the late 1950s, when two of the leading Lutheran publishing houses in the United States, Fortress Press and Concordia Publishing House, began a co-operative venture which eventually led to the publication of the fifty-five volumes of **Luther's Works: American Edition**. These volumes included translations of most of the reformer's writings, and it is anticipated (2017) that more volumes may appear. Throughout this book references to these volumes are given with the abbreviation **LW**, together with the number of the volume, and, where appropriate, the ISBN.

A useful overall compendium of articles about Luther is **The Cambridge Companion to Martin Luther (Cambridge, Cambridge University Press, 2003. ISBN: 0-521-01673-8)**. Edited by Donald K. McKim, it contains eighteen essays by experts in their own fields, grouped under four headings: Luther's Life and Context; Luther's Work; After Luther; and Luther Today.

The texts of the biographies by Melanchthon and Cochlaeus are available in **Luther's Lives**, translated and annotated by Elizabeth Vandiver, Ralph Keen, and Thomas D. Frazel **(Manchester/New York, Manchester University Press, 2002. ISBN: 0-7190-6104-0)**.

For nearly seventy years the standard popular biography of Martin Luther has been Roland H. Bainton's **Here I Stand: A Life of Martin Luther (New York/Nashville, Abingdon Press, 1950. No ISBN)** but although immensely readable and well illustrated, it concentrates on the "exciting" periods of Luther's life and goes into less detail about the later years – this is unfortunate, because it is important to have a good overall picture of the reformer and his theology. To a lesser extent, the same might be said of a more recent biography by the Emeritus Professor of Reformation History at Princeton Theological Seminary, Scott H. Hendrix: this is entitled **Martin Luther: Visionary Reformer (New Haven and London, Yale University Press, 2015. ISBN: 978-0-300-16669-9)**. Dr Hendrix is also responsible for the indispensable book in the Oxford University Press's series "Very Short Introductions", **Martin Luther: A Very Short Introduction (Oxford, Oxford University Press, 2010. ISBN: 978-0-19-957433-9)**. An even more recent book than those of Dr Hendrix is one by the Regius Professor of History in Oxford University, Lyndal Roper: this is **Martin Luther: Renegade and Prophet (London, The Bodley Head, 2016. ISBN: 978-1-847-92004-1)**. Using materials that have only become easily available since the re-unification of Germany, Dr Roper presents a picture of Luther "with warts and all", which not all Lutherans will be entirely happy with. Derek Wilson's **Out of the Storm: The Life and Legacy of Martin Luther, (London, Hutchinson, 2007. ISBN: 0-978-0091-800-017)** is a useful introduction, but it must be remembered that the author, though a leading contemporary historian, is not a theologian. Two other books are recommended to interested readers: Steven Ozment's **The Serpent and the Lamb: Cranach, Luther, and the Making of the Reformation (New Haven/London, Yale University Press, 2011. ISBN: 978-0-300-16985-0)**, and **Brand Luther (New York, Penguin Books, 2016. ISBN: 978-0-3995-6323-2)** by Andrew Pettegree.

An important book for setting Luther in context – though long out of print – is Dr E. G. Schweibert's **Luther and his Times: The Reformation from a new Perspective (Saint Louis, Concordia Publishing House, 1950. No ISBN)**, which deals in great detail with life of the reformer, set within the context of the religion, politics, and economic situation of the first part of the 16th century.

There has recently been a re-evaluation of Luther by Roman Catholic scholars. A very readable book by a well-known Catholic layman is Peter Stanford's **Martin Luther: Catholic Dissident (London, Hodder and Stoughton, 2017. ISBN: 978-1-473-62166-4)**. A book with a slightly misleading title is **The Catholic Luther (New York/Maswah, Paulist

Press, 2016. ISBN: 978-0-8091-4988-9). Introduced and edited by Philip D. W. Krey and Peter D. S. Krey, this contains a selection of texts written by Luther up to 1530.

Countless books have, of course, been written in German, though few of them have been translated into English: two that have been are recommended here. A modern approach to Luther's life was written by the German scholar Bernhard Lohse, who was professor of Church History and Practical Theology in the University of Hamburg. Translated by Robert C. Schultz under the title of **Martin Luther: An Introduction to his Life and Work (Edinburgh, T. and T. Clark, 1986. ISBN: 0-657-09357-3)**, this is a very comprehensive work which not only deals with Luther's life in context, but also tackles some debateable questions, such as when his "reformation breakthrough" (the "Tower Experience"/*Turmerlebnis*) occurred. Of particular interest, in that it provides an alternative view of Luther and his thought, is a book by Gerhard Brendler, who was Professor of History and Director of the Institute for the Study of Church History at the Academy of Science in East Berlin. Entitled in English, **Martin Luther: Theology and Revolution (Oxford, Oxford University Press, 1991. ISBN: 0-19-505112-2)**, this was translated by Claude R. Foster, Jr. The original (*Martin Luther: Theologie und Revolution*), was published in the German Democratic Republic in 1983 at the time of the celebrations of the 500th anniversary of Luther's birth, and it gives a glimpse of how Luther and his place in history were viewed in an avowedly atheist country.

Chapter 2 | Martin Luther: The Years of Obscurity (1483-1517)

Martin Luther (1483-1546) was born into an upwardly mobile peasant family in the small east German town of Eisleben, and he was a Saxon who spoke the dialect of Thuringia. Looking at things from the heights of the 21st century, we know that when he was born the period that we know as the "Middle Ages" was coming to an end. The printing press with movable type had been invented, enabling ideas to spread quickly and effectively. Constantinople had been captured by the Turks in 1451 and the Byzantine Empire had come to an end; scholars from the east had fled westwards, triggering the Renaissance, but, at the same time, the Turkish menace was that much closer to central Europe. Looking westwards, Europeans were about to begin their conquest of the "New World", an event which dramatically changed the economic situation in some parts of the continent.

Although central and western Europe were dominated by the Roman Catholic Church, there were voices across Christendom which had questioned the church's teaching and status. Waldensians, Lollards, Hussites, the Brethren of the Common Life, Beguines, and the scholars who we usually refer to as "Humanists": all of these were part of the background to Luther's 63 year life.

Well educated by late medieval standards, and intended by his father, Hans, for a career in law, Luther, a conventionally pious young man, underwent a profoundly religious experience in early July of 1505, when he was almost killed by a bolt of lightning when crossing heathland near the village of Stottenheim. Reacting emotionally and radically to this, he vowed to give up his legal studies in the University of Erfurt, and, within days, had entered into a strict Augustinian foundation and taken the first steps to becoming a monk. (Luther is almost always referred to as a "monk", although he was, strictly speaking, a "friar".) It is well known that his first years in the monastery were full of struggles and doubts: had he been right to go against the wishes of his father, and could he ever live up to the demands of the monastic life? Fortunately, he had wise guidance from his superiors, including Johannes Staupitz (1469-1524), and they directed him, first of all, towards the priesthood, and then towards the study of theology. As well as developing a reputation as an up-and-coming academic, Luther was regarded as a good administrator and negotiator, and it must have been this latter quality that gave him the chance of a lifetime: internecine feuding among the Augustinians provided him with the opportunity of making his only trip outside Germany, when, in 1510, he visited Rome on behalf of the stricter "Observant" Augustinians.

It is not too difficult for us to imagine the enthusiastic expectation with which Luther set out on this trip to Rome, the spiritual centre of the Roman Catholic Church and the place where many of the earliest Christian martyrs had met their deaths. In 1510, the city resembled nothing more than a gigantic building site: it was being rebuilt after years of neglect, and Luther could not fail but to be impressed by the magnificence of the new architecture that was springing up. He was less impressed by the piety – or lack of it – that he found there, and he is said to have remarked that he went to Rome with onions, but returned to Germany with garlic!

Luther returned to Germany somewhat disillusioned, anticipating that he would resume his life as a monk in Erfurt, but this was not to be the case. The Elector of Saxony, Frederick "the Wise" (1463-1525), was anxious to bring his principality up to the standards of his neighbours – particularly in the field of education – and had established a new university in Wittenberg in 1502. Johannes Staupitz, who was Superior of the Observant Augustinians, was also a professor in Wittenberg, and when the time came for him to retire from the post in 1511, he nominated Luther to be his successor. We do not know exactly what Luther thought of this "promotion" to the struggling infant university, but the town was to become his home for the rest of his life, and today it is proudly known as "Lutherstadt Wittenberg".

From this time on, Luther's life was devoted to teaching and preaching, but his study of theology only served to exacerbate the spiritual doubts which plagued him, and sometime during the years after the trip to Rome, he experienced another important religious experience. Scholars have usually termed this the "Tower Experience" (in German, *Turmerlebnis*), but exactly where and when it took place nobody can be certain: probably it was actually an accumulation of experiences in which Luther came to believe that there were some things profoundly wrong with the contemporary church. Whether this happened earlier or later, we simply do not know, but whenever it took place (if, indeed, it did take place as a single event), it had a profound effect on him and triggered off an avalanche within the church.

At the heart of Luther's spiritual struggle lay a sense of estrangement from God. On the one hand, there was a God who was holy and righteous and who seemed to be demanding holiness and righteousness from those who believed in him, with the threat of punishment if they failed to live up to his demands. On the other hand, there was Luther, a man who knew himself to be a sinner who deserved God's anger and punishment. For Luther, the answer to this terrifying paradox came from studying Paul's letter to the Romans. There, he eventually found the answer he was looking for when he began to understand the phrase "the righteousness of God". Many years later, he is said to have spoken these words:

> The words "righteous" and "righteousness of God" struck my conscience like lightning. When I heard them I was exceedingly terrified. If God is righteous [I thought], he must punish. But when by God's grace I pondered, in the tower and heated room of this building [ie the "Black Cloister"], over the words "He who through faith is righteous shall live" [Rom. 1: 17] and "the righteousness of God" [Rom. 3: 21], I soon came to the conclusion that if we, as righteous men, ought to live from faith and if the righteousness of God should contribute to the salvation of all who believe, then salvation will not be our merit but God's mercy. My spirit was thereby cheered. For it is by the righteousness of God that we are justified and saved through Christ. These words [which had before terrified me] now became more pleasing to me. The Holy Spirit unveiled the Scriptures for me in this tower.
> (From Luther's *Table Talk*, LW. Vol. 54, pp.193-4.)

What Luther discovered was that God's righteousness was one and the same thing as God's love, and that there is no way in which that can be earned. God's love is revealed in the life, death, and resurrection of Jesus Christ, and it is a gift which is freely offered to men and women. God calls them to live their lives, not struggling to gain merit, but trusting in God's daily forgiveness of their sins. This is what is known as "justification by faith".

The crucial, though largely symbolic, date for the unleashing of the avalanche was 31 October 1517 – the eve of the festival of All Saints – when, according to tradition, Luther nailed his 95 academic theses to the main door of the Castle Church in Wittenberg. What prompted him to do this were the activities of a Dominican friar by the name of Johannes Tetzel (1465-1519), who was travelling around the country preaching and selling indulgences. Indulgences were documents which purported to guarantee the purchasers a reprieve from part – or all – of the time that they would have to spend in purgatory after they died. This practice rested on the idea that there was a "Treasury of Merits" – a sort of celestial bank account which had accrued over the centuries and into which had poured the superfluous merits earned by the saints. By buying an indulgence, the purchaser could tap into this and transfer merit, either to themselves, or to their deceased loved ones. What this meant, of course, was that faith had been turned into a business, and Luther, with his new-found theological insights, felt that he had no option but to challenge these practices.

Luther probably never intended things to go the way that they did after this action: publishing these theses was simply an invitation to academic debate, not a slick public relations exercise designed to arouse the passions of the general populace (incidentally, no-one accepted the invitation to debate this set of theses). Whatever the original intention, the effect was explosive, and another storm broke over Luther's head. Unlike the storm near Stottenheim, which drove Luther *into* the monastery, this ecclesiastical storm would eventually drive him *out* of the monastery, and, as his opponents would maintain, out of the Roman church.

FURTHER READING

There is an excellent book which deals in detail with the period covered in the preceding paragraphs – indeed, it takes the story up to 1521: this is the first volume of a trilogy by the German Luther scholar Martin Brecht, **Martin Luther: His Road to Reformation,**

1483-1521 (Minneapolis, Fortress Press, 1985. ISBN: 0-8006-2813-6). Heinrich Boehmer's *Der Junge Luther,* which was translated into English jointly by John W. Doberstein and Theodore G. Tappert, under the title of **Martin Luther: Road to Reformation (Philadelphia, Muhlenberg Press, 1946. No ISBN)**, also makes very good reading. A much briefer book, dealing with Luther from his birth to the Diet of Worms (1521) is by the British Methodist Luther scholar, Dr Gordon Rupp, **Luther's Progress to the Diet of Worms (London, S.C.M. Press Limited, 1951. No ISBN)**.

Studies of the young Luther include Ian Siggins' **Luther and his Mother (Philadelphia, The Fortress Press, 1981. ISBN: 0-8006-1498-4)**, and the rather controversial book by Erik H. Erikson, **Young Man Luther: A Study in Psychoanalysis and History (London, Faber and Faber, 1959. ISBN: 0-571-09885-1)**. Erikson was an American psychiatrist who also produced a book re-evaluating the life and thoughts of Mahatma Gandhi.

Luther might have entered any one of a number of different monasteries in Erfurt, but he chose the stricter version of the Augustinian Order. Interested readers are referred to an English version of the rules of the Order, **The Rule of Saint Augustine (London, Darton, Longman & Todd, 1984. ISBN: 0-232-51617-0)**. Originally based on the Latin version, the original text and a commentary in Dutch by Tarcisius van Bavel was translated by an Australian Augustinian, Dr Raymond Canning. There is a detailed study of the influence of Staupitz on Luther by David C. Steinmetz, **Luther and Staupitz: An Essay in the Intellectual Origins of the Protestant Reformation (Durham NC, Duke University Press, 1980. ISBN: 0-8223-0447-3)**. Luther's *Turmerlebnis* is discussed in detail in a book by Uuras Saarnivaara, a Finnish theologian, entitled **Luther Discovers the Gospel: New Light upon Luther's Way from Medieval Catholicism to Evangelical Faith (Saint Louis, Concordia Publishing House, 1951. No ISBN)**.

Alister E. McGrath's **Iustitia Dei: A History of the Christian Doctrine of Justification (Cambridge, Cambridge University Press, 1986. ISBN: 0-521-37973-3)** provides useful background reading by covering the development of the doctrine during the centuries preceding the Reformation. **Luther on Justification (St. Louis, Concordia Publishing House, 1975. No ISBN)** by Robin Leaver is a brief publication but one which sums the topic up well. Carl E. Braaten's **Justification: The Article by which the Church stands or falls (Minneapolis, Fortress Press, 1990. ISBN: 0-8006-2403-3)** not only discusses the doctrine, but puts it into the context of modern ecumenical debates.

Chapter 3 | The Trials of Martin Luther (1517-1522)

Nearly four years after posting the 95 Theses, Luther was summoned in the early spring of 1521 to appear before the Holy Roman Emperor, Charles V, at the Imperial Diet that was to assemble in Worms. It was here, on the afternoon of 17 April, that Luther was cross-examined concerning books that he had written and the doctrines to be found in them. This dramatic appearance was a turning point in Luther's career, and, although sometimes referred to as a trial, it was just one of the several "trials" that Luther had endured during the years since 1517.

The first "trial" was a public appearance at what is known as the "Heidelberg Disputation", which took place at a meeting of the Augustinian Order in April 1518. Luther's fellow Augustinians were divided over the 95 Theses, but Johannes Staupitz, as Superior of the Order, wanted him to have the opportunity to present his views. Following the normal procedure, Luther drew up 40 theses for debate, 28 of which dealt with theology, and 12 with philosophy. Although these theses represent a development of some of the themes in the 95 Theses, they are, overall, rather moderate and do not challenge the heart of the teachings of the church. Central to them is a theme which was to recur over and over again as his theology developed, namely, the distinction between the "Theology of Glory" and the "Theology of the Cross". In two of the theses he seems to be summing up both his personal experience and his developing theological insights:

> 19. That person does not deserve to be called a theologian who sees the invisible things of God as though they were clearly perceptible in those things that have actually happened (Rom. 1: 20)

20. He deserves to be called a theologian, however, who comprehends the visible and manifest things of God seen through suffering and the cross.
(LW. Vol.31. p.52.)

It is generally agreed that this disputation was a triumph for Luther, and many of the members of the Order – and especially the younger ones – came away convinced by his arguments.

Luther's next "trial" took place just over six months later in October, when he was summoned to appear before the Pope's personal representative, Cardinal Thomas de Vio Cajetan (1469-1532), in Augsburg. The Pope had wanted the Elector Frederick to arrest Luther and send him to Rome for trial, but, although he did not subscribe to his views, the Elector was unwilling to hand over this up-and-coming theologian. The Pope, incidentally, did not want to antagonise Frederick, because he was relying on the Elector's support in the imminent election of a new Holy Roman Emperor. Luther had four meetings with Cajetan, who demanded that he renounce his supposed errors and conform his teaching to that of the church. Although he must have realised the danger he was in, Luther refused to recant, and his supporters had to smuggle him to safety out of Augsburg.

The third "trial" took place in June and July of 1519 in Pleissenburg Castle in Leipzig. Ostensibly, this was to have been a debate between Luther's colleague, Andreas Karlstadt (1480-1541), and a leading member of the Dominican Order, Johannes Eck (1486-1543), but Eck insisted that Luther should take part as well. The original debate was to have been about the relationship between free will and grace, but the discussion was enlarged to include the related topics of purgatory (did it exist, or not), the sale of indulgences, penance, and the authority of the Pope. Ominously, Eck brought the name of Jan Hus (1369-1415) into the debate, accusing Luther of supporting Hus's "heretical" views, to which Luther responded that even church councils can err, and that many of Hus's teachings were true and that he had been wrongly put to death. The other key theme to emerge from this debate – alongside a denial of papal power and of the existence of purgatory – was the assertion that Scripture was the only basis for Christian doctrine. So far as Eck was concerned, this made Luther a heretic.

By this time, the authorities in the church were thoroughly rattled by the rebellious monk, and the Pope, Leo X, decided that the time had come to put him in his place. In June 1520, he issued a papal bull entitled *Exsurge Domine* ("Arise, O Lord"), which identified 41 of the 95 Theses as being erroneous and which forbade either the preaching or writing of Luther's views. Six months later, on 10 December, Luther and his friends threw this document onto a bonfire built near the city gates of Wittenberg, along with books on Canon Law. Undeterred, the Pope issued a second bull on 3 January 1521: the period of grace allowed to Luther had run out and he was declared to be excommunicated. Furthermore, anyone giving him help or harbouring him was placed under interdict.

In between these two papal bulls, Luther had been busy working out the implications of his developing theological position and had produced three very important documents – what are often referred to as the "Three Treatises" of 1520. The first of these was entitled *To the Christian Nobility of the German Nation,* and it was an appeal to the princes and magistrates to take the lead in reforming the church and the institutions of education. Luther also denied that any distinction could be made between "religious" and "secular" men and women – a doctrine which is often referred to as the "priesthood of all believers". The second document, *The Prelude to the Babylonian Captivity of the Church,* attacked the church's teaching that there were seven sacraments (baptism, the sacrament of the altar, penance, confirmation, ordination, matrimony, and extreme unction) and insisted that only baptism and the Mass were scriptural – although he initially thought that penance might be described as a sacrament as well. With the title of *The Freedom of the Christian Man,* the third treatise emphasised what was become the central plank of Luther's theology – justification by faith alone. These three documents represent an important stage in the development of key themes in Luther's theology.

Luther's fourth "trial" took place, as we mentioned above, in Worms in 1521. There he appeared before the Emperor on 17 and 18 April. Leading the questioning of him was the same John Eck who had debated with him in Leipzig. Eck asked him, quite simply, did he acknowledge that he had written the books – 25 in all, there on a table in front of the Diet – and would he retract the teachings in them? Luther did not want to answer immediately and asked for – and was reluctantly granted – 24 hours to prepare a reply. He gave this on the afternoon of 18 April, and stressed that there were three different types of books that he had written. Firstly, there were books that had caused no disagreement and which even his enemies approved of: he could hardly be expected to reject these. Secondly, there were books which attacked abuses in the church and which contained criticisms which he was not prepared to abandon. Thirdly, there were books containing similar criticisms, but which may have offended people because they contained personal attacks: he would apologise for the personal attacks and withdraw them, but not the ideas. "My conscience," he said, "is captive to the Word of God. I cannot and will not recant anything, since it is neither safe nor right to go against conscience. [Here I stand, I can do no other.] May God help me. Amen." The words in brackets, which have become famous, are not to be found in the earliest accounts of Luther's defiance, but were added at a later stage. Eck concluded the questioning by accusing him of being a heretic and likened him to such heterodox teachers as Arius, Pelagius, and Jan Hus, each of whom had been condemned by the church.

Jan Hus, the great Czech reformer, had been influenced by the English theologian, John Wycliffe (1325-1384), and his memory was still alive and well in central Europe. He had made his own protests more than a century before Luther, and had attended the great Council of Constance in 1415: he had gone there under a safe conduct and with the expectation of academic debate, but instead had been condemned and burned at the stake. In 1521, three years after he had posted the 95 Theses, Luther's fate might well have been the same: he attended the Imperial Diet in Worms, made his own protest, but escaped with his life: why? Because, unlike Hus, Luther had a prince, the Elector Frederick, who believed that he had a duty to protect one of his subjects, and especially one who was a professor in his beloved university (and who, incidentally, had been persuaded to pay the fees for Luther's doctorate). As it was, Luther was spirited away from Worms before he could be arrested, and then mysteriously vanished.

From the point of view of the Emperor, this was not the end of the affair, because on 25 May the Imperial Diet issued the so-called "Edict of Worms", which declared Luther a heretic and an outlaw: it was forbidden to read or own any of his books, and, if possible, he was to be apprehended and brought to trial. But immediately after his appearance before the Diet of Worms, Luther, to all intents and purposes, had disappeared from the face of the earth, and no-one seemed to know what had happened to him. Had he been arrested and imprisoned? Had he been killed? The only thing that was certain was that he had not returned to Wittenberg. In fact, the Elector Frederick had had Luther kidnapped for his own safety and taken into protective custody in the Wartburg, the enormous fortress that towers over the town of Eisenach.

Luther arrived in the Wartburg on 4 May 1521, and he remained there until 6 March 1522, when disturbing news forced him to reappear in Wittenberg. These ten months were very difficult ones for him: naturally an active man, who liked to be at the centre of things, his forced inactivity was very frustrating, and he was plagued by ill-health and depression, which he attributed to the work of the devil. It must have been galling for him to be powerless to influence the things that were happening in Wittenberg.

However, this period turned out to be one of great importance because, forced into months of physical inactivity and exile "among the birds", he was able to undertake something that was to prove to be one of his greatest achievements – the translation of the New Testament into German. Using the original Greek text, rather than the official Latin "Vulgate" version, and with the help of books provided by friends who were in on the secret of where he was, it took him only 11 weeks to complete the task. The result was a version of the New Testament that not only provided people with a translation that was in easily accessible language, but which also, as it was to turn out, helped towards the creation of standardised written German.

Luther had been keeping a watchful eye on what was happening in Wittenberg, where tentative steps were being taken to effect practical reforms. At first, these were moderate and conservative: several priests married, and there were minor changes to the public worship of the church. His young co-worker, Philip Melanchthon (1497-1560), professor of Greek in the university, published his *Loci Communes,* which was the first attempt at producing a systematisation of Luther's teachings. But things began to go much further, and, in response to the iconoclastic radicalism of some of his colleagues, notably Andreas Karlstadt, Luther felt obliged to return to the town, though without the Elector's permission. The first thing he did was to preach a series of eight sermons, starting on Sunday, 9 March, in which he made it quite clear that he would not condone violent reformation. It is worth noting here that Luther would have no part in iconoclasm and that in most places Lutheran church buildings retained pictures and statues that more radical reformers such as Karlstadt were only too anxious to get rid of. He expressed himself very fully on this topic in a later treatise (1525), *Against the Heavenly Prophets in the Matter of Images and Sacraments.*

FURTHER READING

There are two books, both with the same title in English, which deal with the "trials" of Luther. The first is by James Atkinson, who was, at the time, Professor of Biblical Studies in the University of Sheffield. **The Trial of Luther (London, B. T. Batsford Ltd., 1971. ISBN: 0-7134-1254-1)** takes the reader through the period from the hearing before Cardinal Cajetan (October 1518), the Leipzig Debate (July 1519), to the Diet of Worms (April 1521), but says little about the Heidelberg Debate. The second book, which is particularly interesting because the author was a Roman Catholic, is Daniel Olivier's **The Trial of Luther (trans. John Tonkin, London and Oxford, Mowbrays, 1978. ISBN: 0-264-66230-X).** Dr Olivier was an Assumptionist Father and Professor of Lutheran Studies at the Institut Superior d'Etudes Oecumeniques in Paris, and his book is interesting because of the numerous "pen-portraits" of important participants in the proceedings. Sadly, for some unknown reason, it lacks an index.

LW. Vol.31 **(Philadelphia, Fortress Press, 1957. ISBN: 0-8006-0331-1)** contains the 95 Theses, the Theses for the Heidelberg Disputation, the Proceedings at Augsburg, the Leipzig Debate, and the text of *The Freedom of the Christian Man.* Volume 32 **(Ibid.1958. ISBN: 0-8006-0332-X)** contains two accounts of Luther's appearance at the Diet of Worms – the first, by an anonymous author, favourable to the reformer, and the second, that of the papal nuncio, Aleander.

The address *To the Christian Nobility of the German Nation,* is printed in LW. Vol.44 **(Ibid. No ISBN)** and the text *of The Babylonian Captivity of the Church* can be found in Volume 36 **(Ibid. 1959. No ISBN)**. *Against the Heavenly Prophets in the Matter of Images and Sacraments* is in **LW. Vol.40 pp.79-223.**

Chapter 4 | Reform, Reconstruction, and Controversy (1522-1530)

The eight years from 1522 to 1530 were busy ones for Luther. He continued to lecture on the Bible; he devised orders of service and wrote hymns; he married and helped to raise a family; with the support of the Elector he organised a church visitation to assess the needs of both priests and people; wrote two catechisms; and translated the Old Testament into German. All of this was undertaken against the threat of reprisals from the Roman Church and its great supporter, the Emperor, and amid profound social and religious upheavals.

Perhaps the most difficult years for Luther during this period were those of 1524-25, when thousands of peasants were slaughtered during what became known as "the Peasants' War".

Unrest throughout the empire had been simmering for decades among the peasants, many of whom were exploited and downtrodden by the landowners and princes in the territories in which they lived. To them, Luther seemed like a godsend, and they believed that his message of freedom not only had a religious meaning, but social implications as well. In 1524 their anger erupted in a series of local uprisings, particularly in the south-west of Germany. Some of Luther's fellow reformers actively supported them, but not Luther. In his 1520 treatise *To the Christian Nobility of the German Nation*, Luther had appealed to the princes of the Empire to take a lead in reforming the church; now, he appealed to them to use every means at their disposal to put down the peasant unrest, and did this with a document entitled *Against the Robbing and Murdering Hordes of Peasants* (May 1525). This open letter, which is couched in the sort of intemperate (and we might add, un-Christian) language that we find elsewhere in Luther, reveals something very important about him: he was a religious reformer who put great faith in those in authority and who had little interest in social reform. After this, his status as a friend of the poor vanished

It was not only exploitation that had fuelled the peasants' rebellion – they had also been affected by the gradual abandonment and closure of the many monasteries and convents that were typical of medieval Europe. In a world of limited medical, educational, and social welfare opportunities, these institutions had gone some way, at least, to filling the gaps, but now they were slowly disappearing. Luther had been a monk, but the monastery in which he lived – the "Black Cloister" in Wittenberg – was almost empty by the time he returned there from the Wartburg in 1522. The monks had deserted the house: some had become parish priests or had taken up secular employment, others, whom we might call "traditionalists" had moved away to monasteries in territories that remained loyal to the Roman church.

It was relatively easy for monks to find new employment, but far more difficult for nuns who left their convents – their only real hope was to abandon their vows of chastity and find a husband. It was in this way that Luther found himself a wife in Katharina von Bora (1499-1552), a nun who, with several of her comrades, had been spirited out of her convent. They ended up in Wittenberg, where most of them – except for Katharina – soon had husbands found for them. Katharina, the last woman of the group to be left husbandless, ended up married to Luther himself, and, although it did not start out as a love match, the marriage blossomed into a real partnership. They married in June of 1525 and over the years produced six children, one of whom died in infancy, and another, Magdalena, who died on the threshold of adolescence. Katharina seems to have been a very competent domestic manager, and she brought a very necessary corrective influence to bear on her husband's rather chaotic approach to household economics.

During the time of the Peasants' War Luther was involved in another conflict, although this time a more peaceful one. His opponent on this occasion was no less a personage than the distinguished Dutch scholar Desiderius Erasmus of Rotterdam (1466-1536). Although regarded with suspicion by many in the Catholic establishment (partly because of his barbed comments and criticisms), Erasmus was recognised as a distinguished scholar whose academic work had contributed greatly to the growth of renaissance learning. Of particular importance was his *Novum Instrumentum* (1516), which provided scholars with a Greek text of the New Testament together with a Latin translation which was more accurate than the official Vulgate version.

Erasmus was also an advocate of moderate reform *within* the Roman Catholic Church, and it was said that it was he who had laid the egg that Luther went on to hatch! There were many who hoped that he would declare his public support for Luther as the Reformation progressed, but he was a peaceable (for which also read "timid") man and the last thing that he wanted was confrontation with the church authorities. However, under external pressure he eventually confronted Luther, but on a subject of his own choosing. This was the question of free will, and he launched his attack in 1524 with a book entitled *Diatribe de Libero Arbitrio* ("A Diatribe on Free Will"), in which he argued that freedom was an essential component of moral responsibility. Luther replied in the following year with his famous *De Servo Arbitrio* ("The Bondage of the Will"), which focused on the Pauline and Augustinian view that, although human beings have freedom to choose in respect of human activities, this freedom did not extend to things relating to salvation. The book quite clearly reflects Luther's years of struggle to find a gracious God, and he regarded it as one of the finest things that he had written. However, it was quite ferocious and Erasmus was deeply hurt by it. Nevertheless, he produced a short response in 1526 entitled *Hyperaspistes,* which Luther ignored.

The other serious conflict of this period focused on the growing difference of opinion between Luther and the more radical reformers of Switzerland on the question of the Lord's Supper. In keeping with his innate conservatism, Luther maintained that Christ was truly present "in, with, and under" the bread and wine of the Mass, whereas the Swiss reformers, and in particular Huldrych Zwingli (1484-1531) and Johannes Oecolampadius (1482-1531), held to a more symbolic understanding. Philip, Margrave of Hesse, summoned a meeting on 1-3 October 1529 at his castle at Marburg-an-der-Lahn in order to try to reach agreement. Prior to the meeting, Philip had asked Luther to draw up articles for debate, and he had produced 15 theses, collectively known as the *Marburg Articles.* Success was almost achieved, and the reformers were able to reach agreement on 14 out of the 15 articles. They were not, however, able to agree on the fundamental question of the real presence, and there is an apocryphal story of Luther drawing a line across the table together with the words *Hoc est corpus meum*, ("This is my Body"). Luther subsequently revised these articles and produced what became known as the *Articles of Schwabach*, which were accepted by several of the Lutheran princes and were later used as a basis for the first part of the *Augsburg Confession* of 1530.

FURTHER READING

Theologians from the former German Democratic Republic had perforce to take an interest in the Peasants' War. A short article on the subject was written by Hubert Kirchner, a pastor in East Berlin, and this was later translated into English by Darrell Jodock and published as **Luther and the Peasants' War (Philadelphia, Fortress Press, 1972. ISBN: 0-8006-3068-8)**. Another East German theologian, Gerhard Brendler, wrote a lengthy study of Luther's theology which was translated by Claude R. Foster Jr. and published as **Martin Luther: Theology and Revolution (New York/Oxford, Oxford University Press, 1991. ISBN: 0-19-505112-2)**. This book has an interesting chapter on the Peasants' War (pp.282-296).

Several books and articles, both factual and fictional, are available about Katharina Luther (née von Bora). One interesting book, which deals not only with her but with other women of the time, is by the writer Derek Wilson and is entitled **Mrs Luther and Her Sisters: Women in the Reformation (Oxford, Lion, 2016. ISBN: 978-0-7459-5640-4)**, and there is an article in Kirsi Stjerna's **Women and the Reformation (Oxford, Blackwell Publishing, 2009. ISBN: 978-1-4051-1423-3)**. There have been several fictional accounts of Katharina's marriage to Luther – not all of them very accurate – but a publication that is obviously based on extensive research is by Anne Boileau: **Katharina Luther (Clink Street Publishing, 2016. ISBN: 978-1-9111-61-3)**.

Luther's *The Bondage of the Will* can be found in **LW. Vol.33**, and the text of Erasmus' *Diatribe on Free Will* is available in **Erasmus-Luther: Discourse on Free Will (New York, Frederick Ungar Publishing Co., Inc. 1961. No ISBN)**. A very readable biography of Erasmus is **Erasmus of Rotterdam (London, William Collins Sons & Co. Ltd., 1969. No ISBN)**, by Roland H. Bainton.

For a treatment of Luther's attitude towards those reformers with whom he did not agree, readers may consult **Luther and the False Brethren** by Mark U. Edwards, Jr. **(Stanford, Stanford University Press, 1975. ISBN: 0-8047-0833-5)**.

Chapter 5 | Luther's Later Years (1530-1546)

There is no doubt that Luther had hoped that the Pope and the Catholic Church would see the truth in his "rediscovery" of the Gospel, and that there would ultimately be a *rapprochement*. In fact, the opposite happened, and positions became entrenched. A key event in this occurred in 1530, when the Imperial Diet assembled in the city of Augsburg. Since the Diet of Worms in 1521, the emperor had been involved in other parts of his extensive territories and in fighting foreign wars, so had had little time for Germany. At Augsburg he tried to bring the princes and imperial cities that had adopted reform into line, but they stood firm and presented a document to the assembly that stated with clarity where they agreed, and where they disagreed, with the traditional teachings of the church. This document, known ever since as *The Augsburg Confession,* was not drawn up by Luther, but by his colleague Philip Melanchthon. As far as the emperor was concerned, Luther was still an excommunicated outlaw, so it was unsafe for him to come to Augsburg in person, and he had to be content with watching events from the castle in Coburg. It would be interesting to see what the confession would have looked like if Luther had written it himself, but, together with his two catechisms, it remains one of the foundational doctrinal statements of the churches that became known as "Lutheran". Interestingly, Melanchthon treated the *Augsburg Confession* almost as though it was a personal statement, despite the fact that it had been signed by representatives of evangelical territories. He subsequently modified some aspects of the original document and produced his own version, which is known as the *Variata,* and which caused ill-feeling among many Lutherans.

Many scholars have commented that the remaining years of his life were disappointing for Luther, and that he became increasingly disillusioned and embittered. As a younger man, he had boundless confidence that his theological discoveries would, self-evidently, be accepted by others, but they were not, and he let his disappointment show. Particularly deplorable to modern ears is what Luther wrote about the Jews in the years leading up to his death. In his early years as a reformer he had written very positively about them, and in his 1523 treatise *That Jesus Christ was Born a Jew* he urged love and concern for them as the people to who Christ belonged.

Twenty years later his tone had changed dramatically and in *Concerning the Jews and their Lies* (1543) he expresses strongly anti-Jewish views in language that is both crude and intemperate. The strength of his language is to be deplored, but probably reflects his disappointment that the Jews had failed to acknowledge their "errors" and had refused to accept the Gospel.

Relations with the Roman Catholics hardened as the years progressed. As with the Jews, Luther had hoped that what he considered to be the self-evident truths of the Gospel would be accepted by the Church of Rome, but this did not happen. The "evangelical" territories, such as his own "Electoral" Saxony, and states such as Hessen and Württemberg, were forced to band together into the so-called "Schmalkaldic League" to defend themselves against the threat of imperial pressure, and, although there were some attempts at discussion, such as that at Regensburg (Ratisbon) in 1541, the situation deteriorated to such an extent that, just months after Luther's death in 1546, war broke out. Although the Schmalkaldic League was defeated and evangelical territories were forced to abandon some of their reforms under the terms of what was known as the "Interim of Augsburg" (1548), a more permanent settlement was reached in 1555 which enshrined the principle that the religion of the ruler should be the religion of the people (*cuius regio, eius religio*).

We have gone beyond Luther's death, which took place on 18 February 1546. In bitter weather the sixty-two year old had gone to his home town of Eisleben to mediate in a dispute between rival Counts of Mansfeld, and, although he was strong enough to preach four sermons there, he caught a chill which proved to be terminal. When the news of his death reached Wittenberg, Melanchthon is said to have drawn a likeness between the old man and the Old Testament prophet, Elijah, and to have said "Alas, gone is the horseman and the chariots of Israel".

FURTHER READING

The period from 1530 to 1546 is covered by the second two volumes of the trilogy by Martin Brecht that is mentioned above. These are **Martin Luther: Shaping and Defining the Reformation, 1521-1532 (Minneapolis, Fortress Press, 1994. ISBN: 0-8006-2814-4)** and **Martin Luther: The Preservation of the Church, 1532-1546 (Minneapolis, Fortress Press, 1999. ISBN: 0-8006-2815-2)**.

There is a straightforward account of how the Augsburg Confession came to be written in Chapter III of Willard Dow Allbeck's **Studies in the Lutheran Confessions (Eugene, WIPF and Stock Publishers, 2002. ISBN: 1-59244-094-0)**, but for a more detailed account see Chapters III-VI **Historical Introductions to the Book of Concord by F. Bente (St. Louis, Concordia Publishing House, 1965. No ISBN)**. Gordon Rupp wrote an article entitled *Luther at the Castle Coburg,* which appeared in **The Bulletin of the John Rylands University Library of Manchester (Volume 61, No.1, Autumn 1978)** and which was subsequently reprinted as a monograph in the same year.

Part 2 | Luther and his Legacy

Having looked at the outlines of Luther's life, we turn in this Part to examine some of the different aspects of Luther's legacy, but we have to record a similar caveat to that in Part One. Just as that was not a biography of Luther, so this is not a compendium of his theology. Rather, it is a selection of topics that seem to be particularly relevant for today, and these include:

- the Word of God;
- the Sacraments;
- the Church;
- vocation, priesthood, and ministry;
- education;
- worship and music; and
- relations with other faiths.

Organ at Den Danske Kirke (the Danish Church) of St Katharine's in London.

Chapter 6 | Luther and Lutherans

We have already used the word "Lutheran" several times in Part One of this book, and, since it is a word that we shall make frequent use of in Part Two, it seems only proper to provide a clear definition of what the word means.

For the past four and a half centuries the name has been borne by a family of churches which emerged from the Reformation of the 16th century, and today over 70 million Christians belong to Lutheran Churches throughout the world. As a working definition of "Lutheran" we shall use that given in the *Encyclopedia of the Lutheran Church* (Volume II, pp.1358-1359) which emphasises two important things. Firstly, it stresses the debt that Lutherans owe to the life and theology of Luther himself: they are, it says, "the followers and spiritual descendants ... of Martin Luther". In other words, using the terminology of this booklet, Lutherans are the heirs of Martin's Luther's legacy. But secondly, it also emphasises the fact that the Lutheran churches are *confessional* churches, appealing, in the final analysis, not to the man Martin Luther, but to the Old and New Testaments and to the consensus of Christian doctrine formally expressed in the three ancient ecumenical creeds and in the Lutheran confessional writings contained in *The Book of Concord* of 1580.

The *Formula of Concord*, which is at the heart of the book, was the result of (sometimes acrimonious) debates which had taken place among Lutherans during the thirty-or-so years since Luther's death in 1546. The differences of theological opinion need not detain us here, but the majority of Lutherans came to accept that the *Formula* settled most of the outstanding issues, although not all Lutherans today accept everything in it. There are two basic documents which are accepted by all Lutherans as summaries of their faith, namely, *Luther's Small Catechism* (1529), and *The*

Augsburg Confession (1530). Alongside these *The Book of Concord* also contains *Luther's Large Catechism* (1529); *The Apology [Explanation] of the Augsburg Confession* (1531); *The Smalcald Articles* (1537); and *The Treatise on the Power and Primacy of the Pope* (1537). These documents were written at different times and places, and they were written for different purposes. The two catechisms were intended as teaching aids to be used in the family and congregation, whereas the remaining six are theological documents which sought to explore and explain Christian doctrine in the sometimes fraught ecumenical context of the 16th century.

It would appear that the name "Lutheran" was first used in a derogatory way in the Leipzig Debate of 1519 to describe the supporters of Martin Luther, and during succeeding encounters it became the normal name to describe them. Its origins as a derogatory nickname are not dissimilar to the first use of the word "Christian", and this is the name that Luther himself would have preferred to use. Writing in 1522 in *A Sincere Admonition ... to All Christians to Guard Against Insurrection and Rebellion,* he says:

> I ask that men make no reference to my name; let them call themselves Christians, not Lutherans. What is Luther? After all, the teaching is not mine. Neither was I crucified for anyone. St Paul, in I Corinthians 3: 22 would not allow the Christians to call themselves Pauline or Petrine, but Christian ... Let us abolish all party names and call ourselves Christians, after him whose teaching we hold.
> (LW. Vol.45, pp.70-71)

However, in spite of what Luther wrote, the name "Lutheran" has an honourable and justifiable use, pointing, as it does, to the work of a man who risked much to preach and teach what he considered to be the truth of the Gospel.

The other name which was frequently used to describe Luther's followers was "Evangelical", and, indeed, this is the name by which some Lutherans in parts of Germany and central and eastern Europe have been known. However, the word throws up some difficulties. In the first place, the German word *evangelisch* was the name favoured by those supporters of the union movements in 19th century German Protestantism who sought to minimise or abolish the differences between the Lutheran and Reformed churches. In the second place, the English word "Evangelical" has specific overtones which were certainly not in Luther's mind when he advocated its use. Perhaps the most accurate title by which the Lutheran churches should be known is that of "Churches of the Augsburg Confession", which is the name used, for example, by Lutherans in Poland, who are the "Evangelical Church of the Augsburg Confession".

Chapter 7 | Luther's Legacy

Dictionaries generally provide two meanings of the word "legacy": it can either mean money or property that is left to someone in a will, or, in a wider sense, it can mean anything that is handed down from, or as from, an ancestor.

Martin Luther had both money and property and he made a will that is now in the archives of the Lutheran Church in Hungary in Budapest. It was, for its day, a rather surprising document, because it bequeathed the management of the Black Cloister – the Luther home in the former monastery in Wittenberg – to Luther's widow, Katharina, together with adequate funds to support both the building and his family. "I do this", he wrote, "because ... as a pious and faithful spouse she has at all times held me dear, worthy, and fine and through God's rich blessings gave birth to and reared for me five living children" (LW. Vol.34. p.295). Not that the lawyers were happy with this arrangement, but Katharina Luther was a formidable woman and she had the powerful support of the Elector.

However, it is with the second meaning of the word "legacy" that we are going to be concerned with in the pages that follow: what is it that Luther handed down to those whom we might describe as his "spiritual heirs", whether they call themselves "Lutheran" or use some other name? And here, we have something of a problem, because we are separated from Luther by five centuries – five hundred years during which the legacy was not only handed down from generation to generation, but, inevitably changed. In 1917, when people were celebrating the 400th anniversary of the start of the Reformation, a humorous little book appeared entitled *Little Ramblings with Brother Martin,* which recounted how a famous statue of Luther came alive. The reincarnated Martin Luther went from one Lutheran church to another, trying to find a spiritual home, but, alas, for some he was too liberal, for others too conservative, for some too "high" and for others too "low". After 500 years it might seem to be impossible to get the "real" Martin Luther to stand up, but in this Part we shall try and let Luther speak in his own words.

However, before looking in detail at the main themes of Luther's legacy, we need to make a few preliminary observations.

The first observation (and in some ways the most important) is that Luther was not a *systematic* theologian. Within his writings we find nothing that corresponds to John Calvin's *Institutes of the Christian Religion,* nor of the many systematic theologies produced in the late 16th and early 17th centuries in the time of so-called "Lutheran Orthodoxy", and there is nothing like the *Church Dogmatics* of Karl Barth (1886-1968). If we want to understand Luther's theology then we have to wrestle with commentaries, lectures, treatises, occasional writings, and the anecdotal evidence of the *Table Talk* recorded by his friends and disciples.

Secondly, we need to point out the obvious fact that these different writings were written in different contexts, and it is also clear that Luther's theology developed and matured during the (nearly) four decades of his career as a teacher and lecturer. This career lasted from his appointment to the chair in Wittenberg in 1511 to his death in 1546, and in a career lasting so long it is only to be expected that there would be differences between his early theology and that of his later years. On the other hand, there is a core of theology which emerged between 1517 and 1521 and it could be argued that his later theology is a working out of these basics.

Thirdly, we need to point out that Luther's theological output is of two distinct sorts: there are the things that he wrote that are the product of his day-to-day work as a teacher and pastor, and there are those things which were written as reactions to events or crises (the latter were often dashed off at great speed). Among the first, we can place the lectures, commentaries, sermons, educational works, and devotional writings, while among the second are such works as the trio of treatises of 1520, the treatise against the peasants' revolt in 1525, and his literature about the Jews.

Luther produced an immense amount of literature and it has not proved easy to encapsulate the essential elements of his legacy in only a few pages. What follows is a distillation of what seem to be the most important features that have been hinted at in the preceding historical section.

FURTHER READING

The selection of books for further reading at the start of Part One includes some titles dealing with Luther's theology, but the following are also of interest. Over the years there were few books by British scholars which dealt with Luther's theological teachings, but after the Second World War there was a renewed interest in him and this resulted in two books which might now be described as classics. The first of these is **Let God be God: An Interpretation of the Theology of Martin Luther (London, The Epworth Press, 1947. No ISBN)**. This was written by Dr Philip Watson, a Methodist theologian, who had a good working knowledge of Lutheranism and who had translated Anders Nygren's *Agape and Eros* from the original Swedish. Another British Methodist scholar, Gordon Rupp, wrote **The Righteousness of God: Luther Studies (London, Hodder and Stoughton, 1953. No ISBN)**. Published in 1963, coincidentally the year in which the Lutheran World Federation held its Assembly in Helsinki, a translation of the Finnish theologian Dr Lennart Pinomaas's book *Voittava usko*, was published in the USA: **Faith Victorious: An Introduction to Luther's Theology (Philadelphia, Fortress Press, 1963. No ISBN)**. Readers might also like to consult two books translated from German: Paul Althaus's **The Theology of Martin Luther (Philadelphia, Fortress Press, 1966. No ISBN)**, and Oswald Bayer's **Martin Luther's Theology: A Contemporary Interpretation (Grand Rapids/Cambridge, William B. Eerdmans Publishing Company, 2008. ISBN: 978-0-8028-2799-9)**. For those who prefer their theology a little lighter, there is **Luther for Armchair Theologians** by Steven Paulson **(Louisville/London, Westminster John Knox Press, ISBN: 0-664-22381-8)**.

The text of Luther's will can be found in **LW. Vol.34, pp.295-297**.

Chapter 8 | The Word of God

A central part of Luther's legacy is the Bible. The Bible is, of course, the common inheritance of all Christians, but Luther's biblical legacy was twofold: there is his translation into German, first of the New Testament in 1522, and then of the Old Testament in 1534, but there is also his particular understanding of how the Bible should be read and understood. The first of these – the German translations – provided the ordinary, literate German, with a version of the Scriptures that was easy to read and which, almost as a by-product, helped to standardise the German language, which, up to that point, had been a jumble of almost mutually unintelligible dialects. The second, what we can term his "exegetical principles", is something that is of fundamental importance if we are to understand Luther's theology.

Luther and the Bible

At the outset, we need to say a few words about Luther's relationship with the Bible. He would have been familiar with it – or, at least, with parts of it – for most of his life. In his early years, growing up as a child and young man, he would have heard, Sunday by Sunday, the texts from the Epistles and Gospels that were read in the Mass, and, although these would have been in Latin and so beyond the understanding of most people, he was one of the privileged ones who enjoyed the benefit of a Latin-based education. This familiarity would have grown by leaps and bounds when he entered the monastery in Erfurt in 1505. The monastery was governed by the Rule of St Augustine, written towards the end of the fourth century (the date that is usually given is 397 AD), and which was a very brief document of roughly 14 pages, full of biblical allusions, and which prescribes the regular reading of the Bible. The community's worship, which centred on the recitation of the daily offices, had at its heart the singing of the psalms, so we can say with certainty that by the time Luther was ordained as a priest in 1507, he would have known parts of the Bible very well.

Eventually, Luther would have come to possess a Bible of his own, and, after being awarded his doctorate, he was expected to lecture on it; significantly, his first lectures were on the Book of Psalms. From then onwards, until his death in 1546, such lectures were at the heart of his activity, and it has been suggested that were he alive today then he would almost certainly be described as a lecturer in the Old Testament.

Of course, his first study was of the Latin version – the Vulgate – which had been translated from the original Hebrew and Greek by the fifth century scholar, Jerome (347-419), and which, by Luther's time, was the official version prescribed for use in the church. However, it would be wrong to assume that there were no translations into the vernacular languages: some countries, such as England, *did* prohibit translation on pain of death, but there were translations into German, which, because of the invention of the printing press, circulated widely. Whether or not Luther was aware of such translations we do not know, but it was certainly the Vulgate that he lectured on for more than a decade.

For people interested in the Bible, this was an exciting time. The great Dutch scholar, Desiderius Erasmus of Rotterdam (1469-1536), was beginning work on a new version of the Latin Bible, based on the oldest texts that he could find. The fruit of his work was published in 1516, and contained not only a Latin text, but also a Greek version and notes. There had also been a growth in interest in Hebrew, and Johannes Reuchlin (1455-1522), a noted Hebraist, produced a number of books, the most important of which was his *De Rudimentis Hebraicis* (1506), which provided scholars with an introduction to Hebrew grammar. Luther certainly developed a good knowledge of Greek, although his knowledge of Hebrew was less good, but fortunately, for more than 25 years he had the help and support of Phillip Melanchthon, who was a talented linguist.

Law and Gospel

The principles of Luther's theology are sometimes summed up under the heading of the "three solas": *Sola Fide, Sola Gratia, Sola*

Scriptura (by faith alone, by grace alone, by Scripture alone), and he came to believe that the Bible was the only source of doctrine. Such a stance meant that he was opposed not only to the Roman Catholic Church, which believed that there was a hidden tradition that had been given to the apostles, but also to the Jews, who believed that scripture had been added to by the Talmud. But Luther was no fundamentalist, and he adhered to strict principles when he came to defining how the Bible should be interpreted: we can sum these principles up as, firstly, the *distinction between Law and Gospel,* and *the centrality of Christ in the scriptures.*

By "the Law of God" Luther meant, primarily, the Ten Commandments, and for him the rest of the Jewish Law had no place in the Christian life. The Commandments are certainly a guide as to how Christians should live their lives, and Luther had no hesitation in putting them as the first section of his *Shorter Catechism,* together with a simple explanation of each one, but for him that is not their primary function. The main use of the Law also has the function of pointing out that Christians, no matter how good they think they are, are actually sinners who need the forgiveness of God: the Law is a mirror in which Christians see themselves as they really are. However, alongside this stands the Gospel, which is the "good news" that God is a loving Father who forgives sinners who repent, and it is this which should be at the forefront of the church's preaching and teaching.

The Law, however, is not synonymous with the Old Testament, nor the Gospel with the New. True, the Old Testament "is a book of laws which teaches what men are to do and not to do ... just as the New Testament is a Gospel or book of grace [which] teaches where one is to get the power to fulfil the Law", but "in the New Testament there are also given along with the teaching about grace, many other teachings that are laws and commandments for the control of the flesh – since in this life the spirit is not perfected and grace alone cannot rule" (LW.Vol.35: pp.236-7).

The second of Luther's basic principles of interpretation is that Christ is central to the whole of scripture. He wrote, "For this much is beyond question that all the scriptures point to Christ alone. Indeed in John 5: 46 Christ says 'Moses wrote of me'. Therefore, everything in the other books is already in the books of Moses, as in a basic source" (LW. Vol.35, p.132). This means that, for him, it is not only the New Testament which has to be seen as a Christian book, but the Old Testament as well: everything, from the story of

Adam and Eve and their fall from fellowship with God, through to the Law and the prophets, point towards Christ. He famously described its books as "the swaddling clothes of Christ".

IMPORTANT NOTE: Lutherans and Roman Catholics differ from most other Christians in the way in which they number the Ten Commandments. They follow the traditional practice of omitting the commandment *Thou shalt not take the Name of the Lord thy God in vain* (it is, in effect, subsumed into the First Commandment), and dividing the commandments about coveting into two – *Thou shalt not covet thy neighbour's wife* and *Thou shalt not covet thy neighbour's goods*. It is important to bear this in mind in inter-church discussions.

Proclaiming the Word

The Word of God, a term alongside of which Luther frequently uses the words *promise* and *Gospel*, is something that we find in the Bible, but the Bible is something that is written down, and he is anxious to emphasise that that the Word in which we meet Christ is primarily something which is spoken and proclaimed. Luther points out that whenever Christ and the apostles refer to the "Scriptures", they are referring to what we term the "Old Testament", and the preaching and teaching of the apostles was focussed on interpreting the Old Testament in order to point out that its scriptures were fulfilled in Christ's life, death, and resurrection. The Old and New Testaments are different in their origins, because whereas the former was written down, so that the Jews were known as "the People of the Book", the heart of the latter, the Gospel, is good news that was proclaimed, openly declared, and reported from mouth to mouth. Christians are, therefore, "the People of the Word". So, why was this Gospel written down, if it was primarily an oral message that is to be proclaimed out loud? The answer to that is that it was written down as an emergency measure, both to ensure its survival when the expected second coming of Christ did not take place as soon as it was hoped for, but also to protect it from heretics who might distort the Gospel's original purity.

For Luther, it is the Word alone that gives the true revelation of God to mankind, but the fact remains that men and women can read their Bibles and still be far away from understanding that revelation. The Word of God is not present in the Bible in such a way that it can be unmistakably understood as Gospel, rather, the tendency is for it to be read as a book of rules to govern human conduct, with examples of people who have lived according to these rules, and, most especially, Jesus Christ; in this way, Christ becomes an example, rather than a saviour. The question that faces us is how to take the Bible and release the Gospel so that it is proclaimed today, just as it was in the time of the apostles? How do the objective facts of the redemptive work of Christ become real for human beings who are separated from them by close on two thousand years of history?

Luther provides an answer to this question when he explains the third article of the Apostles' Creed in his *Small Catechism*. He says:

> I believe that I cannot by my own understanding or effort believe in Jesus Christ my Lord, or come to Him. But the Holy Spirit has called me through the Gospel, enlightened me with His gifts, and sanctified and kept me in the true faith. In the same way He calls, gathers, enlightens, and sanctifies the whole Christian church on earth, and keeps it united with Jesus Christ in the one true faith. In this Christian church day after day He fully forgives my sins and the sins of all believers. On the last day He will raise me and all the dead and give me and all believers eternal life. This is most certainly true.

In this explanation, Luther starts with what seems to be the very negative statement that we cannot believe in Christ or come to him by our own efforts (ie by what we do) or by our understanding (ie by our reason and intellect). Here, Luther is simply reasserting what he says in many different places, namely, that human beings are intrinsically blind to understanding the nature and will of God, and are therefore unable to establish a right relationship with him. Against this, however, he inserts a "but" – the "but" being that God calls people through the Holy Spirit and gives them faith, forgives their sins, and does this day after day. The Holy Spirit creates faith by making the objective facts about Christ of benefit in the here and now: he bridges the gap between the historical works of Christ and our lives today. And this is done in the church by preaching the Word and administering the Sacraments.

How God Reveals Himself to the World

Luther distinguishes very clearly between two different ways in which God reveals himself to the world: there is what he calls the *general knowledge* of God, which is linked to what he calls the *Theology of Glory,* and there is the *specific knowledge* of God, which he calls the *Theology of the Cross.*

Commenting on Galatians 4: 8, Luther describes the *general knowledge* of God, by which he means that everyone knows that there is a God, that he created the heavens and the earth, that he is just, and that he punishes the wicked. However, this *general knowledge* does not give men and women any idea of what God is really like, and he goes on to give an illustration from everyday life. It is as though we know someone by sight, and from our observations we can deduce certain facts about him or her – or, more precisely, we can speculate as to what the person is like: we can build up a picture in our minds, but that picture may not bear any relationship to what the person is really like, nor how he or she feels towards us. This is just like our knowledge of God: we look at creation and we form a picture of how we think God feels and acts, and in this way we ought to be able to form an accurate picture of him. However, this is not the case: we are prevented from knowing God as he really is because mankind has sinned, and the things that we see in creation are actually veils which hide the real God from us.

There are several consequences from this, the most significant being that, although everyone has a *general knowledge* of God, it results in idolatry: the different ways in which human beings worship God come about because, from their vague feelings about a divinity, different peoples speculate what God might be like, and how they should worship him. Luther calls this "pursuing the naked God", in other words, seeking to find God behind the veils. Idolatry for Luther, by the way, is not just making graven images and bowing down to them – whatever human beings put their trust in, be it philosophy, monastic vows, or superstition of any kind, then that is an idolatrous and false god. He goes on to say that the heathen gods were created by a desire for human success, whether it be by being successful in war, or by seeking fertility, beauty, health, or protection from danger.

Luther did not deny that in theory human beings ought to be able to see God as he has been revealed in the works of creation, but, unfortunately, the complication of human sin has meant a dangerous obscuring of the true nature of God. It is not just that sin has hidden God from view, but, from the facts at their disposal, men and women have ascribed to God a character that is totally alien to him. So, far from attaining knowledge of God through creation, human beings become idolaters who create gods to satisfy their own needs and desires, and to Luther's mind the worst forms that such idolatry took in his day was what he regarded as the false piety of the Roman Catholic Church and of the Jews. The question is, therefore, how do we come to see God as he really is?

At this point it might be helpful to look at the reasons why Luther took the decision to enter the monastery in 1505, and how this helped him to answer that question. Of course, there were probably many reasons why he took the decision, but there is one underlying motive that can be clearly distinguished – he desired to find peace with God for his troubled soul. Yet the very nature of the monastic life caused him to find, not peace, but anguish and despair. He was unable to find peace through the usual remedies prescribed by the church and the monastic Rule, things such as penance, meditation, and prayer, but he was fortunate that his spiritual adviser, Johannes Staupitz, pointed him in the direction of study, and it was through this that he eventually found the peace that he was seeking. In his role as a lecturer in the university in Wittenberg, Luther was forced to study biblical texts and wrestle with them so that he could expound them correctly for his students.

The theology of the cross stems directly from I Corinthians 1: 23, where Paul says that although the cross is a scandal and a foolishness to the worldly, it is really a powerful way in which God reveals himself: it stresses the practical, saving revelation of God in opposition to the mysticism and speculation which have their origin in the general knowledge of God. These two sources of revelation – creation and the cross – and the use which man makes of them, are constantly set in antithesis to each other. In a nutshell, what Luther is saying is that we only truly see God when we see Christ on the cross: the whole of the created world is meaningless and useless until it is seen through the perspective of the work of Jesus Christ. But when we read Luther, we become aware of something very startling, namely, that he seldom makes mention of the teaching ministry of Christ; instead, he stresses the objective facts of the incarnation, passion, resurrection, ascension, and second coming.

The Word Today

In all his years at the university in Wittenberg, Luther lectured on the Old and New Testaments, emphasising both the need to study them in their original languages and the need to interpret them according to sound principles. Throughout the centuries, Lutherans have followed this tradition and they have produced outstanding scholars who have contributed to biblical studies, and, in the tradition of Philip Melanchthon rather than Luther himself, they have also produced distinguished systematic theologians. However, the main task of such theologians has always been to produce pastors who can effectively minister in parishes and congregations. All Lutheran pastors receive a thorough grounding in the Bible, and in services of worship they are expected to preach on the text that has been set for the day and to draw out from it again and again the message that God is a loving Father who forgives sinners who repent.

The distinction between Law and Gospel, which was so central to Luther, underpins the church's approach to practical and ethical issues, including such controversial issues as the role of men and women in the church, or heterosexual and same-sex relationships. However, not all Lutherans interpret the relevant passages of the Bible which refer to such matters in the same way, and they can and do hold different attitudes. Although a majority of Lutheran churches now ordain women – which means that the ministry is fully open to women, including becoming bishops – some churches do not. Similarly, many Lutheran churches endorse equal rights for people of both heterosexual and same-sex orientation, including so-called "gay marriage", but there are also many Lutheran churches which take a more traditional view. Sadly, as within some other Christian denominations, these differences can sometimes lead to a breach of fellowship and to mutual condemnation.

FURTHER READING

The primary sources, ie Luther's own writings on the Word of God, are to be found in **LW, Vols. 35-37: Word and Sacrament I-III**. Volume 35 has *A Brief Instruction on What to Look for and Expect in the Gospels* (1521); *How Christians Should Regard Moses* (1525); *On Translating: An Open Letter* (1530); *Defence of the Translation of the Psalms* (1531); and *Prefaces to the Books of the Bible*.

Useful secondary sources are Willem Jan Kooiman's **Luther and the Bible (Philadelphia, Muhlenberg Press, 1961. No ISBN)**; A. Skevington Wood's **Captive to the Word: Martin Luther, Doctor of Sacred Scripture (Exeter, The Paternoster Press, 1969. ISBN: 85364-**

087-4); Thomas M. McDonough's **The Law and the Gospel in Luther: A Study of Martin Luther's Confessional Writings (Oxford, Oxford University Press, 1963. No ISBN)**; and Walter von Loewenich's **Luther's Theology of the Cross (Belfast, Christian Journals Limited, 1976. ISBN: 0-9043-0218-0)**.

A book which was rather controversial in its time is Gustaf Wingren's *Predikan*, translated into English as **The Living Word: A Theological Study of Preaching and the Church (Philadelphia, Fortress Press, 1960. No ISBN)**.

Chapter 9 | **The Sacraments**

Luther was brought up to believe, as a good Catholic, that there were seven sacraments: Baptism, the Mass, Penance, Confirmation, Ordination, Marriage, and Extreme Unction. These were, the Church taught, means of grace which helped Christians through this life to the life to come. As early as 1520, however, Luther wrote his *Prelude to the Babylonian Captivity of the Church*, in which he rejected five of these and advocated that only two of these church ordinances could validly be designated as sacraments. According to his definition of a sacrament, there must be two things: there had to be a promise by Christ, and attached to this, "a sign".

By this definition only Baptism and "the Sacrament of the Altar" met the criteria. Early in the night of his betrayal, Jesus had broken bread and shared wine with his disciples, inviting them to do these things in remembrance of him, and at the time of his ascension, Jesus had commanded them to go into the whole world, make disciples, teach them, and baptise them.

Luther defines a sacrament as being a testament, made by Christ, which is to be distributed to believers, and a testament, he says, is something made by a person who is about to die, and in which three things are involved – the death of the one making the will, the promise of an inheritance, and the naming of an heir. God, says Luther, only deals with human beings on the basis of his word of promise: we are beggars who receive that promise, not because we deserve it, but because it is part of Christ's legacy to us. In *The Babylonian Captivity* Luther asserted that the Roman Church had forgotten the concept of promise, and had "imprisoned" both the laity and the sacraments themselves and had sought to control people's lives from birth to death, through the power of the hierarchical priesthood and its traditions. For Luther, such an "imprisonment" was in clear opposition to what sacraments were really about.

The Sacrament of the Altar

Luther uses several different words to describe the service in which Christians break bread and share wine – in different places he calls it *The Mass,* or *The Sacrament of the Altar,* or *The Lord's Supper*, but the Roman Church had subjected this sacrament to three "imprisonments": it did not allow the ordinary men and women of the church to receive the wine ("withholding of the cup"), it insisted on the doctrine of transubstantiation, and it taught that the sacrament was a sacrifice.

The first "imprisonment" of the Sacrament of the Altar is that only the priest was allowed to receive both the bread and the wine. Like the earlier reformer, Jan Hus, Luther affirmed that allowing the laity to receive only the bread is a clear denial of the words of Christ at the Last Supper: he argues that the accounts of the institution of the sacrament in the Synoptic Gospels show that Jesus gives the whole sacrament – both bread and wine – to the disciples, and that this was confirmed by the apostle Paul. "No-one", says Luther, "has ever had the temerity to say otherwise".

The second "imprisonment" relates to *how* Jesus could be present in the bread and the wine. How these two elements can be the body and blood of Christ is, in the end, a mystery beyond human comprehension, but the Roman Church had attempted to explain it on the basis of philosophical ideas traceable back to Aristotle, and known as "transubstantiation". The basic idea is that the outward appearance of the bread and wine (the "accidents") remain the same, but the inward "substance" of both elements are transformed into the flesh and blood of Christ when the priest says the "words of institution". Luther insists that the incarnate Christ is really present in the bread and wine, but he affirms that we should "not dabble too much in philosophy" – hence it is wrong to say that he taught something called "consubstantiation". On one occasion he did use a graphic description to explain the "real presence": the relationship of the word of promise and the bread and wine was like a piece of iron, heated in the fire so that it glowed with heat – both the fire and the iron were separate until they were united together.

For Luther, with his strong belief in justification by faith, it is the third "imprisonment" which is the most dangerous, because it turned the Sacrament of the Altar into a sacrifice, offered, over and over again by priests, for the sins of the world. Not only did this deny that Christ's offering of himself was something unique, but it had been turned into a business in which those who could afford it paid for Masses to reduce either their own or their loved ones' time in purgatory. Celebrating the Sacrament of the Altar is not something that can be done as a way of placating God, and it is not something that human beings can do for others, because it requires faith, and faith is a personal thing. The Mass is a promise to Christians of the forgiveness of sins, and this promise is confirmed by the death of Christ, and Christians must trust in it.

As time went on, Luther found himself caught between two diametrically opposed positions regarding the Sacrament of the Altar: on the one hand there were the Roman Catholics, with their doctrine of transubstantiation, but there were also the more radical reformers, particularly those from Switzerland, who denied any idea of the real presence in the bread and wine. Their argument seemed to be straightforward: Christ had ascended into heaven, and, as the Apostles' Creed had it, "sits as the right hand of the Father", so, he could not be in two places at once. Luther explained this by asserting that the phrase "the right hand of God" is a description of Christ's power and authority, and, because he is divine, so he can share the Father's "ubiquity", ie his ability to be everywhere, including in the bread and wine of the sacrament.

Attempts were made, particularly at the so-called Marburg Colloquy of 1529, to come to some sort of consensus with the Swiss, but it ended in failure. There were later attempts to arrive at a consensus between Lutherans and the "Reformed" on the question of how Christ is present in the Lord's Supper and, on occasion, attempts were made by the "secular" authorities to force unions between the two confessional groups. Among some Lutherans this remains a lively issue.

The Sacrament of Baptism

The other sacrament that Luther retained was that of Baptism, but, just as with the Sacrament of the Altar, it had also been made subject to an "imprisonment".

Baptism is a sacrament because there is a promise and a sign: in this case the promise is contained in Jesus' words in Mark 16: 16, "He who believes and is baptised shall be saved", and the sign is the water. In contrast with those whom he labelled "Enthusiasts", and who argued that baptism involved a commitment on the part of those who were being baptised, Luther agreed with Roman Catholics that infants should be baptised. He accepts that infants do not understand God's promise and, therefore, cannot have a conscious faith, but they are helped by the faith of those who bring them for Baptism, and by the prayers of the church. The "imprisonment" of Baptism lies, says Luther, in the fact that no-one remembers that they have been baptised, instead everyone looks for other ways of getting to heaven, ie by means of supposed "good works".

The significant point in Luther's ideas about Baptism is that it has a lasting effect because it creates a permanent relationship between the individual and God, and this can only be broken by unbelief. Unbelief is the only sin which can condemn people, and so long as they retain faith in the promises made by God in Baptism, all other sins are blotted out by God's grace. Baptism is not a human activity, but something done by God, who "thrusts you under the water with his own hands and promises you forgiveness of sins, speaking to you upon earth with a human voice by the mouth of his minister", and, while we may wander away from the sign, this does not render it either invalid or useless.

We must remember that *The Babylonian Captivity of the Church* is a relatively early writing, and at this stage Luther still accepted that penance might be a sacrament, but he is already showing signs of subsuming it into Baptism. Like the two sacraments that he has already discussed, Luther maintains that it, too, has been subject to "imprisonment", which, in this case, has been disfigured in such a way that "not a vestige of it remains". The Roman Catholic Church had complicated the idea of penance by dividing it into contrition, confession, and satisfaction, of which it deemed the first to be the most important element. However, by doing that, the emphasis had been placed on how penitent and remorseful the man or women felt, whereas they should have faith in the God who comforts them in their sorrow. This comfort should come, he maintained, through the words of absolution in private confession, which he wanted to retain, even though he could find no direct scriptural basis for it.

FURTHER READING

This section has made frequent reference to Luther's *Babylonian Captivity of the Church* of 1520, the full text of which is available in **LW. Vol.36.** This volume also includes five other of his works on the Sacrament of the Altar, namely *The Misuse of the Mass* (1520), *Receiving Both Kinds of the Sacrament* (1522), *The Adoration of the Sacrament* (1523), *The Abomination of the Secret Mass* (1525), and *The Sacrament of the Body and Blood of Christ – Against the Fanatics* (1529). There are further writings on the same subject in **LW. Vol.35,** in particular *The Blessed Sacrament of the Holy and True Body of Christ, and the Brotherhoods* (1519), and *A Treatise on the New Testament, that is, the Holy Mass* (1520). **LW. Vol.37** contains two treatises: *That These Words of Christ, "This is My Body," etc., Still Stand Firm Against the Fanatics (*1527), and the *Confession Concerning Christ's Supper* (1528).

Two useful secondary sources are **This is my Body: Luther's Contention for the Real Presence in the Sacrament of the Altar** by Hermann Sasse **(Adelaide, Lutheran Publishing House, 1977. ISBN: 0-85910-034-0)** and Marilyn McCord Adams' **Some Later Medieval Theories of the Eucharist (Oxford, Oxford University Press, 2010. ISBN: 978-0-19-959105-3)**.

Luther was less prolific in writing distinctive works about Baptism and Penance, but **LW. Vol.35** contains two writings of 1519 entitled *The Holy and Blessed Sacrament of Baptism,* and *The Sacrament of Penance*. A secondary source on the subject of Baptism is to be found in Jonathan Trigg's **Baptism in the Theology of Martin Luther (Leiden, E. J. Brill, 1994. ISBN: 90-04-10016-4)**, which is a revised version of the author's 1991 doctoral thesis, submitted to the University of Durham in 1991. John W. Riggs' **Baptism in the Reformed Tradition: An Historical and Practical Theology (Louisville/London, Westminster John Knox Press, 2002. ISBN: 0-664-21966-7)** has a brief but useful section on Luther's theology of Baptism, set in the wider context of Protestant thought on the subject. A book which deals with the wider context of the 16th century is J. D. C. Fisher's **Christian Initiation: The Reformation Period (London, SPCK, 1970. ISBN: 281-02433-2)**.

Chapter 10 | The Christian Church

Martin Luther was a churchman, and he was a German. At the time of his birth in 1483 parts of Germany had been Christian for close on a thousand years. Missionaries from many other countries had spread the Gospel in the German-speaking lands, and the country was filled with churches, chapels, cathedrals, and monasteries. Everywhere there were bishops, priests, men in minor religious orders, monks, nuns, and friars, as well as lay church officials.

The church was a visible part of everyday life, and ordinary people were affected by the rhythms of the church year, with its fasts and feasts. Day-to-day life was frequently a miserable struggle, but the church was able to offer people the hope that there was a better time to come in the afterlife. Some aspects of the pains and struggles of this life could be alleviated through the intervention of the saints, and, in particular, Mary the mother of Jesus. Of course, as in many other nominally Christian countries, the faith of the people was intermingled with the remnants of pagan religion and superstition.

The normal German word for "the church" was *Die Kirche*, but this was a word with which Luther was not altogether happy, because he felt that it was open to misinterpretation by ordinary people. It was too easy for them to understand *Die Kirche* as a building in which religious ceremonies took place – a consecrated house or building made of wood or stone. Luther had to wrestle with this fundamental misunderstanding, and although he did not write *The Augsburg Confession* of 1530, it is, in effect, a summary of what he came to believe and teach.

Articles VII and VIII of the confession offer a definition of the Church which corresponds with his understanding: "It is taught among us", states Article VII, "that one holy Christian church will be and remain forever. This is the assembly of believers among whom the Gospel is preached in its purity and the Holy Sacraments are administered according to the Gospel." Article VIII goes on to say that, "The Christian church, properly speaking, is nothing else than an assembly of all believers and saints ... yet ... in this life many false Christians, hypocrites and even open sinners remain among the ungodly". These articles provide us with the main outlines of Luther's understanding of the church, which he sees in personal terms as a fellowship of Christian people. Such a concept placed Luther in opposition to the contemporary Catholic model, which saw the church in institutional and hierarchical terms.

For Luther, the Christian church is an assembly which consists of believers and saints and it is both temporal and eternal. Within this assembly the Gospel is preached and the sacraments are administered: in other words, it is a community in which events take place which have been commanded by Christ, and which is united in faith, hope, and love, under the guidance of the Holy Spirit. This doctrine is rooted, firstly, in his understanding of the credal expression "the communion of saints", which he interprets in personal terms and in apposition to the phrase which precedes it ("I believe in the Holy Christian Church"), and, secondly, in his biblical studies and, in particular, his understanding of the idea of "the people of God".

The Communion of Saints

Just as people misunderstood the word "church", so they misunderstood the word "saint", and thought of saints as men and women who had surpassed what God required of them in terms of goodness and holiness. The traditional medieval idea of sainthood, which had developed over several centuries, was based on the idea of *Verdienst* ("merit"), and had reached its fruition in the concept of the "Treasury of Merits". We might describe this as a "celestial bank account", through which individual Christians could receive help by appropriating to themselves the superfluous merits that had been earned by the "saints" during their lifetimes.

Very early on, Luther's studies in the New Testament – in particular in the writings of St Paul – led him to a radically different understanding of what it meant to be a saint. He came to believe that the Roman Catholic distinction between ordinary Christians and "saints" was invalid, because righteousness and holiness were gifts from God, not things that men and women could earn for themselves. Furthermore, sanctity is not something material or measurable, and it was false teaching to assert that people could invest moral effort (or, in the case of indulgences, financial means), by seeking to buy into the merits of those who had gone before. Luther affirmed that all Christian people are saints: the only valid distinction that can be made is that between the saints in heaven, who need not be our concern, and the saints on earth, who should be. The church is a living community of people who are saints, not because they succeed in living exemplary lives through their own efforts, but because they are sinners who have been made holy by Christ. They share together in Christ's righteousness, serve each other, and bear each other's burdens for his sake, and they live their lives in daily repentance. The Christian church is 'holy', but its holiness does not lie in its individual members, but because it is the body of Christ.

The People of God

The personal nature of the Christian community implied in the phrase *"communio sanctorum"* is reinforced in Luther by his understanding that Christians are "the people of God". This was something that he had to defend on two fronts: firstly, against the Jews, who understood themselves as God's people, and, secondly, against the Roman church, which maintained that it was the true Christian community.

On the basis of his exegesis of Romans 9: 12, he came to realise that the terms "Israel" and "people of God" could be understood in a twofold way. On the basis of Paul's argument in the Epistle to the Romans, Luther understood that there were two Israels – Israel "according to the flesh" and Israel "according to the spirit". Luther was thus able to assert that the blessings given by God to Abraham were spiritual, not physical, and in this way, he was able to find the history of the church in every part of the Old Testament. He conceded that the Jews were justified in claiming that as children of Abraham they were God's people, but he steadfastly maintained Paul's doctrine that the true children of Israel were to be found among those who had faith in God's promises. Christians are children of Israel by faith rather than by physical descent.

However, the real significance of Luther's biblical studies on the idea of the "people of God" does not lie in its application to the Jews.

True, Luther was concerned to demonstrate that Christians were the people of God rather than the Jews, but in practical terms he had little to fear from them, numerically small as they were. No, its true significance lay in its application to the Catholic Church, which maintained that Luther was an innovator and that it alone constituted the "People of God".

Since his heated discussions about papal authority at the Leipzig Debate in 1519, Luther had undertaken extensive research and had come to the conclusion that the Catholic church had abandoned the true meaning of *communio sanctorum*. Both in terms of its theology and its institutionalised existence it had ceased to be faithful to the New Testament pattern, and it was no longer the community of faith and love that Christ intended his church to be. The church needed to be reformed and brought back to a self-understanding that was genuinely scriptural, and this carried with it three implications.

Firstly, the church must take on itself the form of a servant rather than the form of a master. In the same way that Christ was a servant, so the Christian church must stand in the midst of mankind as one who serves. The church, and by implication individual Christians, must be Christ to the suffering and fallen world and be involved in its problems: "I will therefore give myself as Christ to my neighbour, as Christ offered himself to me ... we ought ... each one of us to become as it were ... Christs to one another and Christ may be the same in all, that we might be truly Christians." (LW. Vol.31, p.367.) This is true Christian discipleship or service, and it has as its object the good of one's brothers and sisters.

Secondly, the church has to face up to the possibility that it will share the fate of Christ. In the same way that Christ was mocked, rejected, and killed, so the church, both as a body and through its individual members, has to be prepared for suffering and the cross. In his treatise *On the Councils and the Church,* Luther wrote that "... the holy Christian people are externally recognised by the holy possession of the sacred cross. They must endure every misfortune and persecution, all kinds of trial and evil from the devil, the world, and the flesh ... in order to become like their head, Christ ... enduring this for the sake of Christ, Matthew 5: 11 'Blessed are you when men persecute you on my account.'"

Thirdly, the church is called on to witness. Christ renewed mankind through his death and resurrection, and the church is called on to witness that renewal. It does this by proclaiming the

Gospel and calling on Christians to live their lives in the daily resurrection that is made possible when their sins are forgiven.

There are clear implications here for ecclesiology. If the church is the body of Christ, then not only will its role be to suffer and bear the possibility of rejection and the cross in its service to the world, but its true glory is going to be hidden, just as Christ's was. The true glory of the church will be as hidden as the glory of God is hidden in the shame of the cross.

Clearly, this has implications for any idea of the church as institutional, hierarchical, and triumphant.

The Invisible and the Visible Church

Luther and his fellow reformers took over many ideas about the nature of the church from St Augustine of Hippo (354-439), in particular his ideas concerning the *invisible* and the *visible* church. The *invisible* church consists of true believers: they alone are part of Christ's body and they are known only by God and are destined by him for salvation. This church, which in the fullest sense of the word is the true church, is a communion of the Spirit, created solely by God, who alone bestows faith. The reformers modified this idea to some extent by defining the church as *narrow* or *wide*. In its strictest sense the *narrow* church consists of the faithful and sanctified, who are its members 'nominally and actually'.

Of course, by its very nature, the *invisible* church is something not seen and its members are known only to God. The *visible* church, on the other hand, stands for everyone to see, with all its faults and failings, and it is a mixed community: it is not sinless, but comprises both saints and sinners, good and bad. In this *wide* sense of the word, Luther recognised that the church had to have an external form and be clearly visible, but unlike reformers such as John Calvin (1509-1564) or Martin Bucer (1491-1551), he did not prescribe any specific form of church order. True, many of his colleagues – in particular Johannes Bugenhagen (1485-1558) – drew up church orders for particular territorial churches, but for Luther the important thing was that the church should be identified by recognisable distinguishing marks. Writing to the congregation in Leisnig in 1523, he asserted that, "The sure mark by which the Christian congregation can be recognised is that the pure Gospel is preached there. For just as the banner of an army is the sure sign by which one can know what kind of lord and army have taken to the field, so, too, the Gospel is a sure sign by which one knows where Christ and his army are encamped." (LW. Vol.39, p.305.)

As we have said elsewhere, provided that they were willing to accept the Gospel, Luther would have been happy for the bishops to have continued to lead the church, but few of them did. To provide the church with sound leadership, Luther had to resort to asking the princes and civic authorities to assume authority for instituting and carrying out reform. He did this on the presumption that they were Christian and had the welfare of the church as a principal concern. They were, as the phrase has it, "emergency bishops", given the task of dealing with an unstable situation by providing an authoritative stability. Unfortunately, the emergency never seemed to come to an end, and in most cases the Lutheran churches which emerged from the time of the Reformation were dominated by the secular authorities.

This situation whereby the secular ruler of a territory was regarded as the highest authority in the church (the "*Summus Episcopus*") was further entrenched by the Religious Peace of Augsburg of 1555. As we have already seen in Part One, this established the principle that the religion of the ruler should be the religion of the people (*cuius regio, eius religio*). In fact, this had been a fundamental tenet of Luther's thought all along, namely, that there should be religious uniformity within a given territory. This was one of explanations given for Luther's support of the decisions made by some princes not to allow Jews to reside in their lands.

Of course, arrangements varied from territory to territory, and as time passed and democratic ideas grew in secular society, so Lutheran churches gradually introduced more and more democratic elements into their structures. Naturally enough, this was particularly true where Lutherans were in a "free church" situation, such as the United States, but it was also true of the old homelands of Lutheranism in Germany and the Nordic countries. Today, most Lutheran churches have some sort of structure in which bishops (whether by that particular name or not) and representative synods, exercise authority. The one remaining example where this is not the case is that of the Church of Denmark where the sovereign is still the "*Summus Episcopus*", although it is, in effect, the Minister for Church Affairs who exercises that authority.

It is difficult to find an appropriate term to describe the phenomenon whereby the secular authority exercised supervision of the church. The term that is often used is "state church" or "established church", or, in the Nordic countries, "people's church". The latter is, however, a rather clumsy translation of the term used in the original languages: for example, the Danish term is *Folkekirke* (there are similar terms in the other Nordic languages), but the term "people's church" fails to capture the nuances of the term *"folke"*.

A close relationship with the secular authorities has had both positive and negative consequences for Lutheran churches across the centuries. At its best, it offered protection and stability to the church so that it could pursue its role of providing a pastoral ministry to people in a parish setting. There are good examples of this happening, for instance, through the diaconal work that developed in the Nordic countries, Germany, and elsewhere. However, there could also be a negative side, and this could involve lethargy, self-satisfaction, and a complacent acceptance of the *status quo*, especially on the part of the clergy, who were treated as members of the local establishment. To get a flavour of this, one only has to read the blistering attacks on the Church of Denmark by the philosopher-cum-theologian Søren Kierkegaard (1813-1855).

From Kierkegaard's perspective, the Danish Church had become "a monstrous lie" as the historian Kenneth Scott Latourette puts it, and it had "watered down the Christian law of love and self-denial to a comfortable code of bourgeois ethics". The church's position as a national organisation had given its clergy a security and status which prevented them from being real witnesses to the truth. Kierkegaard wrote:

> A witness to the truth, one of the genuine witnesses to the truth, is a man who is scourged, maltreated, dragged from one prison to the other … and then at last crucified, or beheaded, or burnt, or roasted on a gridiron, his lifeless body thrown by the executioner in an out-of-the-way place, or burnt to ashes and cast to the four winds, so that every trace of the filth might be obliterated.
> (Quoted in Josiah Thompson, *Kierkegaard: A Critical Biography*, p.220)

What Kierkegaard is saying is that the Danish church of his day was not the church of the cross; but there are, of course, many examples of churches and of individual Christians taking up their crosses as witnesses for the truth. As early as 1525, Luther preached a sermon to commemorate the burning of Brother Henry of Zütphen in the town of Ditmarschen, at the beginning of which he said, "In our day the pattern of true Christian life has reappeared, terrible in the world's eyes, since it means suffering and persecution, but precious and priceless in God's sight." (LW. Vol.32, pp.266-267.) Since then there have been many times when the church has suffered persecution, sometimes at the hands of pagan or atheist states, sometimes by other Christians. We can mention, in passing, the persecution of Christians in National Socialist Germany, in German-occupied Norway, in the former Soviet Union, or in present-day Eritrea.

FURTHER READING

Luther wrote extensively on the church and its ministry, and a selection of his writings on these subjects can be found in **LW. Vols. 39, 40 and 41**. Some aspects of his doctrine of the church are discussed in **Spirit Versus Structure: Luther and the Institutions of the Church (London, Collins, 1968. No ISBN)** by Jaroslav Pelikan. For a discussion of the concept of "the Communion of Saints", see Stephen Benko's **The Meaning of Sanctorum Communio (London, SCM Press Ltd., 1964. No ISBN)**.

Fortunately, many of Kierkegaard's writings have been translated into English from the original Danish, but sadly his works are notoriously difficult to read. A good introduction to his life and work is Josiah Thompson's **Kierkegaard: A Critical Biography (London, Victor Gollancz Ltd., 1974. ISBN: 0-575-01718-X)**. There is a short collection of his writings about the church in **Attack Upon Christendom, 1854-1855**, which is a selection of texts by Walter Lowrie, with an introduction by Howard A. Johnson **(Princeton, Princeton University Press, 1968: ISBN: 0-691-01950-9)**.

Chapter 11 | Vocation, Priesthood and Ministry

As we have seen, Luther explained his understanding of Baptism in the *Catechisms* of 1529. We might sum this up as "life in the forgiveness of sins", because, although baptism was a sacrament that was only delivered once, it was something that had to be lived out every day. It can be understood, therefore, as the foundation for Luther's teaching about vocation, priesthood, and ministry.

Christian Vocation

The date that is normally given for Luther's entrance to the Augustinian cloister in Erfurt is 17 July 1505, but this did not mean that he became a monk immediately. Once the monastic authorities were assured that he was who he said he was and that his intentions were sincere, he began a year's novitiate. We know that his novice master was named Johann Greffenstein (dates unknown), and it was his duty to explain the rules of the order, the pattern of daily life in the monastery, and what would be involved in the taking of the final vows. In Luther's case, everything went well and he became a professed monk in July 1506.

Although the Augustinians had their own distinctive rules and practices, they shared some fundamentals with other orders. The common monastic vow was a threefold one and it was intended to be for life: *poverty*, which meant that the individual monk could have no property of his own; *chastity,* which meant the giving up of sexual relations of any kind; and *obedience*, to the monk's monastic superiors. In addition to these three things there was an expectation of stability and that the monastery was to be a monk's home for the rest of his life.

Daily life in the monastery was regulated by the seven daily services (the "monastic hours", or "offices"), the saying of Mass, and mealtimes. In between these, monks were expected to work with their hands and undertake whatever tasks were allotted to them. Bearing in mind his academic background, it is not surprising that Luther was directed to study for the priesthood, although the demands of the monastic life meant that almost all of his brethren were priests.

Apart from the daily community Mass, the monastery had to arrange for priests to say the many Masses that had been endowed by individuals, and also to hear confessions, both from fellow monks and from the local townspeople. The course of study for becoming a priest did not involve an extensive study of theology, but it focused on the Mass and how it should be performed. The textbook that Luther used was entitled *Sacri Canonis Missae Expositio* ("An explanation of the holy Canon of the Mass") which had been written by a theologian of Tübingen, Gabriel Biel (1420-1495), and only published in 1499. Luther set great store by this book and valued it very highly.

The path to final ordination as a priest was marked by several stages, starting with ordination as a sub-deacon, which Luther may have received in the early autumn of 1506. The culmination of the process was ordination to the full priesthood, which probably took place on 3 April 1507 in the presence of his father and family friends. At this time Luther celebrated his first Mass. So, almost two years after entering the monastery, Luther was a fully professed monk and an ordained priest.

14 years later, Luther wrote a lengthy treatise entitled *De Votis Monasticis Martini Lutheri Iudicium* ("The Judgment of Martin Luther Concerning Monastic Vows"), in which he effectively repudiated the vows that he had taken as a monk. Behind the writing of this document lay the fact that a small but growing number of priests and monks were abandoning their vows of celibacy and were marrying, and Luther felt obliged to give theological and pastoral guidance on the subject.

He begins by arguing that it is sinful to go beyond what Christ has commanded and that, since monastic vows are nowhere commanded by him, they must be sinful. Commenting on the vows of obedience and poverty, he asserts that all Christians are called on to be obedient by humbly serving their neighbours, and that true poverty consists of caring for the welfare of others. Taking a monastic vow, he says, conflicts with faith in Christ because it is a form of works righteousness which conflicts with Christian freedom. It is alright, he says, to be a monk, so long as that is something entered into freely and with a concern for God's Word and the welfare of others, but in no way should it be considered superior to other forms of the Christian life. However, Luther maintains that contemporary monastic practices contradict the first commandment because monks honour the founders of their orders above Christ and this prevents them from carrying out the works of mercy and love which are everyone's responsibility. Luther concludes that monastic vows are actually contrary to common sense and reason, and argues strongly against celibacy, which he maintains is a particularly cruel torture. Among the final things that he writes are that no-one should be permitted to enter the monastery before the age of 60, an idea that had also been put forward by Andreas Karlstadt.

Significantly, the treatise was prefaced by a letter to his father. The old man had been present at Luther's ordination as a priest, and although he had been generous in his gifts to the monastery on that day, he had also made it clear what he thought of his son's decision to enter the monastery in the first place. In no uncertain terms he made it clear that he felt that his son had broken the commandment to honour father and mother. In the letter of 1521, Luther admits this and thanks God for delivering him from the vows he had taken.

Priesthood and Ministry

In the treatise that we have just been considering, Luther argued strongly against the teaching and practice of the Roman Catholic Church of his day. Over the centuries the church had come to distinguish between the laity, on the one hand, and the "religious" (priests, monks, and nuns), on the other; but for Luther, this was a false assumption. He drew no distinction between monks, priests, and the laity: Christians are all equal because they have all been baptised. True, he recognised that the works of "the religious" might be "holy and arduous", but they "did not differ one whit in the sight of God from the works of the rustic labourer in the field, or the woman going about her household tasks". Why? Because "all works are measured before God by faith alone". He adds that "... the menial housework of a manservant or maidservant is often more acceptable to God than all the fasting and other works of a monk or priest, because the monk or priest lacks faith".

Central to Luther's understanding of priesthood and ministry was the concept that there was *one* office of ministry, which focuses on the preaching of the Word and the administration of the sacraments of Baptism and the Lord's Supper. Luther also added the exercise of the "Office of the Keys", which involves the granting of absolution in the context of pastoral care. This ministry belongs to all Christians, who, by virtue of their baptism, share in Christ's priesthood and are called on to minister to their fellow believers and to all who are in need. However, sharing in this universal priesthood of believers does not mean that all Christians are called on to preach or administer the sacraments, and Luther was quite clear that no-one should do these things without a call, either from a local congregation or from some other duly authorised body. Such a call should then be publicly proclaimed through the laying on of hands.

The first ordination carried out by Luther was of a man by the name of Georg Römer in 1525. Initially there was something of an *ad hoc* character to such ordinations. It was not until ten years later that the Elector John Frederick prescribed a definite procedure for examining, calling, and ordaining new pastors. It took another four years for Luther to compose his *Ordination for Ministers of the Word* (1539), an order which circulated for several years in manuscript form until it was eventually printed in different Church Orders.

What Luther writes in this order shows a clear differentiation between the Roman Catholic and Lutheran understanding of ordination. The Catholics understood ordination to be one of the seven sacraments, which conferred on the ordinand a special rank that enabled him to offer the sacrifice of the Mass. Luther's understanding was radically different: ordination was a rite which conferred on the ordinand the functions of preaching and administering the sacraments. Luther's drastically different service included scripture readings (I Timothy 3: 1-7, and Acts 20: 28-31), followed by an exhortation to "watch over the congregation of God, purchased with his own blood [and] feed them with the pure Word of God ...". After this, "the whole presbytery imposed their hands on the heads of the ordinands", there was a prayer for the granting of the Holy Spirit, the ordaining minister said the Lord's Prayer, read I Peter 5: 2-4, and blessed the new ministers with the sign of the cross.

Evidence suggests that most parish priests in early 16th century Germany had little or no formal theological education, as Luther discovered in the Saxon Church Visitation (see below), and their ministry was deemed to be valid because of the powers bestowed on them by ordination. He and his colleagues worked tirelessly to rectify this situation through ensuring that candidates for the public ministry were carefully selected, given a thorough theological education, and properly examined before being ordained.

Once ordained, it was the responsibility of the church to ensure that the pastor was supported through appropriate pastoral oversight. Unlike the Roman Church or some of the other reformers, Luther did not believe that the New Testament specified any particular form of church governance. Had the bishops in his day supported the reformation, Luther would have been happy for them to remain in their posts, and this happened in places like Sweden, but it did not happen in Germany, nor in Denmark, and in most cases bishops were replaced by Superintendents.

Today, although an increasing number of Lutheran churches exercise oversight through bishops, this is by no means universally the case. So long as things are done decently and in good order, and that the Word is preached and the sacraments administered in conformity with the Gospel, the specifics of church order may differ from place to place.

As a postscript to this section we might add a word about the diaconate, since this is an important feature of Lutheran churches in some countries. Yet we will look long and hard to find any positive references to deacons in the corpus of Luther's works. In his day the office of deacon was simply a step on the way to becoming a priest, and with his emphasis on the one ministry of Word and Sacrament, Luther simply abandoned the idea of an ordained diaconate. In most Lutheran churches the office of deacon was either abolished, or it was reduced to the lay function of parish clerk or verger.

The diaconate re-emerged in Lutheran churches in the 19th century, and is associated with the names of men such as Johannes Wichern (1808-1881), Theodor Fliedner (1800-1864), and Willhelm Loehe (1808-1872) in Germany. Their influence spread northwards into the Nordic countries, and in particular to Finland and Sweden, and also to the United States. Deacons and deaconesses today are men and women consecrated or commissioned to a ministry that is focused on parish work or social service.

FURTHER READING

The text for Luther's *Ordination of Ministers of the Word* can be found in **LW. Vol.53** (pp.124-126). There are several books in English which deal with Luther's understanding of ministry, in particular **Luther on Ministerial Function and Congregational Office (Philadelphia, Fortress Press, 1981. ISBN: 0-8006-0665-5)**, which is a translation by Ruth C. Gritsch from the German original by Gert Haendler of Rostock University. Two other works of interest are James. H. Pragman's **Traditions of Ministry: A History of the Doctrine of Ministry in Luther's Theology (St. Louis, Concordia Publishing House, 1983. ISBN: 0-570-03900-2)** and Timothy J. Wengert's **Priesthood, Pastors, Bishops: Public Ministry for the Reformation and Today (Minneapolis, Fortress Press, 2008. ISBN: 978-0-8006-6313-1)**. An early exposition of the Lutheran understanding of ministry, designed for the regular examination of pastors, was Martin Chemnitz's **Ministry of Word and Sacraments: An Enchiridion (1593)** translated and annotated by Luther Poellot **(St. Louis, Concordia Publishing House, 1981. ISBN: 0-570-03295-4)**.

For a general discussion of the concept of vocation in Luther, see Carl C. Rasmussen's translation from the Swedish of Gustaf Wingren's *Vår Kallelse*, **Luther on Vocation (Philadelphia, Muhlenberg Press, 1957. No ISBN)**.

Two excellent books on the diaconate have been produced as part of the continuing Porvoo process, both with the general heading of *The Ministry of the Deacon*. The first has the sub-title of **Anglican-Lutheran Perspectives** (eds. Gunnel Borgegård and Christine Hill) **(Uppsala, Nordic Ecumenical Council, 1999. ISBN: 91-85564-10-9)**, and the second is **Ecclesiological Explorations** (eds. Gunnel Borgegård, Olav Fanuelsen, and Christine Hill) **(Uppsala, Nordic Ecumenical Council, 2000. ISBN: 91-85564-10-9)**.

Chapter 12 | Luther and Education

For much of his career Luther was a teacher in the University of Wittenberg, so he was much concerned with theological education. However, his interest in education extended far beyond the university lecture hall and he was dedicated to the idea of sound education for young people (including girls). This interest reflects his own education, but also the state of schooling in his own land of Saxony during the reformation.

The Church Visitations of 1527-1529

Much of what had happened in Saxony (and other evangelical territories) during the 1520s had been on an *ad hoc* basis. Luther's ideas on the reform of the church had been implemented in a piecemeal fashion, and they had spread through personal contacts, writings, letters, and the activities of friends and colleagues. Luther had hoped that the bishops would take a lead in reforming the church, but they had failed to do so and their authority had disappeared. It was the secular authorities and the university that had provided the impetus for reform, but by 1527 events had overtaken them and church order, at both local and regional level, was near chaotic.

The need for church visitations was most apparent after the peasants' revolt, and it was Luther's friend, Nicholas Hausmann, who first made the suggestion that there should be a visitation throughout Saxony in order to ascertain what the situation was in individual parishes, and what help they might need. In October 1525 Luther recommended to the Elector that this should take place and the prince responded by asking Luther to draw up detailed plans for such a visitation, which he duly did. Significantly, the authority for conducting the visitation was to be that of the

Elector. Luther carefully explained to him that he had no church rights as such, and that it was not the task of the secular authorities either to govern the church or control religious teaching. But the Elector was a Christian prince and the most important and powerful layman in the territory, so he had the responsibility for helping in its reorganisation. Furthermore, as the supreme secular authority, the Elector was responsible for preventing discord, faction, and rebellion among his subjects. Accordingly, though after a delay of more than a year, the prince authorised committees of visitors to visit all the parishes of the electorate.

Luther clearly saw this involvement of the prince as a temporary measure to deal with an emergency situation. Since none of the Catholic bishops were prepared to help, the prince had to act as an "emergency bishop", but on the clear understanding that these "episcopal" functions would cease when the emergency was over.

The ecclesiastical visitors were shocked by what they found. Many of the older priests, who had, of course, been in place from pre-reform times, were ignorant, and their education was seldom much better than that of their parishioners. Few of them preached satisfactorily, and in some cases they could not say the Apostles' Creed, the Lord's Prayer, or the Ten Commandments.

Of course, there were honourable exceptions to this, but the overall picture was disheartening. Education at a local level was also in a very bad state: in the villages schools were almost non-existent, and those that existed in the smaller towns were disappointing. It was obvious to Luther and his colleagues that a start would have to be made on improving the standards of both clergy and teachers, so that they could, in turn, raise level of education amongst the laity.

Luther's Catechisms

Luther himself had taken part in the Visitation, and he was shocked by his first-hand contact with the ignorance, superstition, and laxity that he found in many of the priests and people. Returning to Wittenberg, and realising that the crying need was for an improvement in education, he set to work on devising practical ways to do this. The result was the publication, only four months later, of his *Small Catechism*, written largely for the instruction of young people, and the *Large Catechism*, which was intended for pastors and adults.

Although both catechisms are included in *The Book of Concord*, and thereby have the status of confessions of the church, they were not originally intended for theologians, and they were not written in order to define controverted points in theological debates. Luther wrote them with a practical aim in mind: they were intended to be used by pastors for the instruction of the laity, or by schoolmasters or the heads of families.

They speak simply and clearly of the chief articles of the Christian faith – the Ten Commandments, the Apostles' Creed, the Lord's Prayer, Baptism, and the Sacrament of the Altar (together with a short explanation of how to confess one's sins) – in such a way that they can be easily understood by the laity.

There had been catechisms during the Middle Ages, although these had usually been produced for adults, and even before the Saxon Visitation Luther had been aware of the need for something which clearly explained the faith. As early as 1516 he had preached a series of sermons on the Ten Commandments, and he had followed this up in 1517 with a similar series on the Lord's Prayer. In 1525, he had requested his colleagues Justus Jonas (1493-1555) and Johannes Agricola (1494-1566) to undertake the preparation of a catechism, but, from Luther's point of view, their efforts were unsatisfactory. Hence, his decision to write one himself in 1529.

In 1528 the city priest of Wittenberg, Johannes Bugenhagen (1485-1558), who was responsible for delivering regular sermons, was absent from the town. On several occasions Luther substituted for his colleague, and between May and December he preached on the five parts of Christian doctrine that we have already mentioned. The substance of these were eventually printed as a series of charts or placards which sold for a *pfennig* each, and were soon sold out. These formed the basis for the *Small Catechism,* which was first published in booklet form on 16 May, together with a preface and a "table of duties", a brief section (added by the printer) on marriage. It was handsomely illustrated with woodcuts. By this time the *Large Catechism* had been published (21 March), and was being sold at 20 pfennigs a copy.

Although they catechisms are grounded in what Luther saw as the pressing needs of congregations, they also provide us with a clear understanding of how Luther understood the Christian faith. In effect, they are the closest we get to a systematic theology by Luther, and a simple analysis of what he says provides us with the following summary:

- The Ten Commandments are a guide for the Christian life. They tell us what God expects us to do and what we can expect if we fail to keep them. However, their real function is to show us our sin and our need for forgiveness.
- God is our creator and sustainer, a heavenly Father who, out of his goodness and mercy, provides us with all that we need, and protects us from all danger and evil.
- God is also our redeemer, who through the innocent suffering and death of Jesus, and his resurrection and ascension, has freed us from sin, death, and the power of the devil.
- Neither man's own understanding or effort can create faith in Jesus Christ nor bring him to Jesus Christ: it is the Holy Spirit who creates and nurtures faith within the fellowship of the Church.
- Part of that nurturing by the Holy Spirit also includes teaching Christians how to pray, using the pattern of the Lord's Prayer.
- At the heart of the life of the Christian community and of its individual members is the daily and abundant forgiveness of sins, which comes through the proclamation of the Word and the administration of the sacraments.
- In Baptism, Christians are given the gift of faith and new birth, and they are called on to live out that faith through day-to-day repentance.
- In the Sacrament of the Altar (the Lord's Supper) Christians are given forgiveness, life and salvation, by Jesus Christ, who is present in the bread and the wine, just as he promised at the Last Supper.
- The Church, which is the locus for all these activities, has both a *present* and a *future* dimension: the Holy Spirit will, on the last day, bring the living and the dead to eternal life.

Luther and Schools

In our brief introduction to the life of Luther in Part One we observed that, by the standards of his time, Luther was well educated. His education probably started in the elementary school in Mansfeld, the town to which the family had moved in 1484, but at the age of 13 he was sent away to Magdeburg, where he almost certainly studied in the cathedral school. While there, he came under the influence of the distinctive spirituality of the Brethren of the Common Life, a lay movement that had originated in the

Netherlands and which had spread eastwards into the Rhineland and beyond. Though they did not establish schools of their own, many individuals took schoolboys into their homes and provided them with secure lodgings, and in some places the Brethren would establish a *bursa* (hostel) in which pupils could live together. We know that during his year in Magdeburg Luther lodged in the *bursa* in the city, and that he then moved to school in Eisenach where his mother's family lived. After this he was ready to go on to higher studies and he enrolled in the university in Erfurt, a thriving institution of around 2,000 students. We also know that Luther was grateful to his father for providing him with such an education "... [he] lovingly and faithfully kept me at the University of Erfurt, by his sweat and labour to get me where I am". (LW. Vol.46, pp.250-51.)

Luther's education reflects the changes that were taking place in educational provision in the late 15th century. For centuries it had been the monasteries who ran schools, not only to train future members of their Orders, but also to educate children for life in the wider world. But there were also cathedral schools, such as that in Magdeburg, and chantry schools, each of which offered a rather broader curriculum. A very important feature of civic and economic life was the guild system, and merchants and craftsmen who belonged to these guilds often employed teachers – who might be either priests or laymen – to conduct schools to educate their children. While most of these schools were under the intellectual control of the Catholic Church, the growing influence of Christian humanism meant that in some places schools were established which tried to revive education along ancient classical lines.

This system came under threat as the Reformation got under way, and Luther was partly responsible for this – at least initially. In his treatise of 1524 *To the Councilmen of all Cities in Germany that they Establish and Maintain Christian Schools* he offered some devastating criticisms of his day. In typical style, he does not mince his words:

> It is perfectly true that if universities and monasteries were to continue as they have been in the past, and there were no other place available where youth could study and live, then I would wish that no boy would ever study at all, but would remain dumb. For it is my earnest purpose, prayer, and desire that these asses' stalls and devil's training centres should

either sink into the abyss or be converted into Christian schools.
(To the Councilmen of all Cities ... LW. Vol.45. p.352.)

Clearly, Luther was unimpressed by schools in contemporary Germany which failed to educate children effectively, "... to say nothing of the scandalous and immoral life in which many a fine young fellow was shamefully corrupted" (Ibid).

Of course, Luther was not actually suggesting that no education was better than a bad education, but rather that bad education should be replaced by good. He drew the attention of the councilmen to the vast amounts of money being spent on maintaining peace and security so that their cities could prosper, and argued that money should also be made available to reform existing schools or establish new ones. Although the response to this admonition was slow, there was some success and several towns and cities took appropriate steps.

It is one thing to establish schools and another to persuade parents to send their children to them. There is evidence to suggest that many parents simply did not see the point of education and this prompted Luther to write a sermon in 1530 entitled *On Keeping Children in School*. In an earlier sermon *On the Estate of Marriage* (1519), he had stressed how important it was for parents to raise their children properly:

> But this at least all married people should know. They can do no better work and do nothing more valuable either for God, for Christendom, for all the world, for themselves, and for their children than to bring up their children well. In comparison with this one work, that married people should bring up their children properly, there is nothing at all in pilgrimages to Rome, Jerusalem, or Compostella, nothing at all in building churches, endowing masses, or whatever good works could be named. For bringing up their children properly is the shortest road to heaven.
> *(A Sermon on the Estate of Marriage,* LW. Vol. 44. P.12.)

Now, in the 1530 sermon, Luther draws attention to the many different occupations in civic society which require education. Therefore, parents should not despise education but have their children taught so that they can perform the many duties which society demands,

Therefore go ahead and have your son study. And even if he has to beg bread for a time, you are nonetheless giving to our Lord God a fine bit of wood out of which he can carve you a lord.
(*A Sermon on Keeping Children in School*, LW. Vol. 46. p.251.)

But I hold that it is the duty of the temporal authority to compel its subjects to keep their children in school, especially the promising ones we mentioned above. For it is truly the duty of government to maintain the offices and estates that have been mentioned, so that there will always be preachers, jurists, pastors, writers, physicians, schoolmasters and the like, for we cannot do without them.
(Ibid. p.256.)

Luther's attitude towards education was twofold. He was, of course, concerned that the church should train men (and at that time it was exclusively men) for the ministry of Word and Sacrament, but he was also concerned for what we would today call "secular" occupations.

FURTHER READING

The full text of the *Instructions for the Visitors of Parish Pastors in Electoral Saxony* is in **LW. Vol.40, pp.263-320**. An old book, **Luther on Education (St. Louis, Concordia Publishing House, 1889. No ISBN)**, gives an introduction to Luther's understanding of education, together with the texts of two of his educational works, the *Letter to the Mayors and Aldermen of the Cities of Germany in Behalf of Christian Schools*, and his *Sermon on the Duty of Sending Children to School*. A more modern translation of the former can be found in **LW. Vol.45. pp.339-379**, and of the latter in **LW. Vol.46, pp.207-258**. The *Sermon on the Estate of Marriage* is in **LW. Vol.44. pp.3-13**.

A collection of papers presented at the Wittenberg University (Ohio) Luther Symposium of 1983 is to be found in **Luther and Learning (London, Associated University Presses, 1985. ISBN: 0-9416-6413-9)**, edited by Marilyn J. Harrow. **Luther's House of Learning: Indoctrinating the Young in the German Reformation (Baltimore/London, The John Hopkins University Press, 1979. ISBN: 0-8018-2051-0)**, by Gerald Strauss, is a comprehensive study of the topic.

Chapter 13 | Worship, Music and Prayer

Luther's religious conservatism is shown very clearly in his attitude towards public worship and music, which contrasts markedly from that of more radical reformers such as John Calvin (1509-1564) and Huldrych Zwingli (1484-1531). In general terms the Reformed principle was that the only things that were allowed in worship were what were enjoined by Scripture, and that anything else was forbidden. So, Calvin's reformation in Geneva strove to return to a more austere form of worship that he felt reflected the attitude of the early church.

With regard to music, the congregation made use of psalm paraphrases, since these were felt to be scriptural, and therefore permitted. More radical still was the worship which followed the practices of Zwingli in Zürich, where for decades music was frowned upon and not used in public services. Luther's attitude to worship reflects his general principle that if something is not actually forbidden by Scripture, then, provided it is not idolatrous, it can be retained.

The Mass

The principal service of public worship in the Catholic Church of Luther's day was the Mass, and, although there were variations in some parts of the Catholic Church (eg in England), the normal liturgy was what was known as the Roman rite. This had developed over fifteen hundred years and combined elements of Jewish worship, Greek drama, and Roman pagan worship. A High Mass in 1517 was a pageant of spectacular drama which re-enacted the life of Christ, focusing particularly on Christ's sacrifice on the cross. The liturgy moved from the incarnation, through the teaching ministry of Christ, and on to his passion and resurrection, and contained things which remained constant from Sunday to Sunday and elements which changed according to the Church year.

Catholic teaching emphasised the sacrificial nature of the service and taught that when the priest said the words of Christ ("This is my Body" and "This is my Blood") the bread and wine were transformed into the flesh and blood of Christ, and these were then presented to God as a continually repeated sacrifice. Luther came to view this as a "good work", and he realised that the Mass had to be restructured

Luther was concerned with what he saw as the essential theological unsoundness of the Catholic theology of worship, and, in particular, the lack of both preaching and of the active participation of the congregation. The preaching of the Gospel had been replaced by stories and legends, and the congregation had become mere spectators – a fact that was exacerbated by the service being in Latin, which only the most educated could understand.

Luther's writings about worship are not prolific, but they lay down important principles. There are three principal writings about liturgy, two of which, *Concerning the Order of Public Worship* and *An Order of Mass and Communion for the Church in Wittenberg*, both date from 1523, and the third, *The German Mass and Order of Service*, is from 1526.

The first of these documents (*Concerning the Order of Public Worship*) was written in January or February of 1523 against the background of a vacuum that had been created by the reforms carried out by Andreas Karlstadt while Luther was in the Wartburg. Private Masses had been abolished, and, while Luther fully supported that, it meant there was no longer any public worship on weekdays. This document tried to remedy this lack by suggesting orders for daily morning and evening prayer. It is a very brief document (four pages in the American edition of Luther's Works), but lays down the essential principles of evangelical worship.

Luther sets out three principles. The first is that whenever Christians gather together for worship, no matter how few they may be, there should always be preaching, however brief. Secondly, it is appropriate that Christians should gather together in the morning and the evening to hear the Word of God read and explained. Luther recognised that the pressures of daily life would make this impossible for most ordinary people in the congregation, but, "the priests and pupils, and … especially those who … will become good preachers and pastors should be present". Thirdly, the whole congregation should gather for Mass on Sundays (and for Vespers). In both services there should be preaching – in the morning on the Gospel and in the evening of the Epistle – and in the Mass there should be the opportunity to receive the Sacrament of the Altar. Daily Masses should be abolished.

In his more general advice, Luther says that the chants in the services should be retained, but that the majority of saints' days should be discontinued. However, he advocates the retention of some festivals, particularly those associated with the Virgin Mary, such as the Annunciation, the Feast of the Purification, but also, surprisingly, Mary's Nativity and her Assumption. Also to be retained are the Festival of John the Baptist, and festivals connected with Saint Paul.

In this first document, Luther deals in generalities rather than in specifics, but what is obvious is the emphasis which he places on the centrality of the Word, which is essential and which must have free course in the church. On the other hand, in the second document of 1523, issued just before Christmas of that year, he provides a much more detailed outline. This document was written in response to a request from Nicholas Hausmann, a colleague in nearby Zwickau, who wanted to know what steps Luther was taking to reform the Mass.

Traditionally, the order of the Mass could be divided into two parts. The first part ("The Service of the Word") consisted of the lessons from the Bible and the sermon, whereas the second part ("The Canon of the Mass") focused on the consecration of the bread and wine. Luther left the Service of the Word more or less untouched, but the Canon of the Mass was pruned ruthlessly. It was, he said, "an utter abomination ... [and] from here on almost everything smacks and savours of sacrifice". Luther had already made it clear in *The Babylonian Captivity of the Church* that the Mass was not, in his opinion, a sacrifice, so everything suggesting that should be repudiated, while that which was "pure and holy" should be retained.

Luther replaced the traditional Canon with an order which retained the scriptural elements and which focused on Christ's words of institution of the sacrament and the communion of the people (including the distribution of the wine, which the Catholic Church had forbidden). But, let it be remembered, all of the liturgical elements – apart from the sermon – were in Latin, although Luther encouraged the singing of hymns in German.

It was not for another three years that Luther took the inevitable step of producing a vernacular liturgy, *The German Mass and Order of Service*. Other reformers had already produced services in German, but these differed from each other and confusion was growing. Friends encouraged Luther to produce an order of service which might serve as a blueprint for a common liturgy, but he procrastinated, partly because he felt that this was a matter for each local community to decide on.

As well as that, although he was a talented musician, he recognised his own limitations. Fortunately there were others who could help with this, most notably his young colleague Johann Walter (1496-1570). What eventually emerged was something along the lines of a "Hymn Mass" in which many of the liturgical texts were replaced by hymns which could be sung by the whole congregation.

The *German Mass* did not have the effect of standardising the liturgy among the emerging evangelical churches of Germany, or indeed in the churches elsewhere which adopted the Reformation. A whole range of liturgical "families" developed, although scholars classify them according to two main types, based, respectively, on the *Formula Missae* or the *German Mass*. However, to these two we should add a third type, because in south-western Germany (particularly in Württemberg) a form of worship developed which was not based on the traditional Mass, but on the medieval preaching service. This much simpler liturgy was also characteristic of the Lutheran Church in Hungary.

Outside Germany Lutheranism spread northwards into the Nordic countries, which were then divided into two kingdoms. To the west there was Denmark, which also included the Faroe Islands, Iceland, and Norway, and to the west was Sweden, which included Finland. A prime mover in the reformation in the Danish kingdom was Luther's close colleague, Johannes Bugenhagen (1485-1558), who introduced a vernacular liturgy based on the *German Mass*, whereas the liturgy introduced into Sweden by the reformer Olavus Petri (1493-1552) followed the more conservative *Formula Missae*. What is of interest, and what differentiates Lutheran worship from that of the Reformed churches, is the extent to which Latin remained in use alongside the vernacular languages. Luther himself felt that this was important because it ensured that the younger generation in particular would have the opportunity to learn and practise the language.

The Occasional Services

Today, most Lutheran churches have books which contain liturgical orders of service for many different occasions. These are usually referred to as the "Occasional Services", and, while Luther never attempted to compile such a book, he did write orders for baptism, private confession, and marriage. All of these were published as printed texts, but he also wrote an order for the ordination of pastors, although it seems that this only existed in manuscript form. He produced no funeral service, but he expressed his views about how burials should be performed in the preface that he wrote to a collection of funeral hymns produced in Wittenberg in 1542. Completely missing is an order for confirmation: Luther did not approve of the rite of confirmation and was wary of a service which seemed to be adding things to baptism.

Luther produced two orders for baptism. The first was the *Tauff Buchlin Verdeutcht* ("Little Baptismal Book in German"), which was essentially a revised version of the traditional Roman Catholic service. This was the one contemporary Catholic service of which Luther approved, and in *The Babylonian Captivity of the Church* he blessed God that this was the one sacrament which had been preserved "unspoiled and unspotted". Luther's order included a host of ceremonial actions such as breathing under the infant's eyes, putting salt in its mouth, touching its right ear with spittle, several anointings with oil, vesting in a white robe, and the giving of a candle. Luther's justification for continuing with these rites was that he did not want to offend parishioners by abolishing them too precipitously. One innovation, however, was the inclusion of what is known as the "Flood Prayer", in which stories of Noah and the drowning of the Egyptians in the Red Sea were used to prefigure baptism. The second order of baptism appeared three years later, in 1526, and this was a much simpler rite, in which most of the ritual acts described above were omitted. Luther maintained that these were man-made usages which could obscure the real meaning of the sacrament.

As with the baptism service, Luther produced two orders for private confession – one in 1529 and the second in 1531. The 1529 version first appeared in the *Small Catechism* immediately after the section on baptism, under the title of *A Short Order of Confession Before the Priest for the Common Man.* This was a very brief order, but was replaced by the longer 1531 order, Again, this was inserted into the catechism after the section on baptism, but was almost a mini-catechism in its own right, the actual order being prefaced by a series of questions and answers explaining the practice.

The provision of these orders for private confession gives an indication of the value Luther placed on the practice. However, he was clearly unhappy at the way in which things were done in the contemporary Roman Catholic Church. He saw private confession as a privilege which gave Christians the opportunity of receiving God's forgiveness so that their burdened consciences could be relieved, whereas he felt that the Catholic Church, by making confession compulsory and by demanding a complete confession of sins, simply added to the burden.

Finally, under the heading of "Occasional Services" we should briefly mention Luther's 1529 *Traubüchlein für einfältigen Pfarrher* ("The Order of Marriage for Common Pastors"). We know that in *The Babylonian Captivity of the Church* Luther had denied that marriage was a sacrament, but he clearly felt that it was appropriate for the church to continue to bless couples. His service included three parts: the publication of the banns from the pulpit; the marriage, conducted at the entrance to the church; and the blessing of the marriage before the altar.

Hymns

Biographies of Luther from the very earliest testify to the fact that he was musical. He would have been taught music in the schools that he attended and the skills that he acquired there would have been honed during his time as a monk. Tradition has it that he had a good voice and was a competent performer on the lute, and these skills and talents were used in the service of the church through the music that composed for the different liturgical orders and for the hymns which came to characterise the Lutheran church.

Luther began to write hymns after his return to Wittenberg from the Wartburg in 1522. One of the earliest that he composed is *Ein neues Lied wir heben an* ("A new song here shall be begun"), which was written to commemorate the first Lutheran martyrs to die for their faith. These were two Augustinian monks by the names of Hendrik Vos and Jan van Essen, who were burned at the stake in the market place in Brussels on 1 July 1523. Deeply moved by this, Luther composed the hymn, setting his words to a traditional German folk song.

The first collection of hymns appeared in a small book entitled *Das Achtliederbuch* ("The Book of Eight Songs") which contained three hymns by Paul Speratus (1484-1551), four by Luther himself, and one by an anonymous author. A much larger hymnal appeared in the late summer of 1524. This was edited by Johann Walter (1496-1570) and contained 38 chorales, of which 24 were by Luther. Curiously, there is some uncertainty about when Luther's most famous hymn *Ein feste Burg ist unser Gott* (known to British readers in Thomas Carlyles' translation "A safe stronghold our God is still") was actually written, but it was certainly sometime before 1530.

Since these modest beginnings, Lutheran hymnody has grown enormously and Lutheran churches across the world have produced hymns and church music for use in worship. Some of these hymns have become well known across denominational boundaries and throughout the world, eg "Praise to the Lord, the Almighty ..." and "Now thank we all our God ...", whereas others, such as those of the Danish bishop Nikolaj Severin Fredrik Grundtvig (1783-1872), deserve to be much better known.

Lutheran Worship in the 21st Century

At the heart of Luther's reform of worship were the liturgy and the observance of the church year, and, broadly speaking, these continue to be central to Lutheran public worship today. In some countries, churches have strict requirements that all congregations should follow a common pattern of worship, while in others there may be more room for flexibility. However, in all Lutheran churches there is a requirement that the Word should be preached and the sacraments should be administered, and that these activities should normally be undertaken by people who are appropriately qualified and publicly called to the office of the ministry.

Luther said that all Christian worship should include preaching on the Word, no matter how small an assembly or how brief a sermon or meditation it might be. Consequently, preaching is taken very seriously, and although individual ministers will develop their own styles, it is always biblically based and it is usually expected that they preach on the lectionary prescribed by the church. Sermons are usually only delivered by ministers who have received a thorough theological training, which typically includes learning the original languages of the Bible. Only in very particular circumstances are there lay preachers, and there are some churches which provide books of sermons for lay men and women to use if no minister can be present.

Although there have been times when baptism was regarded as a private family matter and it was celebrated in the home, it is usually the case now that infants are baptised publicly in the main Sunday service. Lutherans continue to believe that in baptism God establishes a fatherly relationship with the child that is based on his forgiveness, but that individuals are called on to live out their baptism in daily repentance. In countries where Lutheranism has been the "established" church, this has meant that almost everyone is baptised, but a few voices have been raised which question this practice. One such voice was that of the German theologian Dietrich Bonhoeffer (1906-1945) who raised questions about "cheap grace" in his book *The Cost of Discipleship* (1937).

Lutherans also adhere to Luther's teaching about the Lord's Supper. They believe that when the members of a congregation gather together to break bread and share wine in the way that Jesus commanded, then he is truly present among them, forgiving them their sins. Until recently, most Lutheran congregations only allowed young people to receive the sacrament once they had received instruction from the minister and been received into communicant membership through a service of Confirmation, but it is now becoming increasingly common for younger children to accompany their parents and receive the bread and wine. Sadly, in some places, confirmation has become little more than a rite of passage involving big family parties and expensive presents.

Luther on Prayer

Luther provided Christian congregations with orders of service that they could use in public prayer and worship, but he was also concerned with private prayer and devotion, and much of this was based on his own experience of prayer.

Martin Luther was a child of prayer. Growing up he would have been taught to say the prayers that were common to all Christians of his day, and in particular the *Pater Noster* (the Lord's Prayer) and the *Ave Maria* (the Hail Mary). He would also have been encouraged to pray to the saints, and particularly, in his case, to St Anne, widely believed to be the mother of the Virgin Mary and the patron saint of miners. As we have seen, it was for her assistance that he cried out after he was almost killed by the bolt of lightning near the village of Stottenheim, and it was to her that he made the promise to become a monk.

Prayer filled his life as an Augustinian monk. Together with his fellow friars he joined in communal prayer seven times a day, but he was also expected to engage in private prayer. This was something that he found very difficult because other things impinged on his time. His talents as an administrator were recognised very early on and he was given more and more responsibilities, all of which meant that he got behind in his prayers and drove himself hard to catch up on what he had missed. He was a conscientious monk who suffered great anguish because he felt that he was failing.

As a reformer, Luther was often in danger and he knew that prayer was a great consolation and source of strength. He prayed, and he taught others to pray. After discovering the extent of the ignorance of ordinary people regarding the central teachings of the faith, Luther wrote his two catechisms in 1529 – books that were to be used by the head of the household to instruct members of the family in what they should know. The third section in both catechisms was concerned with the Lord's Prayer, and in *The Small Catechism* Luther explains how people should pray. He does not speak in the abstract or in generalities, but stresses that Christians can pray to God with complete confidence, knowing that he is their Father and that they are his children.

In 1535, Peter Beskendorf, who was Luther's barber, asked him to teach him to pray, and Luther responded with a short booklet which has become a classic. It was entitled *A Simple Way to Pray, for Master Peter the Barber*, and it describes in simple terms how Christians should pray to God. Luther provided simple outlines for individuals to use in their daily worship, including saying the Ten Commandments, the Lord's Prayer, and the Apostles' Creed, together with a psalm "or whatever your devotion may suggest", and contained in this two beautiful prayers – one each for the morning and the evening.

Luther himself did not provide a scheme for daily Bible reading, but over the centuries many such lectionaries have been written and these provide useful meditations on the texts. Very common in some parts of the Lutheran Church is the use of the "Daily Watchwords" (*Die Losungen*) published each year by the Moravian Church, with which Lutherans have often enjoyed close fellowship.

As they exist today, the Watchwords are published in the form of a book, and on each page there are two Bible texts – one from the Old Testament and one from the New – together with a hymn verse and a short prayer.

FURTHER READING

The liturgical writings by Luther referred to above can all be found in **Luther's Works, American Edition, Volume 53: Liturgy and Hymns (Philadelphia, Fortress Press, 1965. No ISBN)**. An excellent introduction to the subject can be found in Vilmos Vajta's **Luther on Worship: An Interpretation (Philadelphia, Muhlenberg Press, 1958. No ISBN)**. Vilmos Vajta was a distinguished Hungarian theologian, living in Sweden, and this is a translation by U. S. Leupold of his doctoral thesis, originally published as **Die Theologie des Gottesdienstes bei Luther**.

A very thorough study of the development of Lutheran liturgies can be found in Luther D. Reed's **The Lutheran Liturgy (Philadelphia, Fortress Press, 1947. No ISBN)**. One of the most thorough treatments of the subject of liturgy is **Christian Liturgy: Catholic and Evangelical (Minneapolis, Fortress Press, 1997. ISBN: 0-8006-2726-1)** by Frank C. Senn. This is a very ecumenical study of the history of Christian liturgy, but Chapters 8, 9, 10, and 12 will be of particular interest to Lutherans.

Readers with a special interest in music are referred to Robin A. Leaver's **Luther's Liturgical Music: Principles and Implications (Grand Rapids/Cambridge, William B. Eerdmans Publishing Company, 2007. ISBN: 978-0-8028-3221-4)**.

The text of Luther's guidance to Master Peter can be found in pp.217-233 of a volume in the series **The Classics of Western Spirituality**. The volume is entitled **Luther's Spirituality (Mahwah NJ, Paulist Press, 2007. ISBN: 978-0-8091-3949-1)**, and is edited by Philip D. W. Krey and Peter D. S. Krey. The complete text of Dietrich Bonhoeffer's **The Cost of Discipleship** is readily available. The text used by the author is available at **London, SCM Press, 1969, ISBN: 334-00259-1**, but a newer edition is now in print.

Chapter 14 | Luther and Other Faiths

Today, that part of the world that we label "the West" is a society that is "multi": multi-ethnic, multi-cultural, and multi-faith. Modern Germany is a classic example of this: because of the *Shoah* (the Holocaust) the number of Jews is now tiny, but its immigrant Muslim (for decades predominantly Turkish) community is large and growing. The situation in Luther's day was rather the reverse: the empire was almost uniformly Christian, with small and scattered Jewish communities but virtually no Muslims. Nevertheless, Luther found time to write about both Jews and Muslims.

Luther and the Jews

Although Luther was a creative figure who made an important contribution to the history of Christianity, it cannot be denied that he could be irascible and that this was often reflected in what he wrote and how he wrote. This can be seen very obviously in his writings about the Roman Church and the papacy, about the peasants, and, most notoriously, about the Jews. Although it does not in any way excuse his tone, it is important to stress that Luther's "anti-Jewish" writings were not based on racially motivated principles, but have a consistent theological basis.

Luther wrote extensively about the Jews and many of his theological writings reflect a dialogue with Jewish thought. He was thoroughly steeped in the teachings of St Paul, and he emphasised the well-known tenets of *Sola Scriptura* (that Scripture alone is the sole authority for doctrine) and justification by faith through grace (*Sola Fide, Sola Gratia*). With regard to Scripture, one of his exegetical principles was his insistence that the Old Testament should be regarded as "the swaddling clothes of Christ", ie that the

Old Testament should be read as a Christian book: its prophecies concerning the Messiah had been fulfilled in Christ, though the Jews denied this. Luther was sharply critical of some of the growing number of experts in the Hebrew language, such as Sebastian Münster (1488-1552), who appeared to deny this fundamental belief and accept rabbinic interpretations of the Scriptures, as expressed in the *Talmud*. A second principle, as we have already seen in a previous chapter, was that the whole of Scripture, be it the Old or the New Testament, can be divided into Law and Gospel. While the Law offers guidance on how we should live our lives, its pre-eminent purpose is to serve as a mirror to show us our sin. The Gospel, on the other hand, is the message that God, for Christ's sake, forgives us our sin and restores us to a relationship with him that is based on faith, rather than obedience to the Law. Such obedience is, for Luther, "works righteousness" and is anathema because it contradicts the Gospel, and he is critical of those who practice it, whether they be Jews, Catholics, or Anabaptists. It can, of course, be argued that these principles might hinder looking at biblical texts in context.

Luther's specifically "Jewish" writings are five in number: *That Jesus Christ was born a Jew* (1523); *Against the Sabbatarians* (1538); *On the Jews and their Lies* (1543); *On the Unknowable Name and the Generations of Christ* (1543); and *A Warning Against the Jews* (1546). To these we can add a letter of 1514 (ie long before Luther became famous) addressed to his colleague Georg Spalatin (1484-1545), who had written to him to ask his opinion of Johannes Reuchlin (1455-1522). Reuchlin was a distinguished jurist who was also a knowledgeable Hebraist, but he had fallen foul of the Dominicans of the University of Cologne and their spokesman, Johannes Pfefferkorn (1469-1523). Pfefferkorn was himself a converted Jew and had suggested that all Jewish books should be seized and burnt.

When asked by the emperor for his opinion about this, Reuchlin had responded in 1511 with a short book entitled *Recommendation Whether to Confiscate, Destroy and Burn all Jewish Books*. Reuchlin, as we might expect from a scholar, comes out strongly against what Pfefferkorn was proposing, but he does not oppose him out of love for the Jews *per se*, but out of concern for learning. In the book he makes a recommendation that teachers of Hebrew should be appointed in some of the principal universities, but his rationale for this is that such a step would make it easier to convert the Jews.

This is an aim with which Luther has sympathy, and he expressed his feelings in his letter to Spalatin:

> I have come to the conclusion that the Jews will always curse and blaspheme God and his King Christ, as all the prophets had predicted. He who neither reads nor understands this, as yet knows no theology, in my opinion. And so I presume the men of Cologne [the Dominicans who were attacking Reuchlin] cannot understand the Scripture, because it is necessary that such things take place to fulfil prophecy. If they are trying to stop the Jews blaspheming, they are working to prove the Bible and God liars ... But trust God to be true, even if a million men of Cologne sweat to make him false. Conversion of the Jews will be the work of God alone from within, and not of man working – or rather playing – from without. If these offences be taken away, worse will follow. For they are thus given over by the wrath of God to reprobation, that they may become incorrigible, as Ecclesiastes says, for everyone who is incorrigible is rendered worse rather than better by correction.
> (*Luther's Letter to Spalatin*, available at https://sourcebooks.fordham.edu/mod/1514luther.asp.)

This early comment on the Jews encapsulates Luther's attitude towards them: they have rejected Christ by refusing to acknowledge him as Messiah, and, though it is to be hoped that they might see the error of their ways and convert, this could only be through the work of God.

Later, as the work of the reformation grew apace, Luther came to believe that the "re-discovery" of the Gospel would naturally lead the Jews to convert, and some of his early writings, such as his *Magnificat put into German and Explained* (1521), and *That Jesus Christ was Born a Jew* (1523), show a genuine love and concern for them and a hope they they will, indeed, be converted. In the former, he insisted that the Jews be treated in a loving and Christian manner, and in the latter he quite clearly demonstrated his *theological* concern. This appears to contrast sharply with his later writings, in particular *Against the Jews and their Lies* of 1543, which we can briefly summarise as follows:

- The Jews bleed the German nation dry because of their extortionate use of usury in their financial dealings; so, their

- gold and silver should be seized and they should be forced to work with their hands;
- The German people should set fire to Jewish synagogues and homes, seize their religious writings, and prevent rabbis from teaching on pain of execution;
- The right of Jews to travel freely on the highways should be abolished, and they should be driven out of the country.

Many writers, such as the historian William Schirer in his *The Rise and Fall of the Third Reich* (1959), have suggested that this is, in effect, a blueprint for the anti-Semitism of the National Socialist state; but what lies behind Luther's vicious attack is disillusionment. He had firmly believed that, once presented with the message of the Gospel, the Jews would recognise the error of their ways and convert.

Although it is no justification, it is worth pointing out that, like many of his theological friends and foes, Luther frequently made use of language both coarse and fierce. By modern standards it is to be deplored, but we should not forget that he was not alone in his attitudes, and there are many stories of Jews in late medieval Europe being victimised. One of the most notorious persecutions of Jews in the 15th century had been provoked in Bohemia (and elsewhere) by the teaching of the Franciscan friar Giovanni da Capestrano (1386-1456), who was canonised by the Roman Catholic Church in 1690. Among the many excesses his preaching inspired was the torture and burning of more than 40 Jews, and the suicide of many more, in Breslau in June 1453. Similarly, 38 Jews were burned in Berlin in 1510, and five Jews in Würzburg were imprisoned and tortured on a charge of ritual murder.

What Luther wrote about the Jews is indefensible: it degenerates into vicious ranting and is inconsistent with his oft-repeated guidance that we should be as Christ to our neighbours. Modern Lutherans have sought to disassociate themselves from his views, and since the end of the Second World War, many Lutheran Churches and representative bodies have issued statements condemning what he wrote, eg the Lutheran World Federation in its *Documentation No 48: Shift in Jewish-Lutheran Relations*.

Luther and Islam

It might be appropriate to add a few words here about Luther's attitude towards Islam, though he wrote much less than he did about the Jews. Luther was able to comment on the Jews and their writings because copies of the Hebrew Scriptures (the *Tanakh*) and of the *Talmud* were available in Germany. Furthermore, there were communities of Jews in different parts of the Empire, and although we do not know if Luther ever met one, we do know that in 1537 he had a correspondence with Josel of Rosheim (1480-1554), who had asked Luther to intervene with the Elector to get permission to travel through Saxony (Luther refused). We might also add that there was a direct link with Judaism because the *Tanakh* had been incorporated into Christian scripture as the Old Testament.

Things were very different when it came to Islam. There were few Muslims in Germany and we can be fairly sure that Luther never met one. On the other hand the threat from the Ottoman Turks cast a constant shadow over the empire and was one of the main preoccupations of the emperor throughout the 1520s and 1530s.

In 1529 the Turks were besieging Vienna, and, as a consequence, Luther produced two writings, *Concerning War Against the Turks,* and the *Army Sermon Against the Turks.* In the former he makes it clear that the military threat from the Turks has to be repulsed, but that such operations were not to be considered as a crusade. Luther sees the Turks in eschatological terms as God's agents against sin and apostasy. "Pastors and preachers", he says, "ought diligently to exhort people to repentance and prayer ... [because] we have earned God's wrath and disfavour, so that he justly gives us into the hands of the devil and the Turk." (LW. Vol. 46, p.171.)

We should note that Luther hardly ever refers to Muslims, but usually to "the Turks", and, as with the Jews, he takes an ambivalent view of their teachings.

Firstly, he takes what appears to be a positive attitude towards the Quran, and he was firm in his assertion that its publication should be allowed. A Zürich theologian, Theodor Bibliander (1504-1564) had produced a reliable and scholarly version in 1543, but the city council of Basel, where it was to be published, forbade its printing and briefly imprisoned the printer, Johannes Oporin. Luther wrote to the council, pointing out that it was important for pastors to know what was in the Quran so that they could strengthen people's faith. Theologians from Strasbourg added their support and the book was finally published with a preface by Luther himself. As we can see, Luther's reasons for wanting the Quran published were identical with his reasons for wanting to preserve copies of the *Talmud* – only when scholars were aware of what was in it could it be refuted.

With regard to the teachings of Islam, Luther approaches these from the same standpoint as he does the teachings of the Roman Catholics and the Jews, ie that of justification by faith. He likens them to the teachings of, "a Papist, a Jew ... and a heretic". Commenting on Galatians 4: 8, he says, "For the Turk thinks the self-same thing as the Charterhouse [Carthusian] monk does: namely, if I do this or that [work], God will be merciful to me; if I do it not, he will be angry" (*Luther on Galatians*, pp.380-381). In other words, Islam is a religion based on "works righteousness". Furthermore, it is a religion which, while acknowledging that Jesus is a prophet, denies that he is divine, and so has a deficient Christology.

Although some research has been done on Luther and Islam, this is a field that needs further investigation. Interested readers might like to start with a readable essay by the American scholar Gregory J. Miller of Malone College, Canton, Ohio, entitled *Luther on the Turks and Islam* (for details, see below).

FURTHER READING

In *The Magnificat Put into German and Explained* can be found **Luther's Spirituality** (Eds. Philip D. W. Krey and Peter D. S. Krey) **(New York/Mahwah, Paulist Press, 2007. ISBN: 978-0-8091-3949-1)**, and the English translation of *On the Unknowable Name and the Generations of Christ* is in Gerhard Falk's **The Jew in Christian Theology (Jefferson/London, McFarland & Company, Inc., 1992. ISBN: 978-0-7864-7744-9)**. The other writings by Luther mentioned above can be found in **Luther's Works: American Edition, Volumes 45 and 47 (Philadelphia/Fortress Press, 1962 and 1971. ISBN: 0-8006-0345-1 and 0-8006-0357-8 respectively)**.

Other relevant literature includes **Martin Luther, the Bible and the Jewish People: A Reader**, edited by Brooks Schramm and Kirsi I. Stjerna **(Philadephia, Fortress Press, 2012. ISBN: 978-0-8006-9804-1)**, and Thomas Kaufmann's **Luther's Jews: A Journey into Anti-Semitism (Oxford, Oxford University Press, 2017. ISBN: 978-0-19-873854-1)**, translated by Lesley Sharpe and Jeremy Noakes.

William Schirer's **The Rise and Fall of the Third Reich (New York, Simon and Schuster, 1959. ISBN: 978-1-4516-5168-3)** is scathing in its comments on Luther (see pp.91 and 230).

Luther's treatise on *War Against the Turk* can be found in **LW. Vol.46, pp.155-205**, and there are numerous references to the Turks in the *Table Talk* **(LW. Vol.54)**. One of the few papers devoted to the subject is by Gregory. J. Miller, *Luther and the Turks and Islam*, in **Harvesting Martin Luther's Reflections on Theology, Ethics, and the Church (Grand Rapids/Cambridge, William B. Eerdman's Publishing Company, 2004. ISBN: 0-8028-2486-2)**, edited by Timothy J. Wengert.

Chapter 15 | Author's Postscript to Part Two

How on earth to sum up the main features of such a prolific and wide-ranging writer as Martin Luther? He wrote extensively on all manner of topics, many of which are of relevance to Christians today but some of which dealt with issues of his own time and which do not mean much to us in the 21st century. The topics selected for inclusion in this Part will not satisfy everyone, and, no doubt, there will be some who question what has been chosen. However, there is so much literature on Luther available that interested readers should have no difficulty in pursuing their own research into areas they feel have been neglected.

How on earth to be even-handed in dealing with Luther? He was a complex character who, it has to be admitted, was obsessed by many things: justification by faith, the Christocentricity of the Bible, and the devil, to name but three. The word "obsessed" in this context is perhaps not the right one and it might be better to substitute the word "overwhelmed": he was overwhelmed by the grace of God as he had experienced it. However, this sometimes made him less than gracious: Luther was no diplomat, and his language about the Papacy, the peasants, and the Jews, as well as about individuals to whom he took a dislike, was sometimes downright un-Christian. In some cases, this has made it difficult to defend what he said and wrote, and there are those who maintain that his legacy in some areas (eg the fate of the Jews in Nazi Germany) was lethal. Although they may not agree that the consequences were as critics make out – there have been many other Christians through the centuries who have been anti-Jewish – modern day Lutherans deplore how he wrote and have sought to distance themselves from it.

Luther's definition of a Christian is that he or she is *simul iustus et peccator* – at one and the same time a saint and a sinner. Luther was certainly both. He was the first to acknowledge that he was a sinner and to admit (some of) his failings, but he also knew himself to be a sinner and a failure who was loved by God and forgiven by him for Christ's sake.

Part 3 | Luther's Legacy in Britain and Ireland

In the preceding two Parts we have looked briefly at the life and times of Martin Luther and then at some aspects of his legacy; now, in the two Parts that follow, we shall be turning our attention to Great Britain and Ireland.

It may come as a surprise to Christians in other denominations to learn that, in one form or another, Lutherans have been in these islands since the time of the Reformation, but by the end of this Part it will not only be clear that this is the case, but that there are actually *three* histories. Firstly, there is the story of the Reformations themselves (in the plural because the experiences of England and Wales and of Scotland were rather different), when individuals came under the influence of Luther and his theology and sometimes died for their beliefs. Secondly, there is the story of the Lutheran congregations established in Great Britain and Ireland after 1669 – a story of people from different parts of the world finding themselves here and wanting to "sing the Lord's song in a strange land" (Psalm 137: 4). Thirdly, there is the story of how men and women of different denominations have been influenced by Luther's legacy and have tried to interpret it in the British and Irish context – a story that deserves a book to itself.

Altar frontal from St Anne's Lutheran Church in London

Chapter 16 | The Reformation

On 30 July 1540, six men were executed at Smithfield, just outside the northern wall of the City of London. They had been strapped, two by two, onto wooden hurdles, which were then dragged by horses through the foul-smelling streets of the capital to their place of execution. None of them had had a trial: the king, Henry VIII (reigned 1509-1547), had had them condemned by a parliamentary Bill of Attainder, which had simply declared them to be guilty. Three of them, Richard Featherstone, Thomas Abel, and Edward Powell, had been found guilty of treason, and they were to be hanged, drawn, and quartered; the other three, Robert Barnes, Thomas Garrett, and William Jerome, had been pronounced guilty of being "incorrigible heretics", and would be burned at the stake. It was a bizarre situation: the "traitors" were traditionalists who remained loyal to the Pope and would not accept that Henry was Head of the English Church; the "heretics" were men who had no difficulty in accepting Henry's title, but who had been influenced by the German reformer, Martin Luther (1483-1546), and who would have liked Henry to have reformed the church more than he had done.

Another bizarre feature in all of this is that Henry, who had been king since 1509, is now often seen as a larger-than-life figure ("Bluff King Hal"), who ruled over a jolly place, often described as "Merry England". In fact, he was, by 1540, a cruel tyrant who might reasonably be called "Harry the Terrible", and, by the time that he died in 1547, he had divorced two wives, executed two more, lost a wife in childbirth, and, at one point, nearly executed his last wife for supposed heresy. He had also executed many of the nobility who actually had a better claim to the throne than him; he had dealt ruthlessly with those who opposed him, or who became "over-mighty"; he had separated the English church from the Roman

Catholic Church; he had destroyed the monasteries, and, at one and the same time seized their wealth and deprived the people of the services they had offered; and he had destroyed the places that people had been wont to visit on pilgrimage. Yet, apart from throwing over the supremacy of the Pope, very little had changed where doctrine was concerned, and the England in which Robert Barnes and the others died had an official formulation of faith – the Six Articles – which was very traditional in what it ordered people to believe. The one big difference, although its significance was perhaps not yet fully appreciated, was that there was now an official Bible in English in every church.

So, by 1540, there had been a church reformation of sorts, but it satisfied no-one. For traditionalists, it had gone too far, and Henry had despatched those who opposed his changes. Some of those who were executed are well-known, such as Bishop John Fisher (1469-1535) and Sir Thomas More (1478-1535), whereas others, like Robert Aske (d.1536) or the nameless Carthusian monks of London, are less familiar. Similarly, some of those interested in reform are well known – Queen Anne Boleyn (1501?-1536) and Thomas Cromwell (1485-1540) both had reformist sympathies; but there are others, such as Thomas Bilney (1495-1531), John Frith (1503-1533), and John Lambert, who are really only known to scholars. The problem was that, whereas the traditionalists more or less agreed on what they believed, those with reformist ideas were divided, and, although often referred to as "Lutherans", they were often far from agreeing with what Luther had said.

But let us backtrack three decades to the time when Henry became king in 1509. When his father Henry VII died, young Henry was just short of his eighteenth birthday, and he succeeded the rather dour and miserly man who had ruled England since seizing the throne from Richard III in 1485. The Tudor claim to the throne was tenuous in the extreme, although it was strengthened when the victor of the Battle of Bosworth married the late Edward IV's older daughter, Elizabeth. The man who eventually became Henry VIII was their second son, so never would have succeeded to the throne had his older brother, Arthur, not died in 1502. Arthur had married the Spanish princess, Catherine of Aragon (1485-1536), and after his premature death a tentative plan was made for Henry, now Prince of Wales, to marry her – full permission for this having been received (or so it seemed) from the Pope. His father delayed putting this plan into action for years, but one of the first things that the new king did was to marry Catherine. If only Catherine had been able to give Henry a son, the whole religious history of England and Wales – not to mention Ireland – might have been different; but she could not, and the only child who lived beyond infancy was a daughter, Mary, born in 1516 (d.1558).

Now, one thing we need to know is that Henry was well versed in theology, although this was to prove a very mixed blessing. After it became clear that Catherine would not provide a son and heir to guarantee the continuation of the Tudor dynasty, he began to question the validity of the marriage, even though the Pope had permitted it. The Old Testament book of Leviticus seemed to contradict itself: one verse forbade a man to marry his dead brother's widow, another verse said it was alright so long as the brother had had no children with her. Henry persuaded himself that it had been wrong to marry Catherine, and he came to the conclusion that he needed an *annulment* of the marriage (not, as is frequently said, a *divorce*). It has to be said, however, that Henry's motives were not entirely altruistic: he had always had a roving eye for a beautiful lady, and had already had several mistresses, one of whom, Bessie Blount, provided him with an illegitimate son, Henry Fitzroy, Duke of Richmond (1519-1536). For a while, a certain Mary Boleyn was the royal mistress, and it was an association with this family which brought about the downfall of Queen Catherine, because Mary had an attractive and sophisticated sister called Anne, who had spent several years at the royal court of France. Henry fell for her in a big way, and since Anne would not, under any circumstances, agree simply to being the royal mistress, he was determined to marry her. So began "the King's Great Matter", which dominated court thinking during the end of the 1520s and was only resolved in 1533 after Henry had renounced the authority of the Pope over the English Church.

If anyone had suggested in 1509 that Henry would disown the Pope and split the English church off from the rest of western Christendom, they would have been laughed at. England may not have been particularly merry, but it was certainly Catholic. And, it was very visibly Catholic: the whole country was divided into dioceses and parishes, and every parish had its church, and every diocese a cathedral. Similarly, there were monasteries, nunneries, and friaries everywhere, and, in a country with no national health system or state education, these institutions provided people – especially in rural areas – with rudimentary medicine, elementary education, and occasional welfare support. If they could afford it, people went on pilgrimages to places like Canterbury, Glastonbury, and Walsingham, they watched or took part in mystery plays, and they worshipped God, week by week, at the celebration of the church's main worship service – the Mass.

There were a few people who dissented from all of this, notably the Lollards – radical followers of the 14th century "heretic" John Wycliffe (1329?-1384), an Oxford theologian-cum-philosopher who had challenged much of traditional Catholic dogma and whose early followers had translated the Bible into English. Incidentally, England was almost unique in Europe in that it had, since 1408, forbidden the translation of the Bible from the official Latin version, the "Vulgate", on pain of death. Faced with the threat of being burned alive, the Lollards kept a very low profile, though we know they still existed in East Anglia, the Chilterns, parts of the West Country, and in south-west Scotland. Far less radical, and very much seeking to reform abuses from within, were scholars who were influenced by what we call the "New Learning" – men like the Dean of St Paul's, John Colet (1486-1519). He was a friend of the towering European intellectual of the day, the Dutchman, Desiderius Erasmus (1466-1536), who had pioneered a new version of the Latin New Testament, with an accompanying critical Greek text based on extant manuscripts.

Henry's support for the Pope was at its most evident in the early 1520s. By this time the Catholic Church was under attack by the hitherto unknown provincial German monk called Martin Luther. As we have seen, he had come to the church's attention in 1517, when he had posted his "95 Theses" onto the door of the Castle Church in Wittenberg, the town where he taught theology in the newly-established university. The theses were originally written in Latin and were intended for academic debate, but, thanks to the printing press, that contemporary miracle of technology, they soon spread across Germany in a vernacular translation. Luther's attack was on what he saw as the scandal of indulgences – official documents which, if purchased, effectively bought you out of the pains of purgatory, the place of purification between earth and heaven – but by 1520 the base of his theology had broadened. In that year he produced three important documents, *The Freedom of the Christian Man; The Prelude to the Babylonian Captivity of the Church;* and *The Address to the Christian Nobility of the German Nation.* Central to these documents was Saint Paul's doctrine of "Justification by

Faith", but, in effect, Luther was attacking different aspects of the whole structure of the medieval church. As far as the church was concerned, this was all very explosive, and when Henry was made aware by his advisers of the threat from Luther, he decided to act.

The contemporary Catholic Church held that there were seven sacraments, church ordinances which, it said, had been instituted by Christ: baptism, the sacrament of the altar (the Mass), penance, confirmation, marriage, ordination, and extreme unction. These were necessary rites which helped Christians achieve the aim of eventually getting to heaven, but in his *Prelude to the Babylonian Captivity of the Church,* Luther asserted that only two of the sacraments – baptism and the Mass – had actually been commanded by Christ. (He did, at first, also include penance, but eventually said that repenting of one's sins was really part of baptism.) Whether or not Henry actually wrote it, or was helped by his theological advisers, a book appeared bearing the king's name and called *Assertio Septem Sacramentorum* ("A Defence of the Seven Sacraments") re-affirming the traditional number of the sacraments. Not a particularly well written or exciting book, it managed to win the king the Pope's blessing and the title of *Fidei Defensor* ("Defender of the Faith"), a title still borne by British kings and queens – though the faith they now defend is not quite the one that the Pope had in mind!

It is clear that there was genuine fear that Luther's ideas and writings might spread to England, as, indeed, they did. John Foxe (1506-1587), who nearly fifty years later wrote a history of the men and women who were put to death for their beliefs – the *Acts and Monuments* (universally known as "Foxe's Book of Martyrs") – tells us that in the early 1520s students in Cambridge University met together at an inn known as "The White Horse" in order to discuss Luther's ideas. Whether this was really "Little Germany", as Foxe and the modern blue plaque on the wall where the inn used to stand tell us, there must be some truth in the story. What we *do* know for certain is that there were book burnings, ordered by the church, and that these took place in both Cambridge and London.

The burning of books was followed by the burning of people, although this did not happen all at once. The first death to become known across the nation was that of Thomas Bilney, a priest from Norfolk who initially fell foul of the king's chief adviser, Cardinal Thomas Wolsey (1474-1530), and, more ominously, of Sir Thomas More, Wolsey's successor. Wolsey opposed heresy, but he preferred to burn books rather than people; not so Thomas More. Bilney was tried, found guilty of heresy, and burned to death in Norwich in 1531. He is sometimes called "Lutheran", but, although he does seem to have believed in justification by faith, he was a traditionalist who believed in the supremacy of the Pope, and the official teaching of the church about the Mass ("Transubstantiation"). What really seems to have annoyed the church were his attacks on the veneration of the saints and their images. Perhaps we can say that Bilney was a sincere man who stands half-way between the traditional church and Luther.

There were others, however, who stood closer to Luther, and in particular, William Tyndale (1494-1535) and Robert Barnes (1495-1540).

Although his roots lay partly in Northumberland and partly in East Anglia, William Tyndale (1494-1536) hailed from Gloucestershire, and has become famous because he translated the New Testament into English, along with six of the books of the Old Testament. He had studied in Oxford, in what is now Hertford College, and after a spell as a tutor to the children of a Gloucestershire landowner, he conceived the idea of translating the Bible into English. He was appalled by the ignorance of many of the clergy that he met, and is supposed to have spoken his famous words to one of the local priests, "If God spares my life, I will cause the boy that drives the plough to know more of the Scriptures than you do". Naively, Tyndale went to London in the hope that its bishop, Cuthbert Tunstall (1474-1559), would support his project, but Tunstall, who was himself something of a scholar, was having none of it. Tyndale decided that discretion was the better part of valour, and went to the continent, spending the rest of his life, first in Germany, and then in Antwerp.

Tyndale was partially successful in his aims, but had to face relentless opposition from Sir Thomas More, whose agents eventually tracked him down and kidnapped him; the local authorities then had him put him to death. He was strangled and then burned on 6 October 1536, at Vilvorde, near Brussels: his last words are supposed to have been, "Lord, open the King of England's eyes". Tyndale, by the way, as well as being a gifted linguist who translated from the original biblical languages of Hebrew and Greek, was a theologian who wrote several treatises, including one which Henry VIII found rather to his liking, entitled *The Obedience of a Christian Man* (1528), and which Anne Boleyn is supposed to have introduced him to. As to whether Tyndale was a Lutheran, scholars fiercely debate this: like Bilney, Tyndale stressed justification by faith, but his great contribution, of course, stems from the belief that he shared with Luther, that everyone (not just ploughboys!) should be able to read the Bible in their own language.

Tyndale translated the Scriptures into a lively and vibrant English which paved the way for the language of later translations and of Shakespeare, but it was only a partial translation; he managed the whole of the New Testament, but only the Pentateuch and the book of Job from the Old Testament. The work had to be finished by others, notably Miles Coverdale (1488-1568), who eventually became Bishop of Worcester, and John Rogers (1500-1555), a man to whose career we shall return below.

And so, we come back to Robert Barnes (1495-1540), one of the men whom we met at the start of this chapter as he awaited death at the stake in Smithfield. Of the "reformists" who were seen to be threats to the church, Barnes is the one of the few Englishmen of the 16th century to whom we can really give the name "Lutheran" – indeed, after his death was reported in Germany, Martin Luther wrote a preface to the story of his martyrdom. Luther knew him personally, as Barnes had visited Wittenberg several times and impressed the reformer and his co-workers.

Born in (King's) Lynn in 1495, he was, like Thomas Bilney, a Norfolk man, who, when he was a child of nine or ten, was sent to the Augustinian priory in Cambridge. Apart from spending some time at the university in Louvain in the Low Countries, he spent around twenty years in the monastery, and after returning from his time abroad became its prior. Barnes was greatly influenced by Erasmus, and he began to introduce a more disciplined study of the classics to his students. He also seems to have been influenced by Thomas Bilney, and was part of the "White Horse" group. His growing interest in reform was first shown openly in a sermon that he preached on Christmas Eve 1525 in St Edward's Church in Cambridge; ostensibly he was following the outline of a sermon by Luther, but he attacked both Cardinal Wolsey and one of the local church officials. The university authorities subsequently questioned him and he was hauled off to London for a hearing before the Cardinal himself. On threat of burning, Barnes recanted from his errors and was forced to do penance at St Paul's Cathedral, alongside some of the merchants of the Steelyard. The Steelyard was the English headquarters of the Hanseatic League, a powerful trading organisation based in north Germany, but embracing much of northern Europe; it seems that the London merchants had been smuggling forbidden books into England – initially some of Luther's works, but later, Tyndale's New Testament.

At this point, Barnes escaped being burnt, but he was confined in the Fleet Prison for six months, and then transferred to a sort of "house arrest" in the Augustinian priory in London. Conditions there cannot have been too severe, because he apparently did some trading in Tyndale's New Testament himself, and there is a story of him selling a copy to a group of Lollards from Essex. However, the authorities got wind of what was going on, and he was removed to the Augustinian house in Northampton. This was probably a prelude to burning, so, with the help of friends he staged a fake suicide and escaped, first to Antwerp, and then to Wittenberg, where he matriculated in the university and began his acquaintance with Luther and his friends. It was in Wittenberg that he became convinced of the soundness of Lutheran theology and where, in 1530, he wrote his first academic work, which was a Latin *Loci Communes* (a set of theses setting out important theological principles), and which was almost immediately translated into German. This became the basis for his *Supplication unto King Henry the Eighth* (1531), in which Barnes protested his loyalty to the king, spelled out his Lutheran theology, and recounted his hearing before Wolsey five years before.

Like other reformists, Barnes had to tread carefully with Sir Thomas More, who certainly had him in his sights, but, armed with a royal safe-conduct, he was able to return to England and begin several rather uneasy years in the service of the king. However, he must have realised that as long as More was around, he could not feel completely safe, so he returned to Germany, where he served as an assistant to a Lutheran pastor in Hamburg, Johannes Aepinus. After this, he moved back to Wittenberg, where he wrote a history of the Popes, which Luther greatly admired.

During the years between 1535 and 1540, Robert Barnes travelled back and forth between England and Germany. Some scholars have suggested that these years represent the high water mark of the influence of Lutheran theology in England. Thomas Cromwell, a self-made man who had served Cardinal Wolsey and then gone on to become Henry VIII's principal adviser, was sympathetic to reform, and, indeed, had overseen the severance of the English church from Rome and the dissolution of the monasteries. He was in favour of an alliance with the German Lutheran princes, who had created a defensive alliance called the Schmalkaldic League, but this came to nought, partly because Henry, being a king, felt that he out-ranked the princes and should, therefore, have led it.

There were two other reasons that it failed: the first was that Henry refused to sign the *Augsburg Confession,* the principal statement of faith which the princes had presented to the Holy Roman Empire in 1530, and the second was that Henry hated Luther. His *Assertio Septem Sacramentorum* had been followed by an acrimonious exchange between Henry and some of his advisers on the one hand, and Luther on the other. Harsh words had been said on each side, and there was little forgiving or forgetting. However, Henry was prepared to discuss things, so long as Luther was not involved, and Cromwell managed to achieve an agreement with the Germans known as *The Wittenberg Articles,* which encouraged Parliament to adopt a statement of faith for the English church known as *The Ten Articles,* which were broadly Lutheran in tone, particularly Article V, which dealt with justification by faith.

Ironically, bearing in mind his own eventual fate, Barnes got involved in the trial, conviction, and death in 1533 of John Lambert, a reformist who denied the real presence of Christ in the Lord's Supper, and whom the king was determined should die. This highlights the issue that, for some people, became crucial in the debate about reform: was Christ present in the bread and wine, and if so, how? Lambert, like John Frith, was a brilliant young theologian who, and along with many others, were termed "sacramentarians" – men and women who denied the real presence of Christ in the sacrament.

Barnes' downfall came with that of Thomas Cromwell. After nearly two decades, Henry had finally got himself a son, Prince Edward (1537-1553), but his mother, Jane Seymour (1508-1537), Henry's third wife, had died a few days after his birth. By the way, Henry's second wife, Anne Boleyn, who was almost certainly interested in reform, had committed the sin of failing to produce a son, as well as (possibly) committing several other sins as well, and she has the distinction of being the first English queen to be executed. Now Queen Jane was dead, and, after a suitable interval, Henry began to look for a fourth queen. An opportunity to kill two birds with one stone, reasoned Cromwell: find a German bride, and you provide the king with a wife and cement an alliance with the

German princes at the same time. His gaze rested on Anne (1515-1557), sister of the duke of Cleves – or, rather, it rested on her portrait, specially painted by Hans Holbein. Cleves was a territory in north Germany, close to the Dutch border, and it was not quite Lutheran, since its previous ruler had favoured a religious policy rather like Henry's own. What happened is well known: Henry liked the portrait but did not like the lady, refused to consummate the marriage, and demanded that Cromwell secure an annulment. Cromwell managed it, but had fallen out of favour with the king: his enemies from among the nobility, who resented that an upstart like him should have wielded such power, pounced, had him condemned by Act of Attainder, and hurried him off to the scaffold on 28 July 1540. Robert Barnes, who had played a part in the Cleves negotiations, died two days later. Even before Cromwell and Barnes died, a religious reaction had set in: in 1539, Henry VIII repudiated the *Ten Articles* and had instead issued *The Six Articles of Religion*, which re-emphasised some of the traditional Catholic beliefs, making England's religion "Catholicism without the Pope".

A lesser known, but ecumenically significant reformist figure in the first half of the 16th century is John Rogers (1500-1555), who assisted Miles Coverdale in completing William Tyndale's Bible translation, and who had the dubious honour of being the first martyr to die in the reign of Mary I. Rogers was a native of Deritend, then a small village near Birmingham. Like so many people of the time, we do not know very much about his early years, but he seems to have been educated in Cambridge, where he graduated in 1526. There is silence until 1534, when he became chaplain to the English merchants in Antwerp, where we know that he met both Tyndale and Coverdale and, according to Foxe, helped them with their Bible translation. Apparently, Tyndale entrusted his unfinished Old Testament translations to Rogers, and, after Tyndale's death, Rogers completed the work. Thomas More had died on the scaffold in 1535, but it was still dangerous to use Tyndale's name, so this Bible was attributed to an anonymous "Thomas Matthew" – hence the name it is usually known by, "Matthew's Bible". It was brought to England and, via a route which included Archbishop Thomas Cranmer (1489-1556) and Thomas Cromwell, came to the attention of Henry VIII, who authorised its publication and ordered that a copy should be put into every parish church. However, this state of affairs did not last long because it contained too many reformist-orientated introductions to the biblical books, and "Matthew's

Bible" was replaced in 1539 by the "Great Bible", which was a revision of Rogers' work, minus the offending notes.

Rogers had returned to England from Antwerp, but seeing the traditionalist reaction of 1540 and the fates of Robert Barnes and the other martyrs, he went to Germany where, on the recommendation of Philip Melanchthon, he became pastor of a Lutheran parish in north-western Saxony, and he stayed there until the death of Henry VIII in 1547. It would be fascinating to know what he preached during this time, but sadly none of his sermons have survived. Back in England, he served in a parish in London, lectured in St Paul's Cathedral, and translated some of Melanchthon's works into English. Like Robert Barnes before him, Rogers also became caught up in a heresy trial, this time of a women called Joan Boucher, who was an Anabaptist, part of a radical reformist group who denied the validity of infant baptism. She was tried and with Rogers' concurrence sentenced to be burned – a fact which shocked John Foxe enormously.

Rogers had returned to England when Edward VI came to the throne in 1547, and the six years of his reign were later seen as a "Golden Age" by Englishmen who wanted reform. For some unknown reason, Henry VIII, a staunch traditionalist, had had his young son brought up by reformists, with the result that the new monarch was fully in favour of reform. Under the political leadership of his uncle, Edward Seymour, and his successor, the Duke of Northumberland, and the spiritual leadership of Thomas Cranmer, reform came fast: an English service book, *The Book of Common Prayer*, was produced in 1549, with a second version in 1552, and books of sermons were produced for priests to use. It is the two versions of *The Book of Common Prayer* which really show how any Lutheran influence was being replaced by the influence of more radical Swiss reformers such as Huldrych Zwingli (1484-1531) and Heinrich Bullinger (1504-1575). The communion liturgy of the 1549 *Prayer Book* is quite Lutheran in its structure and ethos, whereas that of 1552 is much more "Reformed", and this reflects how Thomas Cranmer's theology – especially his understanding of the Lord's Supper – was changing. This was partly because a number of well-known continental theologians, such as Peter Vermigli (1500-1562), John à Lasco (1499-1560), and Bernardino Ochino (1487-1564), came to England to escape persecution, and they brought their Reformed ideas with them. John à Lasco was actually made Superintendent of a "Strangers' Church" – a congregation worshipping in Dutch and French, and outside the jurisdiction of the local bishop – and Bernardino Ochino, occasionally described as "a Lutheran", held services in London in Italian and Spanish. The "Strangers' Church" was Reformed, but it represents an important link as a precedent for the first Lutheran congregation, established in London in 1669. By far the most important of these continental reformers, however, was Martin Bucer (1491-1551), the reformer of Strasbourg, who came to Britain in 1549 and was appointed as Lady Margaret Professor of Theology in Cambridge. He took a mediating view of the Lord's Supper, somewhere in-between the Lutherans and the Reformed, and, had he lived, he might have exerted a considerable influence, but unfortunately he only survived for two years in the cold and damp of the Fens.

John Rogers would have witnessed all of this, but we do not know what he made of it. We do know, however, that he witnessed the "Golden Age" come toppling down. Edward VI died on 6 July 1553 at the tender age of 15, and, after a failed attempt to put his cousin, Lady Jane Grey (1537-1554) on the throne, he was succeeded by his half-sister, Mary, a devout Roman Catholic who was determined to take the church back to the days before her father's breach with Rome. She has gone down in history as "Bloody Mary" because of the sustained reign of terror which saw around 300 reformist martyrs perish before she died in 1558. On 4 February 1555, John Rogers was to be the first of those who died.

There are other people that we could have mentioned in this section – Thomas Hytten, John Bale, Anne Askew – or people like John Frith and Miles Coverdale, about whom we could have said more, but there is one person whom we obliquely mentioned early on, Henry VIII's sixth and last queen, who nearly got herself arrested for heresy. Always known by the name she was born with, Katherine Parr (1512-1548), she had already been married twice when, at around thirty years of age, she caught the attention of Henry. It could be said (charitably) that Henry had been unlucky in love, and after the fiasco with Anne of Cleves, he had bounced back and married a teenager named Catherine Howard (1520-1542), niece of the Duke of Norfolk. This turned out to be another fiasco, and Catherine was executed in 1542 on a charge of adultery. What Henry needed at this point was a mature and experienced wife who could cope with an increasingly irascible husband who stank – literally – from an old wound to his leg and which caused him enormous pain and discomfort. Katherine, whose family had always been on the fringes of court life, fitted the bill very well. Left to her own devices, she would probably have married Thomas Seymour (d.1549) – brother to the late Queen Jane, and therefore uncle to the next king, but when Henry proposed marriage to her, she had little choice but to accept. The marriage took place in the early summer of 1543.

John Foxe tells us that Katherine was noted for her learning and her piety, but this almost caused her downfall, because there is no doubt that she had reformist sympathies. Knowing the king's interest in theology, she seems to have discussed religious matters with him from time to time. While the king usually appears to have enjoyed this, Katherine occasionally went too far, suggesting that he might go further with his reforms of the church. The king complained to his advisers about being lectured to by a woman, and some of them, being anti-reformist traditionalists, hatched a plot to get rid of her. They persuaded Henry to sign a warrant for her arrest, but he seems to have been playing some macabre game and, when Thomas Wriothesley, the Lord Chancellor, came to arrest her in the king's presence, Henry gave him a firm dressing down. From then on, it was the Chancellor and his allies who were out of favour, although Katherine had learned a salutary lesson, and henceforth she was far more circumspect in expressing her religious beliefs to the king.

Katherine's faith was expressed in two books that she wrote, making her the first queen to be a published authoress. The first book, *Prayers and Meditations,* appeared to be conventional in its piety, so could safely be published in 1545, but the second, *The Lamentation or Complaint of a Sinner* (to give it its abbreviated title), was so clearly influenced by Martin Luther and other reformists that it had to wait for the rather safer times of Edward VI, and was published in 1547. If we can call any publication in the time we are considering to have been Lutheran, then it is *The Lamentation*: the queen writes movingly about her previous life of ignorance, about her need for repentance, emphasises justification by faith, and echoes Luther's "Theology of the Cross". Like Robert Barnes or John Rogers, Katherine was not a Lutheran in any formal sense, and she outwardly conformed to whatever the current religious situation happened to be – but her theology was clearly Lutheran. And by the way, reader, she married him (Thomas Seymour) after the death of Henry VIII in 1547.

Queen Mary died in 1558 and was succeeded by her half-sister Elizabeth (1533-1603), daughter of Henry VIII and Anne Boleyn. Elizabeth's private religious views have prompted unending arguments among historians: she was probably Lutheran in her sympathies, but she was a woman who, above all else, wanted peace and quiet. The church, which we now call "Anglican", that emerged as the result of the "Elizabethan Settlement", a long drawn out process, represented a middle-way between the old and the new. It had the "old" church order of bishops, priests, and deacons, but a "new" theology which owed much to continental Reformed thinking.

A few people with Lutheran views remained: Elizabeth's former tutor, Roger Ascham (1515-1568), wrote a treatise (which has only recently been published) on the Lord's Supper which emphasised the "real presence", and this view was also held by the Bishop of Gloucester, Richard Cheyney (1513-1579). If Lutheran views had ever been alive in England during the early stages of the Reformation, by Elizabeth's time they were peripheral to the mainstreams of Christian thought in the country. The distinguished Reformation scholar, Alec Ryrie, has characterised this as "the strange death of Lutheran England".

However, there was one interesting event which was to have an effect later on in our story, and this was a translation of Martin Luther's *Commentary on Galatians.* Strictly speaking, this was not a commentary as we might understand the term today, written systematically by an author as an exegesis of a biblical text, but a record based on student notes of lectures given by Luther in 1531. Luther had, as was customary at the time, lectured in Latin, and a text in that language was first produced in 1534: a second, revised edition appeared in 1538, and a version in German in 1539. In 1575, forty-one years after the first Latin version, an English translation appeared with a foreword by the then Bishop of London, Edwin Sandys (1516-1588), who was a firm Protestant. In the foreword, Sandys not only gave his permission for the book to be published, but also commended it to its readers, but, rather mysteriously, noted that the translators refused to be named: their purpose, he wrote, was neither "their own gain nor glory", but to "relieve afflicted minds, and do good to the Church of Christ". Although the translators, who were probably much influenced by Swiss theology, omitted a few things – especially where Luther touched on sacramental theology – scholars are generally in agreement that they did a good job of transmitting the spirit of the commentary.

This, then, brings us to the end of our section dealing with Lutherans and the Reformation in England and Wales. Unlike many parts of Germany and unlike the Nordic countries, the Tudor kingdom did not become Lutheran: Henry VIII's reformation was idiosyncratic and overwhelmingly coloured by his personal aims and ambitions, but there were men and women who personally embraced Luther's teachings in some form or another, some of whom died for their faith. Remote as they may seem, and disconnected as they may be from the subsequent history of the Lutheran Churches in Britain, these individuals played an important part in the Reformation and can be counted among the spiritual ancestors of Lutherans in these islands. One very important thing to emphasise is the international flavour of the events in which they were involved: there was a constant coming and going between Britain and Europe, firstly with Germany, but later with Switzerland, and this resulted in a cross-fertilisation of ideas which profoundly affected the English church.

FURTHER READING

There is no shortage of general books about the Reformation in England and Wales, and it would be impossible in a brief history like this to mention more than a few of them. Alec Ryrie's book **The Age of Reformation: The Tudor and Stewart Realms 1485-1603 (Harlow, Pearson Education Limited, 2009. ISBN: 978-1-4058-3557-2)**, offers a comprehensive survey of the period, but for a much longer work readers should consult G. W. Bernard's **The King's Reformation: Henry VIII and the Remaking of the English Church (New Haven and London, Yale University Press, 2005. ISBN: 978-0-300-12271-8)**.

There are a number of books of particular interest to Lutherans. Henry VIII's relationship with Luther and Lutherans is covered by Erwin Doernberg's **Henry VIII and Luther (London, Barrie and Rockliff, 1961. No ISBN)**, and **Henry VIII and the Lutherans (Saint Louis, Concordia Publishing House, 1965. No ISBN)** by Neelak S. Tjernagel. The Tyndale scholar, David Daniell, has written what is, at present, the "standard" life of the Bible translator, **William Tyndale: A Biography (New Haven and London, Yale University Press, 1994. ISBN: 0-300-06132-3)**, and Korey D. Maas has published **The Reformation and Robert Barnes (Woodbridge, The Boydell Press, 2010. ISBN: 978-84383-534-9)**. There is much debate about whether or not Thomas Cromwell was "Lutheran", and an interesting contribution is made by John Schofield in **The Rise and Fall of Thomas**

Cromwell: Henry VIII's Most Faithful Servant (Stroud, The History Press, 2008. ISBN: 978-0-7524-4604-2). Dr Schofield has also written **Philip Melanchthon and the English Reformation (Aldershot, Ashgate Publishing Limited, 2006. ISBN: 0-7546-5567-9)**, which has a particularly interesting section on Lutheran influence on Elizabeth I.

There has recently been a renewal of interest in Katherine Parr, and the full texts of her two books are now available in **Katherine Parr: Complete Works and Correspondence (Chicago and London, The University of Chicago Press, 2014. ISBN: 978-0-226-21379-8)**, edited by Janel Mueller.

The 1575 edition of Luther's Commentary on Galatians, in a version revised and completed by the Luther scholar Philip S. Watson, was published in the early 1950s: **A Commentary on St Paul's Epistle to the Galatians by Martin Luther (London, James Clarke & Co. Ltd., 1953. No ISBN)**.

Since it was first written, **Foxe's Book of Martyrs** has never been out of print. A selection of narratives is available in the Oxford World Classics series edited and produced by John N. King **(Oxford, Oxford University Press, 2009. ISBN: 978-0-19-923648-8)**.

Chapter 17 | The Hidden Years (1575-1669)

It simply would not do, in a book like this, to have a couple of blank pages, but that is what the years from 1575 to 1669 feel like for anyone writing a history of Lutherans in Great Britain. Of course, 1575 is a rather arbitrary date, but the few examples of Lutheran thinking among English Protestants really came to an end with the English translation of Luther's *Commentary on Galatians*. 1669, on the other hand, is the year in which, for the first time, a Lutheran congregation was established in Britain. So what of these "unknown years"?

The first thing to say is that there were certainly Lutherans in Britain during that time. Trade between Britain and northern Europe continued to flourish, and there were continental merchants, diplomats, and artisans in the country throughout the whole period. The Hanseatic merchants maintained their presence in London and elsewhere; true, Queen Elizabeth had closed them down towards the end of her reign, but James I allowed them to re-establish themselves, but where did they, and other foreign Lutherans, actually worship? The answer to that question is that we cannot be sure. The Steelyard had a small chapel, but it could not have accommodated a sizeable congregation – which leaves two possibilities. Firstly, it could be that the Hanseatic merchants worshipped in their local parish church, which was All-Hallows-by-the-Tower, but it is also possible that they attended the Strangers' Church, which had been established in the days of Edward VI, exiled in the time of Queen Mary, and then re-established when Elizabeth came to the throne. But – and this is an important factor to bear in mind – this was a time when confessional differences were becoming more sharply differentiated, and the Strangers' Church was Reformed, and the Lutherans of north Germany might not have wanted to worship there. Incidentally, when John à Lasco and his congregation were forced to leave England in 1553, they were regarded with great suspicion by Lutherans and no major Lutheran territory would give them a home, until they were eventually allowed to settle in Frankfurt-am-Main.

For a number of reasons the Strangers' Church in London was in a very interesting ecclesiastical situation. Firstly, it was the only non-Anglican religious community to have a legal existence in England; secondly, although it had its own Superintendent, from the time of Queen Elizabeth it was officially under the jurisdiction of the Bishop of London; and thirdly, only non-English citizens could be members of the congregations, which worshipped either in Dutch or French. For the most part, these arrangements worked well, although Archbishop William Laud (1575-1645), who more than anything else wanted religious uniformity, interfered with the autonomy of the Dutch and French congregations scattered across the country. However, from a Lutheran point of view, the Strangers' Church in London was to go partway to providing a model for the first Lutheran congregation, established in the early years of the reign of Charles II. But, before turning to 1669 and all that, there are a few passing references to Lutherans which deserve a word or two.

First of all, there is the story of Captain Henry Bell, under whose name an edition of Martin Luther's *Table Talk* was published in 1651, with the express permission of Parliament. The *Table Talk* is a collection of anecdotes and sayings that purport to have been made by Luther during meals in the family home in the former monastery in Wittenberg, and there had been a collection of these sayings in existence since 1566, when they were first published in Germany. It seems that Henry Bell was sent a copy by a certain Caspar van Spaar, with the request that he translate it into English; Bell agreed, but kept putting the task to one side. According to the story, Bell was eventually persuaded by a ghostly apparition that he must complete the task, and, said the ghost, he would be provided with time and space in which to do it. Several years in prison (we do not know what he was charged with) seem to provide the right setting for the work, and, after being freed, the completed manuscript was sent to Archbishop William Laud, who thoroughly approved of the work and handsomely rewarded Bell with a gift of £40. Laud was executed in 1646, but the puritans in Parliament also approved of the translation and authorised its publication. There is much that is legendary in this story, but there is no doubt that the English translation of the *Table Talk* was published in 1651.

Secondly, there is Reverend John Durie (1596-1680), who has been described as the "grandfather of ecumenism". Of Scottish background, but educated in the Netherlands, Durie had been a member of the French-speaking congregation in Cologne, where he had got to know several prominent churchmen of different confessional backgrounds. He moved to the Polish city of Elbląg, which was then under Swedish rule, and in 1628, through King Gustavus Adolphus' Minister, Axel Oxienstierna, petitioned the king for help in securing unity between Lutherans and the Reformed, although the petition did not get very far. However, Durie got support from George Abbot (1562-1633), the Calvinistically-inclined Archbishop of Canterbury, and he was ordained as a priest in the Church of England. Unfortunately, Abbott's successor in Canterbury, William Laud, had little interest in church unity – unless it meant conformity to the Church of England – and he declined to support Durie's schemes. However, as the political situation in England deteriorated and the country drifted towards civil war, Durie grew close to Oliver Cromwell (d.1658), who was to eventually end up as Lord Protector during the country's decade or more of experimenting with republicanism.

In 1641, Durie published a tract entitled *Concerning the Work of Peace Ecclesiastical* in which he urged Protestants – defined by him as Anglicans, Lutherans, and Presbyterians – to find ways of uniting, but the times were hardly propitious for such a proposal: the British civil wars began in 1642 and lasted for a decade, and Germany was being devastated by the final years of the Thirty Years' War. However, Durie's ideas did not fall on completely deaf ears, and they found support from Johannes Matthiae, who was Bishop of the Swedish diocese of Strängnäs, though ultimately they came to nothing.

Although the first sixty-or-so years of the 17th century saw little direct Lutheran activity in Britain, there was some British interest in Luther and Lutherans, as we have seen with Henry Bell and John Durie, and Gustavus Adolphus was regarded as a great Protestant hero because of his achievements before his death at the battle of Lützen in 1632. However, a more direct influence, perhaps, came in the form of John Bunyan, the "Tinker of Bedford".

John Bunyan (1628-1688) is one of the great heroes of English Protestantism: reared on the Bible, John Foxe's *Book of Martyrs,* and some other Puritan writings. He is perhaps best known for his classic book, *The Pilgrim's Progress,* first published in 1678.

However, it is an earlier book, *Grace Abounding to the Chief of Sinners* (1666), written while a prisoner in Bedford gaol, that is of interest to us. In this book, Bunyan tells of how, "God ... did cast into my hand, one day, a book of Martin Luther; it was his comment on the Galatians ... [and] this, methinks, I must let fall before all men, I do prefer this book of Martin Luther upon the Galatians, excepting the Holy Bible, before all the books that I have seen, as most fit for a wounded conscience". What is interesting is that Bunyan's knowledge of Luther was only a partial one, and there is no indication that he either knew or understood anything of the reformer's ecclesiology or sacramental theology; certainly, as a Baptist, he would have little sympathy with Luther's theology of baptism. What seems to have been significant for Bunyan was the way in which Luther struggled with temptation.

FURTHER READING

The definitive work on William Laud is by Hugh Trevor-Roper, and is simply entitled **Archbishop Laud (London, Phoenix Press, 1962. ISBN: 1-84212-202-9)**. There is also an article on Laud entitled *William Laud and the Outward Face of Religion*, by J Sears McGee, in **Leaders of the Reformation (Richard L. DeMolen, Ed., Selinsgrove, Susquehanna University Press, 1984. ISBN: 0-941664-05-8)**. Sadly, neither of these books devotes any space to Laud's attitudes towards Lutherans, but Dr Trevor-Roper's book does devote some space to his attitude towards the Strangers' Churches around England. There is a lengthy description of the career of Captain Henry Bell in Gordon Rupp's **The Righteousness of God: Luther Studies (London Hodder & Stoughton, 1953. No ISBN)**, pp.56-57. For information about John Durie, see Ruth Rouse and Stephen Charles Neill, **A History of the Ecumenical Movement, 1517-1948 (London, SPCK, 1967. No ISBN)**.

There are several biographies of John Bunyan, but Principal Gordon Wakefield's **John Bunyan the Christian (London, Harper Collins, 1992. ISBN: 0-00-627840-X)** is both brief and very readable. Both **Grace Abounding**, and **Pilgrim's Progress** are readily available in both hardback and paperback versions. The distinguished historian Christopher Hill, has written **A Turbulent, Seditious, and Factious People: John Bunyan and His Church (London/New York, Verso, 2016. ISBN: 978-1-78478-686-1)**, and this gives much useful information about Bunyan's attitude towards Luther.

Chapter 18 | The First Lutheran Congregations in Britain and Ireland

It is accurate – if rather poetic – to begin this chapter by saying that just as many British Lutherans in the first 60 years of the 16th century perished in fire, so it was fire which led to the establishment of the first Lutheran congregation in England in 1669: in this case "The Great Fire of London".

It was just over six years since the brief experiment of an English republic had come to an end and the Stuart family had been restored to the throne in the person of King Charles II (reigned 1660-1685). Things had not gone particularly well for the new king; personally inclined towards Roman Catholicism, he had, nevertheless, promised religious toleration in the "Declaration of Breda", which he had issued from his exile in the Netherlands, but die-hard Anglicans in Parliament had thwarted this, and in 1662 ministers who would not conform to the teaching and practices of the Church of England were forced to leave their parishes in what became known as the "Great Ejection": conformity was the order of the day.

There had been war with the Netherlands, which so recently had provided Charles with a refuge, and then the plague had struck London in the hot summer of 1665. Now, sometime during the night of 1-2 September 1666, a fire broke out in a bakery in Pudding Lane in the heart of the City of London, and by the time it was under control several days later, much of the city had been destroyed – houses, shops, churches, and other public buildings – and thousands of people were homeless.

The king himself, together with his brother, James, Duke of York (1633-1701), behaved with great bravery during the Great Fire, but then were left with the tremendous task of re-building the city.

Money for the royal administration was always a problem, and here was an added burden: where was the money to come from to pay the architects, suppliers, and workmen needed for the task? Paradoxically, for a Catholic-leaning king, this dilemma was to lead Charles to permit the establishment of the first Lutheran congregation in Britain, because it was to the cities of north Germany, and, in particular, Hamburg, that he turned for help. The Germans had the money and other resources, but, in effect, they made the stipulation that they would need to have a place to worship according to their own, Lutheran, beliefs. The German and Nordic merchants in London petitioned the king, using the good offices of the Swedish ambassador, Baron Johan Barkman Leijonberg, and Charles granted their request in a series of documents dating from 1669. They were permitted to build a church and were granted a piece of land on which one of the London parish churches – Holy Trinity in Trinity Lane – had stood, but there was a clear stipulation that this was to be a foreign congregation, like the Dutch and French Strangers' Church and that anyone who took English nationality should become a member of their local Anglican parish. The new church was dedicated on 21 December 1673, the Fourth Sunday in Advent; and the sermon preached on Ezra 6 by the first pastor, Gerhard Martens, is still extant – all 30 pages of it. This church, although officially named "Holy Trinity", is always known as the "Hamburg Church", and this is the name which is used below.

The members of this first Lutheran congregation were a very mixed bunch of people: there were Germans, Dutch, and people from what we would now term as the Nordic countries. They undoubtedly had different interests in the world of commerce, but what united them was their allegiance to the Lutheran confessions. This was a genuinely international and multilingual congregation, and, although the common language of worship was German, regular services may also have been held in Danish.

The insistence – in theory, at least – that all English men and women should belong to the Church of England, was a reflection of the concept prevalent on the continent of *cuius regio, eius religio*, that is to say, the idea that the religion of the prince should be the religion of the people. This had meant that non-Anglican church groups were not tolerated and suffered serious penalties; the Strangers' Churches at Austin Friars and elsewhere, and the Lutheran Church in the City of London, could only exist because they had royal permission. This situation was alleviated somewhat after the "Glorious Revolution" of 1688, which deposed the Roman Catholic King James II and brought his daughter and son-in-law to the throne as William III and Mary II. William, a Calvinist, had played a leading role in the Dutch "United Provinces", which were, by the standards of the day, quite liberal. One of the earliest pieces of legislation passed by the new monarchs' first parliament was the Toleration Act of 1689, which enabled English Nonconformists to have their own places of worship and their own ministers, provided they took oaths of allegiance to the king and queen, although they were still denied access to political and civil offices and to the universities of Oxford and Cambridge.

For Lutherans, the Toleration Act meant that they could establish new congregations, mostly in London, but also across the sea in Dublin, and between 1692 and 1763 no less than six new congregations were established. Four of these congregations – three in London and one in Dublin – were German-speaking, one used Danish, and the sixth used Swedish as its language of worship.

The first new German-speaking congregation was that of St Mary-le-Savoy, founded in 1694 and given a home in a chapel in the Savoy Palace, between what are now the Strand and the Embankment, just to the west of the boundary of the City of London. The reasons for the establishment of this congregation are obscure, but disagreements within the Hamburg Church, and the distances some people had to travel to worship, probably played a part. Interestingly, the liturgy used in St Mary's was used by the first organised body in the American colonies, the Ministerium of Pennsylvania, as its approved order of service in both German and English.

The next German-speaking congregation was also founded within a royal palace and was the direct result of royal influence. After William III's death in 1702, the crown passed to his sister-in-law Anne (1665-1714), whose husband was George of Denmark (1653-1708). George, who was naturalised in 1689 and given the title Duke of Cumberland, was a staunch Lutheran, and pressed for the establishment of a court chapel, which was eventually established in 1700 in St James's Palace. Two things made this different from the other German-speaking congregations: it was placed under the supervision of the Bishop of London and used a German translation of the Book of Common Prayer for its liturgy. The congregation continued to hold services in the Chapel Royal until the early 1900s, when services were transferred to the newly-built Christus Kirche in Knightsbridge.

A fourth German-speaking Lutheran congregation was established in 1763 in the East End of London to cater for the growing number of German residents there. By this time, German influence in London was strong, partly because of the fact that Queen Anne had died with no living children in 1714, and, according to the Act of Settlement of 1701, the succession had passed to the family of the Electress Sophia of Hanover (1630-1714). Sophia died before Anne, so it was her son who succeeded to the throne as George I (reigned 1714-1727), and a sizeable train of German courtiers followed him to England, to be further followed by merchants and artisans. No new German-speaking congregations were established in the first decades of Hanoverian rule, but, several short-lived German-speaking congregations were established in the latter half of the 18th century. The only one that survived was St George's, and its building in Alie Street, although no longer used for regular services, is now the oldest surviving Lutheran church building in Britain. Interestingly, the first pastor, Gottfried Wachsel, got into difficulties when he tried to introduce English into his ministry, and eventually a London magistrate ruled that worship in St George's had to be in German.

The only Lutheran congregation outside London was that established in Dublin in 1696, and, like Holy Trinity, this was an international and bi-lingual congregation, using both German and Danish. Many German and Nordic soldiers had fought as mercenaries in the army of William III, which had defeated the Roman Catholic king, James II, at the Battle of the Boyne, in 1689, and when hostilities ceased some had decided to stay in Ireland. Two of the chaplains to these mercenaries stayed on as well – Iver Brink, who was a Dane, and who later achieved fame as a writer of hymns, and Esdras Marcus Lichtenstein, who was a German of Jewish background. Both men had been ordained as chaplains in the Hamburg Church in London, and both had a hand in establishing the congregation in Dublin. Eventually, the congregation was able to build a church – dedicated in 1725 – and this was the spiritual ancestor of the present-day "Lutheran Church in Ireland". Incidentally, there was a considerable influx of refugees from the area in west Germany known as the Palatinate into parts of southern Ireland after 1708, and several villages in the Republic of Ireland still have a distinctly German look to them. These immigrants were largely Calvinist, and they did not identify themselves with the congregation in Dublin.

The other two Lutheran congregations established in London were not German-speaking, but served people of Nordic background who had settled in the capital. One of the things which Charles II needed to re-build the city after the Great Fire was timber, which Denmark – whose territories included Norway – had in abundance, and the consequence was that many Danes, Norwegians, and Swedes came to live in London. Of course, these were Lutherans, and they worshipped in Holy Trinity, which, as we have noted, may have held services in Danish for them, but eventually they migrated to establish their own congregation, which built a church in Wellclose Square. This church was granted Letters Patent from the king in 1692, and one of its first pastors was the Iver Brink who had helped to establish the congregation in Dublin. Although the congregation worshipped in Danish, it inevitably included people from the whole Nordic area.

Nowadays, the Nordic countries are a byword for peaceful international co-operation, but their history has sometimes been somewhat bloody, and in the late 17th and early 18th centuries the kingdoms of Denmark and Sweden crossed swords more than once. On one such occasion, when the Danish king, Frederik IV, seized back Schleswig and Holstein, which had been occupied by the Swedes for a decade, one of the pastors of the Danish congregation, Jørgen Ursin, preached a sermon and said prayers in which he appealed for God's protection and for a victory for the Danish king. The Swedes upped and left and established their own congregation in 1710, which by 1728 had its own church in Prince's Square.

These, then, were the first Lutheran congregations to be established in Great Britain and Ireland, and, apart from the handful of short-lived German-speaking congregations which sprang up briefly towards the end of the 18th century, they were the congregations which survived – though often with difficulty – until the 19th century, when things changed dramatically.

We cannot leave the 18th century without mentioning some of the wider Lutheran influences on British society, making some reference to Georg Friedrich Handel (1685-1759), John Wesley (1703-1791), and the Lutheran involvement in British missionary activity.

Lutherans have always been a "singing" church; Luther himself had written hymns, often using well known popular melodies, and these became a noted feature of Lutheran worship. Others followed his example and a substantial corpus of Lutheran sacred music had grown up by the beginning of the 18th century, typified, most characteristically, by the work of Johann Sebastian Bach (1685-1750). Much modified by Italian influence, this musical tradition was brought to Britain by Handel. Not himself a writer of hymns, Handel popularised the musical form known as the "oratorio", and his prolific output was sung in both church and concert hall. His most famous piece is, of course, the "Messiah", beloved of choirs today, but he also wrote "Zadok the Priest", which has been sung at the coronation of all British monarchs since that of George II in 1827.

There was also an important Lutheran influence in the story of John Wesley, the founder of the Methodist movement. Wesley, the son of a Church of England country priest from Lincolnshire, was himself ordained and became a convinced high church man. In the 1730s he was sent out by the Society for the Propagation of the Gospel to Georgia, and it was there that he first came across Lutherans. At this time he placed great emphasis on the apostolic succession, which, he maintained, had been preserved in the Anglican churches, and in his view this prevented him from enjoying altar fellowship with both Lutherans and Reformed, because neither had (in his view) valid ordination and, therefore, valid sacraments. On the other hand the Moravians, whom he had first met on his voyage to North America, did. Spiritual descendants of the Hussites of 15th century Bohemia and Moravia, this church fellowship had been rescued from near oblivion by a Lutheran nobleman, Nicholas Ludwig von Zinzendorf (1700-1760), who let them settle on his estates in Saxony. There they established a community known as Herrnhut, where he strongly influenced their theology and practice along pietistic and mystical lines. Wesley was very impressed by their quiet faith and trust during the long and arduous voyage across the Atlantic, and during the voyage he not only learned something of their beliefs, but also took the opportunity to learn German. While in the Americas he translated several Lutheran hymns into English.

Wesley's Christianity at this time was high church, somewhat rigid, and rather legalistic, but a slow process of change, which involved Luther, began after his return to England. Firstly his brother Charles introduced him to Luther's *Commentary on Galatians,* which he read with enthusiasm, but the real breakthrough came on 24 May 1738, when he attended a religious meeting in a Moravian Chapel in Aldersgate Street in the City of London. During the meeting someone read part of Luther's *Preface to the Commentary on Romans,* in which the reformer described the effects which God works in human beings when they have faith in Christ, at which point Wesley underwent a mystical experience, which he later described as like having his "heart strangely warmed".

Although Wesley owed a great debt to Luther, his theology developed along rather different lines, and he did not understand the sentiments that Luther expressed, for example, in works such as *The Bondage of the Will.* Wesley stressed the idea of sanctification and the possibility of Christian perfection, ideas which reflected a fusion of his own earlier thinking and Lutheran pietism. There is no space here to discuss the merits of pietism, which in historic terms owes its origins to German theologians such as Philip Jakob Spener (1635-1705) and August Hermann Francke (1663-1727), men who believed that, by stressing the importance of doctrinal orthodoxy, the Lutheran territorial churches had failed to serve their people. They wanted to restore a Christianity which was more vital and personal, and they developed the idea of the *collegia pietatis* (religious meetings alongside formal church services), and the establishment of educational and missionary institutions. Scholars debate how far the pietists departed from Luther, but there is no doubt that much of what Wesley understood of Luther was filtered through their eyes. Incidentally, as we shall see below, British Methodist scholars were to play a significant part in the modern rebirth of interest in Martin Luther and his theology.

The third area in which there was a Lutheran involvement in British Christian life was that of overseas missionary activity. Although it was the 19th century that was to be the great century of missionary endeavour, a start had been made in the preceding hundred years. The first English mission society to be founded (1701) was the Society for the Promotion of Christian Knowledge (SPCK), and among its earliest overseas involvements was support for the mission work that had been started by the King of Denmark in the small Danish colony of Tranquebar in southern India. Two German missionaries sent out by the king, Bartholemaeus Ziegenbalg (1682-1719) and Heinrich Plütschau (1688-1747), had begun work among the Tamil-speaking indigenous people of Tranquebar and had, between them, produced a Tamil translation of the Bible: the SPCK provided a printing press and a trained printer to publish this. Subsequent German missionaries ended up serving in a dual capacity: they were Lutherans, supported by an Anglican missionary society (and a rather high church one, at that), trying to evangelise local people, but they were also employed by the British East India Company to serve as chaplains to its troops. In this latter capacity, these Lutheran pastors used the *Book of Common Prayer* for services, and employed Anglican rites for both the Lord's Supper and Baptism, and, it should be noted, nobody questioned the fact that they had not been ordained in the "apostolic succession".

A little under a hundred years later, in 1799, an evangelical Anglican mission society – the Church Mission Society (CMS) – was founded, but, to begin with, it faced the serious problem that it could find no Anglican priests willing to go to the mission field. In desperation it approached Dr Steinkopf, the pastor of the St Mary-le-Savoy Lutheran congregation, and asked for his help in finding suitable candidates: the result was that the CMS's first two missionaries in what is now Sierra Leone were Lutherans. Again, no questions were raised about their non-episcopal ordination – although they were asked that, when in England on leave, they should avoid preaching in Nonconformist chapels! Incidentally, when the British and Foreign Bible Society (BFBS) was founded in 1804, Dr Steinkopf was among its committee members and served as its first foreign secretary.

These early missionary endeavours are an early – and very interesting – example of the extent to which the Church of England regarded Lutherans as belonging to sister churches. Lutheran pastors from Germany and Denmark, who had not been ordained by churches claiming the "historic episcopate", were, nevertheless, recognised as ministers of Word and Sacrament, without any suggestion that they needed to be re-ordained.

FURTHER READING

2016 marked the 350th anniversary of the Great Fire of London, and numerous books and learned articles were published to commemorate it. One publication is by Rebecca Rideal and is entitled **1666: Plague, War, and Hellfire (London, John Murray Publishers, 2016. ISBN: 978-47362-355-2)**. Samuel Pepys' diary for the years of the plague and the Great Fire is easily available.

Susanne Steinmetz has a good outline of the early history of the German congregations in London in Chapter 4 of **Germans in Britain since 1500**, (edited by Panikos Panayi) **(London, The Hambledon Press, 1996. ISBN: 1-85285-126-0).** The Hamburg Church, St Mary's, and the Danish and Swedish Churches, have all published books describing the history of their respective congregations, and details are available from the churches concerned.

A brief introduction to the life of George Frideric Handel is **Handel (London, Cassell Publishers Limited, 1990. ISBN: 0-225-66595-6)** by the Roman Catholic scholar, Hamish Swanston, and many recordings of his work are available on CD.

Frank Baker's **John Wesley and the Church of England (London, Epworth Press, 1970. ISBN: 0-7162-0538-6)**, is a source of information about Wesley's early attitudes to Lutherans. There is a useful history of the Moravians by J. Taylor Hamilton and Kenneth G. Hamilton: **History of the Moravian Church: The Renewed Unitas Fratrum 1722-1957 (Bethlehem Pa., Interprovincial Board of Christian Education of the Moravian Church in America, 1967. No ISBN).**

For a comprehensive description of the growth of Christian missions, see Stephen Neill's **A History of Christian Missions (Harmondsworth, Penguin Books Ltd., 1964. No ISBN).**

Chapter 19 | From the 19th Century to the Outbreak of the First World War

Apart from the Lutheran congregation in Dublin, which seems to have died out by the mid-19th century, all the Lutheran churches established in Britain since 1669 had been centred in London, although none of the congregations established there after St George's in 1763 had survived more than a few years. The 19th century, however, witnessed a significant growth in the number of Lutheran churches, most of which were to be found in the north of England and in Scotland. The majority of these congregations were German-speaking, catering for the significant number of immigrants from different parts of Germany, but there were also new Danish, Finnish, Norwegian, and Swedish churches to cater for visiting seamen and small, but influential, trading communities in the larger seaports.

Very recently, in the first part of the second decade of the 21st century, there has been much talk of the "Northern Powerhouse" proposing the area become a centre for economic and industrial development, but the term could well have been used to describe the north of England – and Scotland – during the 19th century. What we now refer to as the "Industrial Revolution" started in various different parts of Britain, but the north rapidly became a centre for the development of many different sorts of industry – including, among others, coal mining, steel manufacturing, ship-building, and textile manufacture. The north of England suddenly became very attractive to immigrants from northern Europe, although it has to be said that they sometimes ended up there when they were actually intending to go somewhere else.

There were many different reasons why people began emigrating from Germany, but for most people the driving force was economic. In the 1840s, some parts of the country experienced very poor harvests, and many people, especially in rural areas, were reduced to poverty. The situation was not helped by the sub-division of land into smaller and smaller units, nor by the process of industrialisation, which drew people into increasingly overcrowded towns and cities. Many people felt that the only remedy was to emigrate, either to other parts of Europe, or further afield to the United States, South America, or Australia. Great Britain, which was in the throes of the Industrial Revolution, needed skilled workers for its factories, but also offered opportunities to people who were prepared to work hard and establish small businesses, and it is interesting how often we read, for example, of German butchers and bakers.

For those people who decided to emigrate beyond Europe, Great Britain played a key role: would-be emigrants took ship from the seaports of Hamburg and Bremen, landed in ports such as Hull or Grimsby, and then made their way by train or canal to Liverpool or Southampton, from which they could embark on ships carrying them further afield. Many of these migrants arrived in Britain and simply abandoned their plans to go further, and they helped to swell the numbers in the German communities that were being established in different towns and cities.

The first German-speaking congregation to be established in the north of England was in Liverpool, and dates from the 1820s, and by the time of the outbreak of the First World War in 1914 there were congregations in Manchester (which at one time had no less than three), Bradford, Hull, and Newcastle-upon-Tyne, as well as congregations in Edinburgh and Glasgow. These congregations flourished alongside the original congregations in London, and although they greatly valued their independence, by the beginning of the 20th century they had established an Association of German-speaking Congregations in Britain, which organised annual conferences for the pastors.

The 19th century also saw the blossoming of work by the Nordic churches in the north of England and Scotland. Today, the Nordic countries enjoy high standards of living and are among the world's most prosperous societies, but this was not the case in the 19th century. What was true of Germany was also true of Denmark, whose territories included the Faroe Islands, Greenland, and Iceland; of the kingdom of Sweden-Norway; and of the Grand Duchy of Finland, which was then part of the Russian Empire. Parts of these countries were desperately poor and many people decided that emigration was the only possibility, and, as with their German counterparts, the majority of these emigrants crossed the Atlantic by way of Great Britain.

At the same time, however, trade between the Nordic countries and Great Britain was increasing. British industrialisation had led to an increase in shipping across the North Sea, and ships carrying timber and wood pulp from the forests of Norway, iron ore from Sweden, or agricultural products from Denmark brought migrants and seamen to British ports. The need to cater for both the migrants and visiting seamen led to churches being established in all the major seaports. The first such church was established by the Norwegians in Leith (the port of Edinburgh) in 1864, but within a few years there were Danish, Finnish, Norwegian, and Swedish churches in all the major seaports from Aberdeen southwards along the east coast, and across the country on Merseyside. At one time these was even a seasonal Swedish church in Shetland on the island of Unst – which is as far north as you can go in Britain – catering for the summer herring fishermen. There was also trade with what are now known as the "Baltic States", but which were then part of the Russian Empire, and it is known that a Latvian pastor was resident in South Wales at the dawn of the 20th century.

The life of these congregations and missions continued uninterrupted into the 20th century, and in the early 1900s there were nearly thirty "foreign" Lutheran churches in Great Britain, although in some cases their membership included families that had been settled in this country for generations. The German-speaking congregations were independent of each other but had a relationship with the churches in Germany; the Nordic congregations were either part of the church of their homeland, or were related to their respective seamen's missions.

There is no doubt that these Lutheran congregations, scattered across the country and worshipping in different languages, would have interacted with the local indigenous communities, but there are some examples of a wider Lutheran influence on British Christianity during the 19th century. Of these, we might mention two examples: the "Jerusalem Bishopric" and the ways in which the Lutheran musical tradition became better known in these islands.

Firstly, then, the Anglo-Prussian Bishopric in Jerusalem, which was created in 1841 and continued until 1886. This institution had its genesis in the mind of King Frederick William IV of Prussia, and it envisaged the establishment of a bishopric in Jerusalem whose incumbent would alternate between a representative of the Prussian Union Church – a body which had come into being in Prussia by royal edict in 1817 and which united Lutherans and Reformed congregations into one church – and the Church of England. Although evangelical Anglicans supported this move, it faced all sorts of problems and there was strong hostility from other quarters: Prussian clergy objected to the Anglican insistence on episcopacy, and many high church Anglicans objected to what they saw as a form of union with a Protestant church without any guarantees over questions of either doctrine or church order. One of its fiercest critics was John Henry Newman (1801-1890), one of the leaders of the "Oxford Movement" in the Church of England, and it was a contributory factor in his decision to join the Roman Catholic Church. The joint bishopric survived for over forty years, until the two churches divided responsibility for mission and ministry in Palestine between them, with the Anglicans covering Jerusalem and the northern half up to Lebanon, and Lutherans covering Jerusalem and the southern half. The division stands to this day. The Lutherans also wished to focus on social work and education, while the Anglicans were more focused on conversion, although now both churches are involved in social work, education and advocacy as well as parish ministry.

As we mentioned above, Lutherans developed a strong musical tradition, starting, indeed, with Martin Luther himself. His great and much beloved hymn, *Ein feste Burg ist Unser Gott*, was, however, unknown in Britain until it was translated into English as "A safe stronghold our God is still" by the Scottish historian and man of letters, Thomas Carlyle, in 1831. Carlyle had a high opinion of Luther, whom he regarded as one of history's great leaders. More important, perhaps, were the Winkworth sisters, Susanna (1820-1884) and Catherine (1827-1878), who were from Berkshire, and of Anglican background, but whose family moved to Manchester in 1829, where the two girls came under a strong Unitarian influence. Both girls eventually spent time in Germany, where they discovered Lutheran spirituality and hymnody. Susanna went on to translate the *Theologia Germanica*, (published 1874), which Luther himself had translated some three hundred years before, and which had greatly influenced him, along with the writings of some other German mystics. Catherine's work is probably better remembered today because of her love of music: in 1853, she published *Lyra*

Germanica, a translation into English of well-known German hymns, including *Nun danket alle Gott* ("Now thank we all our God"), which was followed up by a collection of the music to go with it, published in 1862 as "The Chorale Book for England". She also wrote some biographical works, including a life of Theodor Fliedner (1800-1864), one of the pioneers of the deaconess movement in Germany.

Fliedner was a parish pastor in Kaiserswerth, a village close to Düsseldorf and in the heart of a Roman Catholic community. In the mid-1830s he had made a fund-raising trip to the Netherlands and there encountered the work of Mennonite deaconesses. After his return to Germany he determined to establish a similar sort of work among Lutherans, and in 1836 set up a deaconess house close to the church. This was something new and experimental, but it quickly became accepted as a work of the church and similar houses were established, such as that by Pastor Wilhelm Loehe (1808-1872) at Neuendettelsau in Bavaria. Visitors from Britain were impressed by what they saw and brought the idea of deaconesses back with them, and several denominations – notably the Church of England, the Church of Scotland, and the Methodist Church – each established deaconess orders in some form or another.

FURTHER READING

An indispensable book covering part of this period is **The History of German Lutheran Congregations in England, 1900-1950 (Frankfurt am Main, Verlag Peter Lang GmbH, 1987. ISBN: 3-8204-0971-8)**, written by Friedeborg L. Müller, whose husband, Jörg Müller, was, at one time, pastor of the German-speaking Lutheran congregations in the West Midlands. This contains an excellent section on the early history of the German Lutheran congregations in Britain up to 1914. A detailed history of the Diocese in Jerusalem can be found in Rafiq A. Farah's **In Troubled Waters: A History of the Anglican Church in Jerusalem, 1841-1998 (Bridport, Christians Aware, 2002. ISBN: 1-873372-16-7)**.

Susanna Winkworth's original translation of the **Theologia Germanica** was out of print for many years, but was eventually reprinted **(London, Vincent Stuart and John M. Watkins Ltd, 1966. No ISBN)**. A newer translation is now available in the *Classics of Western Spirituality* series **(London, SPCK, 1980. ISBN: 0-281-03762-0)**.

Chapter 20 | From the Beginning of the First World War to the Present Day

The outbreak of the First World War in 1914 brought serious difficulties for all the Lutheran churches in Great Britain, but it was a major blow to those which used the German language. There was very strong feeling against anyone who was seen to have a connection with Germany, however tenuous it might be. "German" businesses and property were attacked, many people of German background were interned, and even the royal family had to change its name from Saxe-Coburg-Gotha to Windsor. Pastors were repatriated to Germany, church services could no longer be held, and church buildings were confiscated.

The First World War created difficulties for the Nordic churches as well. Denmark, Iceland, Norway, and Sweden were neutral, whereas Finland and the Baltic provinces, which were part of the Russian Empire, were part of an alliance which included Great Britain, France, and Italy, along with some smaller nations. Anglo-Nordic trade suffered, as trade through the U-boat-infested waters of the Baltic and the North Sea became increasingly difficult.

What is apparent from all that has been said about Lutherans in Britain since the first congregation was established in 1669 is that their congregations all used languages other than English for their worship and pastoral service. Pastors may, on occasion, have used English on special occasions, but, as we saw in the case of St George's congregation in the late 18th century, the use of the language was frowned upon. Lutheran congregations and seamen's missions in Great Britain were here to serve people who wished to use their mother-tongues, and there was no idea of mission within British society, but the seeds of an indigenous Lutheran Church were quietly planted towards the end of the 19th century.

Not all of the German migrants who left their homeland in the 19th century did so because of economic reasons; there were some who emigrated to the United States or Australia in order to escape from religious persecution. The reason for this is that they were "confessional" Lutherans, which is to say, Lutherans who set great store by their adherence to the Lutheran Confessions and who wished to retain their Lutheran identity and traditions. In some parts of Germany this became increasingly difficult as the 19th century progressed, because the rulers of some individual states imposed unions between Lutheran and Reformed congregations. The first major attempt at this occurred in Prussia as a result of a decision by its king, Frederick William III, following the Reformation celebrations of 1817, and as Prussia grew in size as the century progressed, so more and more parts of Germany were drawn into such politico-ecclesiastical unions. However, in some areas, such as Saxony and Silesia, there was resistance to these trends, and this eventually resulted in congregations which became known as "Old Lutheran", or in emigration.

For most of these confessional Lutherans, Britain was a staging-post on the route to somewhere else, but a small group settled in London and eventually established two small congregations in the northern part of the capital. The older of the congregations, known originally as Immanuel Church, was founded in Kentish Town by six German-speaking bakers and their families. They were unhappy at what they thought of as the non-confessional stance of the German-speaking churches which then existed in London, and they appealed for help to an American body, the Lutheran Church–Missouri Synod (LCMS). This body sent them a young pastor who, within five years had laid the foundations for organised church life and also helped them to establish a second congregation in Tottenham: these became the founding churches of the Evangelical Lutheran Church in England (ELCE) to which we will return below. These remained predominantly German-speaking congregations, but gradually introduced English into their ministry, and were thus able to escape the worst effects of the anti-German feeling which exploded after 1914.

The other German-speaking congregations faced an uphill struggle to re-establish themselves after 1918: church property had been confiscated, and it was not always possible to get it back; the few pastors who remained were concentrated in the London area, and, in general, people of German background were not happy to identify themselves as German. Something of a revival took place between 1925 and 1939, although the congregations faced unexpected challenges in their relationships with the church authorities in Germany.

Before, During and After the Second World War

The twelve years after Adolf Hitler's accession to power in 1933 – the years of the so-called "Third Reich" – saw an influx of Lutherans into Great Britain. Before the outbreak of the Second World War in 1939, hundreds of German-speaking Lutherans, often of supposed "non-Aryan" (ie Jewish) background, fled to Britain, and many of these found a home in the German-speaking congregations that had survived the First World War. Among the pastors who ministered to them in London was Dietrich Bonhoeffer (1906-1945), later to become famous as a theologian and martyr.

A key figure, and one who came to act as a bridge between churchmen in Germany and Great Britain, was George Bell (1883-1958), who, after several years as Dean of Canterbury, had been Bishop of Chichester since 1929. Bell was a convinced ecumenist who was active in the more practical side of ecumenical activity, and particularly in what had come to be known as "Life and Work", an organisation of which he was to become President. In this capacity, he had been present at a conference in Berlin in February of 1933, just days after the National Socialists took power in Germany, and thus had first-hand experience of the atmosphere in the country. Over the following months he became increasingly aware of the repressive measures being brought in – in particular, the anti-Semitic legislation – and continuously sought to make the British churches aware of what was happening. He became a staunch supporter of the *Bekennende Kirche* ("The Confessing Church"), the movement which had organised itself in opposition to the growing centralisation and nazification of the Protestant churches in Germany.

Bishop Bell got to know Bonhoeffer during the period between 1933 and 1935 when the young theologian was pastor of two German congregations in London: Sydenham and St Paul's, and a firm friendship was established between them. As had been the case throughout their history, the German-speaking congregations in Great Britain had operated largely independently of each other, and, although their pastors met together from time to time, there were differences between them as to what attitude to take towards events in Germany. However, at meetings in Bradford in November 1933, and in London in the following February, the pastors affirmed unequivocally that the heart of the church's message is Christ and the doctrine of justification by faith alone. Bonhoeffer returned to Germany in 1935, where he was asked to be the leader of one of the five new pastoral seminaries, established by the Confessing Church, and he continued to provide Bell with information about what was happening in the Third Reich.

The steady stream of refugees from Germany to Britain continued, among them Jews, Protestants, Roman Catholics, and people of no faith, and as Chairman of the *International Christian Committee for German Refugees,* Bishop Bell sought means of providing support for them, including giving help to "non-Aryan" refugee pastors. How to help them became a particularly crucial question because, after the outbreak of hostilities, hundreds of people were detained in camps across Britain, and, in particular, the Isle of Man, but, as the war proceeded increasing numbers of prisoners-of-war, among whom were many ordained pastors, were also held in camps. Eventually, Bishop Bell was able to secure the services of a Swedish pastor, Birger Forell, to serve as chaplain to the POW camps. Pastor Forell had been chaplain to the Swedish Embassy in Berlin from 1929 to 1942, so knew very well how the church had suffered and its pastors had been persecuted. The outcome of his work was the setting up of a theological school at a POW camp at Norton, in Nottinghamshire, which had the task of preparing pastors and teachers for service in post-war Germany. It flourished between 1945 and 1948, and among those who lectured there was Dr Anders Nygren (1890-1928), the Swedish theologian who became Bishop of Lund in 1949 and was the first President of the Lutheran World Federation (LWF) after its establishment in 1947. He contributed to an LWF report on "The Word, the Sacraments, and the Church" which used materials that he had delivered as lectures in Norton Camp. One of the camp's best known alumni is the distinguished theologian Jürgen Moltmann.

There are two other educational endeavours in which Bell played a part. The first of these was known as the *German Confessional Institute,* which was based in London and which was promoted strongly by a Presbyterian minister, William Paton, with the aim of preserving the work of the *Bekennende Kirche* in post-war Germany. Its life-time was quite short, but much longer lived was the *Training Centre for post-war Christian Service,* based in an old manor house at Wistow, just south of Leicester. Although not having exactly the same aims – the *Institute* was specifically theological, whereas the *Training Centre* was practical – they provided important opportunities for men and women to prepare themselves for service to the church in Germany after the war ended.

The *Training Centre* at Wistow was initially led by Dr Gunther Schweitzer: it trained many people to be parish workers, but after Dr Schweitzer returned to Germany in 1947 it gained a new leader and changed the focus of its work. The new warden was Willi Baermann, a refugee who had served as the *Centre's* treasurer, and a new name was adopted: *The Wistow Centre for International Christian Fellowship and Service,* and from this time onwards its main aim was to provide visitors with experience of communal life and ecumenical reconciliation. Incidentally, Mr Baermann has the distinction of being the first Lutheran pastor to be ordained in Britain – in St George's Church on 12 December 1948 – after the Second World War. After Wistow was closed in the summer of 1959, Pastor Baermann and his family moved to Leicester, where he served the German-speaking Lutheran congregation there.

In the preceding paragraphs, our emphasis has been on the refugees from Germany, but during the war itself, military personnel from countries such as Norway and Poland were stationed in Britain. The Norwegians were, of course, predominantly Lutheran, and not only did the Norwegian churches scattered across Great Britain provide them with a home from home, but new communities came into existence, particularly in Scotland. Units of the Polish army also found their way to Britain, and although Lutherans were only a tiny minority in pre-war Poland, there was a handful of Lutheran military chaplains, several of whom opted to stay on in Britain after the war. Included among these was Pastor Władysław Fierla, who, in addition to speaking Polish, also spoke Slovak. After 1945 most – but not all – of the Norwegians returned home (some had married British women and chose to stay here). Many demobilised Poles decided to remain rather than return to a homeland increasingly under the influence of the Soviet Union.

Only a handful of German-speaking congregations had managed to struggle on through the years of the Second World War, mostly in London, but also in Oxford and Liverpool. Life had not been easy for the Nordic congregations either, but they had survived in spite of the air-raids and other deprivations of wartime.

Towards the end of the war there had been a fierce attack on Lutherans – or at least on Martin Luther – in the form of a pamphlet written by Peter F. Wiener, a teacher of German in a well-known public school. Entitled *Martin Luther: Hitler's Spiritual Ancestor,* this publication, which ran to over eighty pages, emphasised the less savoury aspects of the reformer's theology, and, in particular, his anti-Semitism. In the aftermath of the war this brought forth a response from Lutheran pastors currently serving in Great Britain – Danish, Finnish, German, and Swedish – and it took the form of a book entitled *Luther Speaks,* containing a series of essays "for the fourth centenary of Martin Luther's death". Although it did not directly address the issues raised by Mr Wiener, the foreword, written by the distinguished Norwegian bishop, Eivind Berrgrav, mentioned the anger that the pamphlet had provoked among Lutherans, so it was certainly present in the back of the authors' minds. It was present in the minds of others as well, particularly that of Rev'd E. Gordon Rupp (1910-1986), a Methodist minister in south-east London, who had studied on the continent before the war and had a strong interest in Luther and his theology. In 1945 he responded to Mr Wiener's pamphlet with an erudite publication entitled *Martin Luther: Hitler's Cause or Cure?* in which he firmly rebutted the accusations that had been made. It is worth mentioning at this point that Dr Rupp went on to write one of the first books to deal comprehensively with Luther's theology: *The Righteousness of God: Luther Studies* (1953).

The Lutheran Council of Great Britain

In the years following the end of the Second World War, large numbers of refugees from Europe, many of whom were Lutheran, came into exile here. Many of these came from the Baltic States: thousands of people had left their homes rather than stay under Soviet re-occupation, and they found themselves living in camps for "displaced persons" scattered across Germany. In Estonia and Latvia the Lutheran churches had been established bodies embracing a large part of the population, but Lithuania, which, like Poland, was overwhelmingly Roman Catholic, also had a small, multilingual, Lutheran church. All three countries had enjoyed independence between the two world wars, but they had now been absorbed into the Soviet Union, and few of the refugees wanted to return to their homelands in these circumstances. Britain, which had seen large parts of its cities destroyed and many of its people killed, either in air raids or on active military service, was desperate to re-build its economy, and needed the human resources to help achieve this. The British government recognised the potential of the thousands of displaced persons living in the German camps, and in 1947 started recruiting "European Volunteer Workers" (EVWs) to come and work in Britain.

The situation that these EVWs found themselves in was often very difficult. Only in rare circumstances could whole families come: the authorities recruited single people, who were lodged in hostels and who were assigned work in factories, hospitals, and coal mines – irrespective of their previous experience and qualifications. Often working reluctantly in their assigned jobs, it was only after three years that they were permitted a wider choice and could look for more congenial employment. Gradually, however, the situation improved and families could be reunited. Naturally enough, having lost everything else, these men and women wanted to preserve their languages and cultures, and the church was an important way of doing this. Among these refugees were several pastors, and although in the early days they had to do manual work of different sorts, help from Lutherans in Sweden and the United States eventually made it possible for them to be released so that they could concentrate on pastoral work and gather people together in congregations. These were people of many different national backgrounds, but all shared the common experience of being displaced from their homelands, and shared the same Lutheran faith. Right from the start, in spite of the differences of language, culture, and tradition, Lutherans recognised their need for each other, and as early as 1948 they came together in "The Lutheran Council of Great Britain", which still serves as a co-operative agency for the majority of Lutherans in this country. The original groups which founded the Lutheran Council were The Evangelical Lutheran Church of England (ELCE), and the Estonian, German, Latvian, and Polish churches, but they have been joined over the years by the Lutheran Church in Great Britain and by several other language groups (Danish, Finnish, Hungarian, Icelandic, Norwegian, and Swedish), although the ELCE withdrew in 1956.

From the time of its establishment in 1948, the Lutheran Council of Great Britain was the primary agency for co-operation between

Lutherans in the United Kingdom. At first, its aims were strictly practical: it was the channel by which aid and assistance from Lutherans abroad could be brought to exiled pastors who were trying to gather their people together into congregations and establish some sort of congregational and synodical structures. Initially, this aid had come mainly from different Lutheran Church bodies in the United States and from Sweden, but after the establishment of the Lutheran World Federation (LWF) in 1947, the new body served as a distribution agent for this support.

At a very early stage the LWF appointed a "Senior Representative" to Great Britain, the first of whom was a clergyman from the United States, Rev'd David Ostergren. He and Dr George Pearce, pastor of the two ELCE congregations in north London, took the initiative in bringing together the leaders of the different exile groups to establish the Lutheran Council. Soon, influential people in the Council's founding leadership wished to broaden its aims from the practical, towards full unity and the establishment of one single united Lutheran Church in Great Britain, incorporating all the German, Nordic, Baltic and any other Lutherans in these islands, as we shall return to .

From the outset, the Lutheran Council took the view that its members should, as far as possible, do everything together, and the period from 1948 to the mid-1970s saw many different co-operative ventures. In addition to such practical matters as ensuring that pastors received regular salary subsidies, the Council set up a pension scheme, and established a fund to provide pastors with cars. It also provided bricks and mortar, such as the purchase of a Lutheran Church House in South Kensington, and the establishment of Hothorpe Hall in Northamptonshire as a Lutheran Youth and Conference Centre, and, eventually, the setting up of a Lutheran Student House in the Notting Hill area of London. At a local level, the Lutheran Council was able to direct funds to many congregations so that they could purchase or construct buildings, which meant that, by 1970, many major towns and cities had a visible Lutheran presence.

The significance of Hothorpe Hall in late 20th century Lutheran history cannot be exaggerated. Situated around five miles from the Leicestershire town of Market Harborough – geographically close to the heart of England – it was, for many Lutherans, a tangible reflection of both their diversity and their unity. Situated in 12 acres of land, the Georgian manor house, with its own late Victorian chapel, was purchased in 1955 for the princely sum of £3,400. This stately home, once the property of the de Trafford family, had been used for several different purposes since the Second World War, and although far from derelict a lot of work needed to be carried out before it could become fully habitable. The Lutheran Council's Youth Director, Rev'd Lloyd Swantz, was appointed as its Director, and he recruited volunteers, both from Britain and abroad, to come and help in restoring the house, which was eventually dedicated in 1956. From then, until it was sold in 1985, it provided a focus for Lutheran activity and a reminder to minority communities which were little known in Britain, that they were a part of a world-wide communion. It had a small permanent staff, supported by volunteers from all parts of the world, including, for many years, students from Luther College in Decorah, Iowa, two of whom would come for a year's placement as part of their study programme. For many years it had a language school providing instruction in English for overseas missionaries, led by Eva Stead, a refugee from the Third Reich who had been a member of St Mary's German-speaking congregation in London. Throughout its time as a Lutheran property it played a major role in providing a centre for youth activities, a highlight being a "Youth Festival" in 1965, which drew together more than a hundred young people of many different national backgrounds to discuss the theme of "Faith Victorious".

The Lutheran Council established a Lutheran Youth Association and a Women's Association, both of which held regular national and regional conferences, and it published a regular quarterly magazine called *The Lutheran in Great Britain*.

It is now nearly seventy years since the Lutheran Council was established, and, on the whole, it has been successful in carrying out its agreed tasks, although from time to time there have been the sort of frustrations that naturally occur when people of very different cultural and historical backgrounds work together. Inevitably, there have been many changes, but the membership of the Council has grown and it now brings together most of the Lutheran church bodies in Great Britain. Sadly, two former members, the Chinese Rhenish Church in London and the German-speaking Protestant Synod, have left the Council. Both of these church groups were bodies that had strong Reformed or *Unierte* ("United") connections, but two Lutheran congregations in the German-speaking Synod (St Mary's with St George's in London, and the German-speaking congregation in Liverpool) joined the Council in their own right. Also, the Danish church in London, which had never been a member but had always co-operated with the Council, became a member.

One significant feature of the work of the Lutherans during the period after 1970 was the way in which their presence became less visible. We noted above that around that time there was a concrete Lutheran presence in many major cities in the country, but in the years following there was a gradual selling off of church property. Church buildings in places such as Corby, Hull, Liverpool, and Middlesbrough were sold, as were church houses in South Wales, Bristol, and Leicester. Similarly, the Lutheran Council sold Hothorpe Hall and the Church House in South Kensington.

One success story was the building of the International Lutheran Student Centre (ILSC) in the Bloomsbury area of London, on the post-Second World War site of St Mary's German-speaking congregation, in-between St Pancras Railway Station and the University of London. Systematic work among overseas Lutheran students had originally begun at the beginning of the 1960s when the Lutheran Council appointed a Finnish woman, Aili Rytkonen, to work among them. She began what became known as "Open House" at the Lutheran Church House in Collingham Gardens, and these modest beginnings blossomed into a major investment by the Council. A house was bought in Pembridge Gardens, close to Notting Hill Gate underground station, and Edvin and Sylvie Eding, who were of Estonian background and members of St Paul's Lutheran Church in Corby, were appointed as its first wardens. In the 1970s, an agreement was reached with St Mary's to re-develop the Thanet Street site, using funds from the LWF (channelling donations from its member churches, including German, Nordic, and American Churches), the British Council, and the sale of LCGB properties. An efficient and striking piece of architecture was built, which continues to provide accommodation for over eighty students, as well as providing the headquarters for the Lutheran Council of Great Britain and Lutheran Church in Great Britain, and church premises for St Mary's with St George's Lutheran congregation.

English-speaking Lutheranism

To many British people, "Lutheran" meant something strange and foreign, but after the Second World War English-language Lutheranism began to develop. We have already seen how the two "confessional" German congregations in north London had switched to English, but until the 1950s they had not sought to expand their work. This changed in the mid-1950s when, with the help of the Lutheran Church–Missouri Synod and under the leadership of Dr George Pearce, the ELCE drew up a "Master Plan" which envisaged the planting of new congregations, not only in Greater London, but in selected places around the country. Not all of these congregations flourished and some of them eventually closed, but several of them grew and developed. Particularly important was the purchase of Westfield House in Cambridge to be a Lutheran House of Studies. Originally intended to train Lutheran pastors for work in the ELCE, it has diversified and now also provides a range of courses, including successful programmes for overseas students (see below).

Quite independently, Lutheran mission work had also been started in Cornwall. A native Cornishman, Joe Pedlar, had discovered Lutheranism while in the United States, and had eventually persuaded The Evangelical Lutheran Synod (ELS), an American Lutheran body of Norwegian background, to support his mission work. Eventually, the ELS sent an ordained pastor to work in Cornwall, but the mission only had limited success and was eventually absorbed into the ELCE towards the end of the 1950s.

Several of the German-speaking congregations around the country began holding occasional (sometimes monthly) services in English, with the intention of ministering to English-speaking partners in mixed marriages, and to the second and third generations who did not speak German. In one congregation, Bristol, the ministry became bi-lingual, with regular services alternating between German and English, whereas in some other congregations, such as Middlesborough, every service included both languages. One congregation, however, actually gave birth to an English-speaking congregation.

St Mary-le-Savoy had had a continuous history since its foundation at the end of the 17th century, although it had lost its home in the Savoy Palace when that building was bombed during the Second World War. Re-housed in a former Anglican parish building close to St Pancras railway station, it was served in the post-war years by Pastor Hans-Herbert Kramm, who had previously ministered to the German-speaking congregation in Oxford and whose Ph.D. thesis was published in 1947 under the title of *The Theology of Martin Luther*. Dr Kramm realised that there were increasing numbers of Lutherans in London for whom English was the *lingua franca,* and for many of whom the different language congregations could not provide a home. He began regular services in English, which, in turn, led to the eventual establishment of a separate congregation – this is now St Anne's Lutheran congregation in London, a member of LCiGB.

Subsequently, English-language Lutheran congregations were founded in High Wycombe, Hothorpe Hall, and Corby, a new town in Northamptonshire which had the largest number of Lutherans *per capita* of anywhere in Britain (around 500 in a town of 50,000) – although the congregation is now one of the smallest in LCiGB. Eventually, these four congregations came together in 1961 to establish the "United Lutheran Synod in Great Britain". Within a few years these had been joined by congregations in Birmingham, Leicester, and Leeds, to form the nucleus of what is now the Lutheran Church in Great Britain (LCiGB), to be later joined by Chinese, Swahili and Polish Lutheran congregations, to which we shall return in more detail below.

One reason for the development of the congregations in Birmingham, Leicester, and Leeds, was the adoption by the Lutheran Council of a "Development Plan", which envisaged increasing co-operation between Lutheran congregations at a local level, and even the eventual possibility of a united Lutheran church embracing most of the Lutheran congregations in the Great Britain. However, for many of the Lutherans in Britain, these were steps that were far too ambitious, and seemed doomed to failure. Most Lutherans were wedded to their mother tongues and, surrounded by friendly "Protestant" churches, could see no reason why they should develop English-language work when they and their children could go to local Anglican or Free Churches. In recent years an attitude of cooperation has been reinforced by the different international agreements that have come into being, such as the Meissen Agreement between the *Evangelische Kirche in Deutschland* (EKD) and the Church of England, and the Porvoo Agreement between The Nordic and Baltic Lutheran Churches and the Anglican Churches in Western Europe. Evidencing closer relationships with other Churches, these agreements provide great opportunities to work together, including mutual recognition of baptism and ministry under Porvoo.

FURTHER READING

There is a general book about immigrants to the United Kingdom by Francesca M. Wilson: **They came as Strangers: The Story of Refugees to Great Britain (London, Hamish Hamilton, 1959. No ISBN)**.

The Manual of Lutheran Activity in Great Britain (London, Lutheran Council of Great Britain, 1951), is long out of print, although it is hoped that the Council of Lutheran Churches might be able to make photocopies available to interested readers. Copies of the 1975 book, **The Lutheran Council of Great Britain**, and its 2004 booklet **Lutheran Churches in Great Britain: An Introduction**, are still available on request from the Council. The Lutheran Church in Great Britain published a booklet by Roy Long and Sarah Farrow in 2010 entitled **Lutherans in London: A Walk Exploring the History of Lutherans in London**, and this is available from the church office. There is a chapter on Lutherans in Britain in Roy Long's **The Lutheran Church (Exeter, Religious and Moral Education Press, 1984. ISBN: 0-08-029305-0)**. Dr George Pearce's booklet **The Story of the Lutheran Church in Britain Through Four Centuries of History (London, The Evangelical Lutheran Church of England, 1969. No ISBN)**, contains lots of interesting information, but concentrates primarily on the history of the ELCE.

Friedeborg Müller's book on the German-speaking Lutheran Congregations in Britain up to 1950 (mentioned at the end of the preceding section) actually takes the story forward beyond that date, and gives a distinctive interpretation of events. Readers interested in the background to the effects of the Third Reich on German-speaking Lutherans in Britain, and of related matters, can consult any one of a number of books about Dietrich Bonhoeffer, of which one of the most recent is Ferdinand Schlingensiepen's **Dietrich Bonhoeffer: 1906-1945 (London, T&T Clark International, 2010. ISBN: 978-0-567-03400-7)**.

There is a fascinating account of the early history of the Wistow Community, which takes the story from the beginnings to around 1950. This was written by Lisbet Baermann, wife of Pastor Willi Baermann, and is entitled **The Wistow Story: A Venture of Faith, Part One**. This was printed privately and lacks publication details, including the date it was published. Its interest lies in the fact that it gives very interesting background material to the situation of refugees of "non-Aryan" background in Great Britain.

Chapter 21 | Theological Education

With one exception, Pastor Willi Baermann, all of the Lutheran pastors who came to Britain as "displaced persons" as a result of the Second World War had received their theological education in their country of origin. For most of them, this meant an education that was very largely influenced by German theology: it was heavily academic, and practical training was rather limited. By the mid-1950s it was also becoming clear that a shortage of pastors was beginning to develop: several pastors from the Estonian, Hungarian, and Latvian churches had left the country and moved on to serve congregations elsewhere – mostly in North America. This meant that congregations in Britain would either have to call pastors from abroad, or that some sort of theological training would need to be developed here.

Mansfield College

It was against this background that the LWF, in co-operation with the Lutheran Council, decided to establish a Lutheran tutorship in Mansfield College, Oxford. At the time (the mid-1950s), Mansfield, which was a Congregationalist foundation, was not a full college of the university, but a "Permanent Private Hall", which was, however, able to enter students for university degrees. (Mansfield became a full college in 1995.) As well as helping in the training of pastors, The LWF tutorship provided a Lutheran theological presence in the University and a chaplaincy to Lutheran students there. In total, a dozen pastors were trained there, including students of American, British, Estonian, Hungarian, and Latvian background. Once trained and ordained, most of these pastors not only served in their own national language congregations, but in English-speaking Lutheran congregations as well. Not all of these theological students actually took degrees: several of them had had their education interrupted by the events of the Second World War and so were not able to meet the matriculation requirements of the university. However, they were all given a full three-year theological education, which contained a significant element of practical pastoral training. Interestingly, one of the LWF tutors, Dr Jan Womer, served as Principal of the College from 1986 to 1988.

Studying in Mansfield College brought with it many significant opportunities. Because it had provided a home for some pre-Second World War Lutheran refugees from the Third Reich, the college was very sympathetic towards Lutherans, and it had a number of well-known theologians on its staff who were well acquainted with Lutheran theology (Dr John Marsh, Principal from 1953 to 1970, had translated some of the German theologian Rudolf Bultmann's works into English). Lutheran students were able to attend lectures given by some of the best contemporary British theologians, and there was a Lutheran tutor to provide a confessional input to their studies. Overall, the course was rigorous, demanding, and, in the fullest sense of the word, ecumenical. There were Lutheran services of Matins and Vespers once a week in the college chapel, and twice a term the college's Sunday Service took the form of a Lutheran celebration of the Lord's Supper.

The LWF ceased to provide a tutor in the late 1990s, and with that the formal Lutheran contact with Mansfield College came to an end.

The Selly Oak Colleges in Birmingham

Theological education of a rather different flavour was developed in the Selly Oak Colleges in Birmingham. These institutions had a long and honourable history as providers of education for people who wanted to train as missionaries abroad, or in different aspects of service in their churches at home, such as teacher training or youth work. Administered by different denominational bodies, they had developed a good working relationship and had established a Federation with a Central Council.

As long ago as 1910, after the Edinburgh Missionary Conference, the Selly Oak Colleges had welcomed missionary candidates from Lutheran Churches in Germany and the Nordic countries, and this Lutheran presence continued, despite the interruptions of the two world wars: it grew in importance, and in the late 1960s it resulted in Lutherans being appointed to the central staff of the colleges. The first of these was Dr Johannes Aagaard, who was seconded from his post in the University of Aarhus for the academic year 1967-68, to be followed the next year by Dr C. F. Hallencreutz, who was from the University of Uppsala. These appointments were jointly funded on a temporary basis by the Mission Councils in Germany and the Nordic countries, but thanks to the energy and enthusiasm of Dr Sigvard von Sicard, a Lutheran academic of Swedish background and an expert in Islamic Studies, the LWF held a consultation in Copenhagen in 1970, and this took the step of establishing a permanent lectureship in Selly Oak. This continued under the leadership, first of all, of Dr von Sicard, then of a German missiologist, Dr Gottfried Rothermundt, and finally of a Norwegian, Dr Aasulf Lande. Although the successive lecturers in Selly Oak interpreted their task in different ways, they all maintained links with the Lutheran Council of Great Britain.

There were three significant features of this work. Firstly, from an ecumenical perspective, the Lutheran presence in Selly Oak helped to strengthen the connection between British missionary activity and that of the Lutheran churches around the world; secondly, the lecturers provided pastoral care for the growing number of overseas students in the higher education institutes in Birmingham and the West Midlands; and thirdly, the lecturers were able to make a distinctive contribution to the teaching in the colleges. Sadly, in 1997, the LWF decided to withdraw its support and the lectureship came to an end.

Westfield House, Cambridge

From an early stage in its expansion, the ELCE recognised that it would need to establish a centre where it could train pastors and conduct research, and such work started in 1956, when Dr William Arndt, who had worked as professor of Greek in Concordia Seminary in Saint Louis, Missouri, came to Cambridge. Initially, the ELCE came to an arrangement with Fitzwilliam College, whereby candidates for the Lutheran ministry could study there for a degree in theology, with Dr Arndt providing some distinctively Lutheran elements. Sadly, Dr Arndt died in February of 1957 and Pastor Norman Nagel was called from the Luther-Tyndale congregation in London to be his successor. His priority was to study for a doctorate, which he was eventually awarded for a thesis on Luther's

Doctrine of the Lord's Supper, but at the same time he had a pivotal role in establishing a more permanent place for potential ordinands to study. Westfield House, a short walk from the centre of Cambridge, was purchased in the summer of 1960, and, after being thoroughly refurbished, was dedicated in February 1962: an inaugural lecture entitled *The Freedom we have in Christ*, was delivered as part of the celebrations by Bishop Bo Giertz of the Church of Sweden Diocese of Göteborg. After more than half a century, Westfield House is still flourishing, and over the decades has diversified its programme to not only train students for the ministry of the ELCE, but also to provide a place for overseas students to pursue their studies.

Ecumenical Ordination Courses

Of course, Lutheran pastors coming to serve in Britain from their home churches abroad had received a thorough theological education in their country of origin, but the end of the Lutheran lectureships in Mansfield College and Selly Oak in the late 1990s meant that, apart from Westfield House, there was no longer any formal Lutheran presence in institutions of higher education in Great Britain. This also meant that there were no places where potential ordinands could have a full-time theological education with a distinctively Lutheran input, and several recent candidates for the ministry have either taken part-time courses in non-Lutheran colleges, such as Oakhill College in North London, or have availed themselves of the opportunities provided by ecumenical ordination courses. The prototype for these courses was the "Southwark Ordination Course", but individuals wishing to receive a theological education by this route have participated in the Northern Ordination Course, which was based in Manchester, the Yorkshire Ordination Course, based at the College of the Resurrection in Mirfield, or the South East Institute for Theological Education (SEITE), based in London. These courses, which are part-time, can be very stressful for the participants, but they have the advantage that they are ecumenical. The disadvantage is that any Lutheran input can only come from the candidates' own churches.

Chapter 22 | Lutherans in Scotland and Wales

Inevitably, much of the discussion so far has concentrated on England, but England is only one of the four countries that make up the United Kingdom, and Scotland, Wales, and Northern Ireland also have Lutheran congregations. In this chapter we shall concentrate on Scotland and Wales and give a brief glimpse into the historical background of the Lutheran presence there, and then, in the next chapter, look at the Lutheran Church in Ireland.

Lutherans in Scotland

With something over 5.5 million people, Scotland is the second largest of the nations which make up the United Kingdom, and it has a very distinctive social and religious culture. The crowns of the two countries were united in 1603 when James VI of Scotland (d.1625) succeeded his cousin, Elizabeth I, and became James I of England. The actual political union of the two countries did not occur until 1707, although that did not prevent the Stuart monarchs – including both James I and his son Charles I – from interfering in the country's religious affairs and causing turmoil and insurrection.

Scotland, in the early 17th century, was essentially two cultures within one nation. Broadly speaking, there was the country south of the "highland line", which spoke Scots, a distinctive language similar to English, and which had embraced reform along Presbyterian lines, and there was the area to the north and west, which spoke Gaelic and which had preserved the old Celtic and Catholic culture. The Scottish Parliament had formally adopted the Presbyterian system of church government in 1560, but there were still bishops, and it took almost a century and a half before the Church of Scotland emerged as fully Presbyterian.

There were no Lutheran congregations in Scotland until the second half of the 19th century, but that is not to say that there had been no Lutheran influence in the country, and, indeed, the first Lutheran martyr in these islands was a Scotsman with connections to the royal family. He was Patrick Hamilton (1504-1528), a second cousin of King James V (reigned 1513-1542), who, after studying in St Andrew's and then in Paris and the Low Countries, returned to Scotland and taught in St Andrew's. However, he was coming under the influence of Martin Luther and, recognising that discretion was the better part of valour, he escaped to the continent, travelling first to Wittenberg, where he met Luther and Melanchthon, and then on to Marburg, where he studied in the university that had recently been established by the Margrave, Philip of Hesse. While in Marburg he wrote (in Latin) a brief summary of the relationship between Law and Gospel, which was subsequently translated into English by John Frith, and which has come down to us as "Patrick's Places". Subsequently, Hamilton returned to Scotland, fell foul of the authorities, was arrested, tried, and speedily executed on 29 February 1528.

"Patrick's Places" is a tantalising document: it is undoubtedly Lutheran in its theology, but it is a very short document which focuses on the distinction between Law and Gospel, but which gives no clues as to what Hamilton thought about such matters as the church or the Lord's Supper. But he was not the only Scottish Lutheran: one of the men who examined him before his trial, Alexander Alesius (1500-1565), was so moved by his death that he adopted Lutheran ideas: he moved, first to England, but then, eventually, to Germany, where he became a professor in a Lutheran university. John Macalpine was another Scottish reformer who was eventually to serve the church abroad: the brother-in-law of Miles Coverdale, the Bible translator, he ended up teaching in the Danish university of Copenhagen. And there were others: John Gau (or Gaw), John Johnsone, and the Wedderburn brothers, James, John, and Robert. John Gau and John Johnsone both wrote popular explanations of Lutheran theology, and the Wedderburns put together a collection of hymns. After this, there is a gap in the history of Lutherans in Scotland, largely because the religious influences were predominantly Calvinist, although we might just mention that James VI's wife Anne (1574-1619), was a Danish Lutheran princess, although she eventually converted to Roman Catholicism.

The first Lutheran congregations in Scotland date from the 1860s and were German and Norwegian. Although we do not have a lot of evidence about German immigration to Scotland, we know that some small communities were established in the country, although settlement was never on the same scale as that in London or the north of England. A German congregation was established in Edinburgh in 1863, to be followed a few months later by a Norwegian chaplaincy for seamen. The Norwegian work, which eventually led to the establishment of a church building in Leith, was actually the first Nordic seamen's mission to be established, although it is now an arts college and the Lutheran congregation meets in St Mary's Episcopal church. This congregation was served in the beginning by Pastor Johan Cordt Harmens Storjohann, whose first service, in a hired schoolroom next to the Mariners' Church in Leith, was held on Whit Sunday in 1864. Further Norwegian work was started in several other places during the decades that followed – Glasgow, Greenock, Grangemouth, Methil, Burntisland – places which featured in the considerable trade between Scotland and Norway. More German congregations were established, too, in Glasgow, Dundee, Aberdeen, and Perth, and Swedish seamen's missions appeared in Aberdeen and Baltasound.

All the German-speaking congregations ceased their ministries at the outbreak of the First World War, and, so far as we know, there was no attempt to revive them at any point between then and the years after the Second World War. However, the period between 1940 and 1945 was a time of considerable Lutheran activity in Scotland. Early in April, 1940, Norway was attacked by Germany, and, although the Norwegian armed forces put up a determined resistance, they were no match for the German invaders and King Haakon and his government were forced to flee to Britain. Although the government-in-exile was in London, the Norwegian armed forces that had escaped were stationed in Scotland, and, in particular, in Dumfriesshire, Clydeside, Moray, and Shetland, where they were served by military chaplains who had accompanied them. The little Moray town of Buckie was a major centre of activity for escaped fishing boats, and became known as "Little Norway": church work was begun there in 1942 by the Norwegian Seamen's Mission and continued under the supervision of the pastor from Leith until 1946. Norwegian activity in Shetland became well known after the end of the war because of the "Shetland Bus", the name given to the operation to transport military hardware and personnel to Norway to help the resistance movement. Almost all of this military chaplaincy work in Norwegian ended shortly after 1945, and most Norwegian military personnel returned home, but the seamen's chaplaincies continued until the 1980s, and the seamen's church in London now serves the Norwegian communities in Scotland.

The other foreign military presence in Scotland during the wartime years was Polish, and escaped Polish servicemen were organised into fighting unites as early as 1940. Of course, the majority of Poles were Roman Catholic, but a small percentage was Lutheran, and there were at least three Lutheran army chaplains who conducted services for their co-religionists. Many of the Poles remained in Scotland after the war, and, although there was no resident pastor, pastors from England travelled north to conduct regular services, and work continues in both Edinburgh and Glasgow up to the present day.

German-speaking church activity re-emerged in Scotland after 1945 for much the same reasons as in other parts of the United Kingdom, and congregations were eventually established in several of the major cities in the country. In one respect, however, they were different from the congregations elsewhere, insofar as they were quite consciously Reformed, rather than Lutheran, although every congregation had within it people of Lutheran background.

Just as in the rest of Great Britain, there was also an influx of Baltic Lutherans into Scotland after 1947, and statistics from 1951 suggest that there were around 250 Estonian and 200 Latvian Lutherans in Scotland, each with a resident pastor, but work among these people slowly declined, and today no services are held there in either language. Scotland does, however, have one English-speaking congregation. This is located in East Kilbride, a new town to the south-east of Glasgow, where the Evangelical Lutheran Church of England established a parish in 1962, and although it no longer has a resident pastor (it is served from Sunderland), it continues to minister to a small but faithful congregation.

Lutherans in Wales

The principality of Wales, lying in-between the English Midlands and the Irish Sea, has an ancient and distinctive Celtic language and culture. Although both of these have been threatened for centuries by the predominance of English, they have survived and, with the advent of political devolution at the very end of the 20th century, they have grown and flourished.

Wales has been Christian for over 1,500 years and most of the mainstream denominations are represented there. The time of the Reformation coincided with the country's legal and political integration into the Tudor kingdom, which meant that the church underwent the same changes as the church in England, although there is no record of any Lutheran influence, such as there was in England in the time of Henry VIII. Industrialisation on a massive scale began towards the end of the 18th century, particularly with coal mining and steel making in south Wales, and this was accompanied by the growth of the Nonconformist churches, whose chapels became an important feature of Welsh life.

Lutheran activity in Wales seems to have started in the mid-1860s, and by the end of the 19th century there were churches and congregations in several places in south Wales. The first church to be established was Norwegian: it was built at West Bute Dock in Cardiff and was dedicated in 1868, and was soon followed by churches in Barry and Newport. The need for these churches was directly related to the enormous growth in trade between Wales and Norway, particularly in the export of coal from the burgeoning seaports along the coast of south Wales. Norway was covered in forests and its timber helped to meet the need for the pit-props that were used to support the roofs of the tunnels in the coal mines. Norwegian ships were a common sight in these south Welsh ports, but there was also a growing resident community which involved itself in the welfare of the visiting sailors. The Norwegian churches were not only centres of spiritual life, but provided reading rooms and hospitality for men who might often be away from home for months at a time. Prominent among the Norwegians who had settled in Wales was a certain Harald Dahl, whose son, Roald, went on to become the world-renowned author of books for children.

These churches continued their ministry until the 1970s, and were particularly active during the dark days of the Second World War, when many Norwegian sailors were prevented from returning to occupied Norway. However, massive changes took place in international trade as traditional practices were replaced by fast turnaround on-off container ships, and there was less need for the sort of ministry that the seamen's churches had provided. The surviving churches in Cardiff and Swansea became redundant and there was every danger that both of them might be demolished, but vigorous action by the local Norwegian communities and their friends meant that they were saved. The church in Cardiff was rebuilt in a prominent position on the waterfront of Cardiff Bay and now houses the Norwegian Church Cultural Centre, and the Swansea Church (originally built in Newport, but transported in its entirety to Swansea in 1909), is now in the heart of a redeveloped area of the city.

A Lutheran ministry in the German language started in South Wales a little while after the one in Norwegian. Initially, the work was inter-denominational, and was begun by a Baptist by the name of James Schmutz, who was able to build a small "German Church" in Cardiff in 1882. Specifically Lutheran work was undertaken by the German Seamen's Mission across the whole of the Bristol Channel area, and an organised congregation covering Bristol, Cardiff, and Swansea was established on 21 March 1909, but, like most of the other German-speaking congregations in Great Britain, its work came to an end with the outbreak of the First World War in 1914. Between the end of that war in 1918 and the end of the Second World War in 1945, there was no church work at all in the German language.

The post-war years saw the same sort of influx of German-speaking Lutherans into Wales as into the rest of the United Kingdom – released prisoners of war who either did not want to return to Germany, or who came from areas that were no longer German, eg East Prussia or western Poland; German women who had married soldiers from the British Army of the Rhine; and a small number of students, au-pairs, and others. Informal meetings were held in different places in the immediate post-war years, and in 1948 church services had been held in Cardiff, Swansea, Carmarthen, and Llanelli, conducted by the pastor in Bristol. Eventually, in 1956, a congregation covering the whole of south Wales was established, distinct from that of Bristol, and within months a Lutheran Church House had been purchased in the western side of Cardiff. The next year, 1958, a small Lutheran Church House was also purchased in Llanelli, and the work in west Wales was organised as a separate congregation. In 1978, thirty years after the first service had been held, the German-speaking congregations published a commemorative book outlining the history of the work over the preceding century, and could report that congregational activities of different sorts were taking place in Cardiff, Swansea, Llanelli, Port Talbot, Newport, and Cwmbran. But, as elsewhere, diminishing numbers of members and financial support led to a restructuring of German-speaking church work across the whole country, and in the second decade of the 21st century the pastor is again resident in Bristol and services are restricted to Cardiff and Swansea.

Alongside the German-speaking population that arrived in south Wales after the Second World War came displaced persons from eastern and central Europe, and particularly from the Baltic States and Poland. In the case of the Latvians and Estonians we can trace the presence of individuals and communities earlier than the late 1940s. Although little is known of his activities, a Latvian pastor, Konstantīns Ūdris, lived and worked in the Bristol Channel area in the early years of the 20th century, serving Latvian seamen who worked on ships transporting goods between Riga and Cardiff. He seems to have lived in Cardiff, but worked across the whole area. It seems likely that a few Latvians were resident in south Wales after this, but nothing is known for certain. We do know, however, that there were some Estonians living in the area throughout the Second World War – ships' crews (and in some cases their families) who were prevented from returning to Estonia when the country was occupied by the Soviet Union in 1940, and who made their permanent home in and around Cardiff. The number of Latvians and Estonians in the area was swelled considerably by the men and women who arrived after 1947, and Latvian congregations were established in several places, served by a pastor resident in Bristol; the same was true of the Estonian community, which was also served by a pastor from Bristol. These congregations flourished from then until the 1980s, by which time many of the older generation had passed away and younger people had either lost interest in church activities, moved away, or been assimilated into the wider community. Today, there are no Estonian services in the area, and Latvian services are restricted to twice-yearly gatherings in Swansea.

Similar things happened with the Polish Lutherans who found themselves in south Wales, but here things were exacerbated by the minority situation which Lutherans had found themselves in in Poland, and by the very wide parishes which Polish pastors in Britain had to serve. A map showing Polish Lutheran activity from 1951 shows that the pastor resident in Birmingham, who served south Wales, had to travel as far north as Manchester and as far south as Plymouth, ministering to eleven congregations or preaching stations. Much later on, in the 1970s, responsibility for the Polish Lutherans in Wales – which actually, by this stage, meant Cardiff – was transferred to a pastor from London and is now merged into the LCiGB.

Cardiff has also seen two examples of ministries in the English language. The first example of this was started in 1964 on the initiative of the then pastor of the German-speaking congregation, Bernd Krug, who was instrumental in setting up an "Inter-Lutheran Church Committee". This came to an agreement with the Norwegian Seamen's Mission to refurbish the redundant church in Bute Docks and begin monthly English services there for people from the different Lutheran groups in the area. These services flourished for a dozen or so years, but eventually came to an end in the late 1970s. The other English-language ministry was begun by the ELCE in the 1960s, when a mission was started in the Fairwater district of Cardiff as part of the church's Mission Plan. This eventually led to the establishment of St David's Evangelical Lutheran Church, which continues its ministry to this day.

FURTHER READING

There is no official history of Lutherans in Scotland, but with the assistance of pastors serving the congregations there, Roy Long produced two papers, both of which were printed privately. These are entitled, respectively, *Some Early Scottish Lutherans*, and *Lutherans in Scotland: A Brief Introduction*. Both of these were revised and updated in 2016 and are available from the author at roy.long485@btinternet.com. There are two invaluable sources of information about Lutheran ministries in Wales. The first, published in German and English by the German-speaking congregations in South and West Wales, is entitled **Gemeinden in Wales 1948-1978**, and contains a mixture of historical information and personal reminiscences. Similarly, there is an excellent booklet about the Norwegian churches, written in English, Norwegian, and Welsh: its English title is **A Little Bit of Norway in Wales: Recollections of the Norwegian Seamen's Churches**. This was produced to accompany an exhibition at the Norwegian Cultural Centre in Cardiff in 2006.

Chapter 23 | The Lutheran Church in Ireland

In a booklet that is concerned with charting the history of Lutherans in Great Britain, it might seem strange to include a brief section on the Lutheran Church in Ireland. The twenty-six counties which today make up the Republic of Ireland (or Éire, to give it its name in Irish) first became independent as the Irish Free State in 1922, but eventually left the British Commonwealth in 1949. However, like all other denominations, the ministry of the Lutheran Church in Ireland covers the whole island, including Northern Ireland, which is part of the United Kingdom, and it seems appropriate, therefore, to include a few words about it.

The principal congregation of the Lutheran Church in Ireland is in Dublin, where it worships in St Finian's Church in the south of the city, but services are also held on a regular basis in Belfast and several other places across the country. The work of the congregation began in the mid-1950s, and the first pastor was Pastor Hans Mittorp, who was installed in his post on 17 April 1955 by Dr Hans Lilje, Bishop of Hanover. St Finian's, which had been used by the (Anglican) Church of Ireland for many years, was made available to the Lutheran community in 1960 through the good offices of Archbishop George Otto Sims (whose mother was Lutheran), and was dedicated on 21 May 1961. The church has a longer and interesting history, having been built originally in 1863 for use by a sect known as the "Catholic Apostolic Church" – sometimes known as the "Irvingites" after its founder Edward Irving.

Although the present Dublin congregation is only a little more than sixty years old, it is actually the spiritual descendant of the Lutheran congregation established in the time of King William III, which has been described earlier. That congregation eventually had its own church in the centre of Dublin, but by the middle of the 19th century the Lutheran community had ceased to exist and, according to some reports, the church burned down.

Since the congregation was re-established in the middle of the 20th century, it has always been open to the use of the English language, and today St Finian's has three German services a month, and one in English. Services are also held from time to time in Latvian, Polish, and Swedish. Today, with a new "Luther House" adjacent to St Finian's, the Lutheran Church in Ireland is an active and flourishing community with strong ecumenical links to both the Protestant and Roman Catholic churches.

The congregation in Belfast has survived, despite suffering – as many others did – during the time of "The Troubles". Although it is German-speaking, like the congregation in Dublin, it has also been willing to use the English language, and, indeed, had an English-speaking pastor for a couple of years in the early 1960s. He was David Hoecker, an American theological student, and was ordained in St Finian's on Reformation Day, 31 October 1961, specifically to serve in Belfast. There is some uncertainty about how long he remained in Northern Ireland, but it is believed that he returned to the United States after about eighteen months.

As in Scotland and Wales, there are Swedish and Latvian Lutheran congregations that meet in borrowed premises, served by their pastors who visit from London.

FURTHER READING

On the occasion of the celebration of the 300th anniversary of the founding of the congregation in Dublin, a bilingual book was published, entitled **Evangelisch-Lutherische Kirche in Ireland – 1697-1997 – The Lutheran Church in Ireland**. A similar booklet was published in October 2009 with the title **Lutheran Church in Belfast and Dublin – 25 Years Joined Together**, commemorating the association of the Belfast and Dublin Congregations in 1984.

Chapter 24 | Author's Postscript to Part Three

The one thing that is immediately obvious from this history of Lutherans in Britain is that there are, in effect, *three* histories. The first is that of the Reformation itself, when there was a brief flowering of what we might call "indigenous" Lutheran thinking, typified in England by men and women such as Robert Barnes and Katherine Parr. But Henry VIII, with whom power in England ultimately lay, was personally ill-disposed towards Luther and his ideas, and by the time that conditions were favourable to reform – during the reigns of Edward VI and Elizabeth I – the stronger reformist influences were coming from Switzerland rather than Wittenberg. The story in Scotland was much the same: Patrick Hamilton died before his theological potential could mature, and the other Scots who held Lutheran views, such as Alexander Alesius and John Macalpine, were forced to work abroad. Although Lutherans in Britain can claim these men and women as their spiritual ancestors, there is no direct historical continuity between them and later Lutheranism.

The second history is that of Lutherans in Britain and Ireland from the second half of the 17th century, and that history is largely one of "foreign" Lutheran congregations and chaplaincies. These congregations, which have come into existence since Charles II issued his Letters Patent to the group of North European merchants and traders who formed the nucleus of the Hamburg Church, have always consisted of people whose origins lay outside these islands. True, there have frequently been strong links with local people and churches, but the Lutheran congregations using languages other than English have never seen themselves as being directly involved in any form of mission work within the wider community. On the other hand the ELCE and the LCiGB both use English as their primary language, and are very much involved in mission.

The third history is that of Lutheran influence in Great Britain and Ireland. Over the centuries this has waxed and waned, but it has always been present in one form or another. There was, obviously, the influence that Martin Luther and Lutheran theology exercised on individuals and events at the time of the Reformation and afterwards. There was also the interest shown by individuals – such as John Bunyan, John Wesley, and Thomas Carlyle – in Luther's theology (although it has to be said that their understanding of it may have been partial). There are also those British theologians who have, particularly since the end of the Second World War, sought to make Luther better known in these islands: among others, Philip Watson, Gordon Rupp, James Atkinson, John Schofield, and Alec Ryrie. And – difficult to assess – there is the influence that Lutheran pastors and lay people have had within their local communities.

Yet still, Lutherans are sometimes referred to as *Lutherians*, or assumed to take their name from the late Dr Martin Luther King. A lot still needs to be done to ensure that Lutherans are better known in Britain.

Part 4 | Lutherans in Britain Today

In Part Three we have looked at Lutherans and Lutheran activity in Britain since the time of the Reformation. Now, in Part Four, we shall bring the story up to date by looking at the distinctive language groups which make up the Lutheran communities in Britain, setting them, where applicable, in the context of the church situation in their homelands. The method employed is the simple one of using the 1951 *Manual of Lutheran Activity in Great Britain* as a source of information and statistics for the post-Second World War Lutheran presence in these islands, and trying to sketch in the history of the intervening years down to the present time – a convenient cut-off point being 2011, sixty years after *The Manual* was published.

Sjømannskirken St Olav's Norwegian Church in London

Chapter 25 | Nordic and Baltic Lutherans

Chronologically, some of the first Lutheran congregations in Britain were established by Lutherans from the Nordic countries. The third Lutheran congregation in London, the "Danish Church", was built in Wellclose Square in the 1690s, and a Swedish congregation was established in 1710. Further Nordic churches were established in the 19th century, including Finnish and Norwegian seamen's churches, and an Icelandic congregation came into being towards the end of the 20th century. The Baltic congregations, on the other hand, came into being as a result of the mass displacement of their populations after the Second World War. However, although they originated at different times and for different reasons, it is appropriate, because they now all adhere to the Porvoo Agreement, that we treat them together.

The Porvoo Agreement

On 28 November 1996 a service was held in Westminster Abbey in the presence of the Queen and the Duke of Edinburgh. The procession of clergy that made its way down the aisle towards the chancel included ministers and moderators, priests, bishops, and archbishops, drawn from all the major Christian churches of the world, but a look at the Order of Service indicates a predominance of Anglicans and Lutherans from northern and western Europe. This was a service to celebrate "*The Porvoo Agreement between the British and Irish Anglican Churches and the Nordic and Baltic Lutheran Churches*", which, the "Historical Note" at the beginning of the Order of Service observed "is the most significant ecumenical agreement into which these churches have ever entered". It was also noted that this service in Westminster Abbey had been preceded by similar services in the Norwegian city of Trondheim on

1 September 1996, and in Tallinn, the capital of Estonia, seven days later on 8 September. At each of these services, copies of the Agreement were signed by representatives of the churches, though not by those of the Church of Denmark or the Evangelical-Lutheran Church of Latvia.

The Porvoo Agreement of 1992 was the culmination of more than a hundred years of inter-church dialogue. Starting in the last decades of the 19th century, the Nordic and Baltic Lutheran Churches had begun to develop an interest and involvement in ecumenical matters, and this took two forms – their relationships with each other and their relationships with other churches. By the end of the 20th century they had established strong links with each other and with Lutherans elsewhere, and they had joined the Lutheran World Federation when it was established in 1947, although the political situation in the Baltic States made active participation difficult for the churches there.

An ecumenical enthusiast of the early 20th century, Nathan Söderblom (d.1931), Archbishop of Uppsala, was a pioneer of inter-Lutheran co-operation with neighbouring churches. He seems to have been fond of referring to the Baltic Sea as *Mare Lutheranum* ("The Lutheran Sea") and he spent much time trying to bring the Lutheran churches in the nations surrounding it into closer fellowship, based, among other things, on the concept of bishops in what is usually referred to as "apostolic succession", ie the unbroken historic succession of bishops from early times down to the present day. As we shall see, as Archbishop he consecrated an archbishop in the church of Estonia and a bishop in Latvia (whose successor adopted the title Archbishop), but less well known is that he also blessed the Bishop of the Lutheran Church in Slovakia.

But the Nordic and Baltic churches also began to forge links with other denominations, most notably the Church of England – and, by extension, the other Anglican churches in Europe. From the 1880s, the Church of Sweden began to develop closer ties with the Church of England, and other Lutheran churches followed suit. Granted, with the similarities in church structure between these churches and the Church of England, it was almost natural that strong relationships should have developed between the Nordic Lutherans and the Church of England and other Anglican Churches in Europe. Bi-lateral agreements were reached in the 1920s between the Church of England and the Church of Sweden, and then subsequently with the Lutheran churches in Finland, Estonia, and

Latvia, and in the early 1950s there were theological discussions between the Church of England and the Churches of Denmark, Iceland, and Norway (1953). Although these were, in their different ways, official moves, at a less formal level a very significant role was played by the Anglo-Scandinavian Theological Conferences, which began in 1929 and, with a break during the Second World War, have continued every two or three years down to the present day. Each of these distinct and separate initiatives can be seen as a forerunner of Porvoo.

The city of Porvoo (in Swedish, Borgå), from which the Agreement takes its name, lies some thirty miles east of Helsinki, the capital of Finland. It is a very historic city – the second oldest in the country – and it started out as a trading centre in the 13th century. Its ancient cathedral has witnessed many significant events, including the first Imperial Diet after Finland's annexation by Russia in 1809, at which Tsar Alexander I confirmed the basic laws of the newly established Grand Duchy. From an ecumenical point of view, a date of great importance in the cathedral's history was Sunday, 10 October 1992, when David Tustin, Bishop of Grimsby, preached at a Lutheran Service of Holy Communion. This was attended by the men and women who were participating in a conference in Järvenpää, a few miles north of Helsinki – the fourth in a series of conferences that had begun in 1989 on the initiative of Robert Runcie, Archbishop of Canterbury, and his Swedish counterpart, the Archbishop of Uppsala, Bertil Werkström. The aim of these conferences was to move forward from the individual agreements between different Anglican and Lutheran churches in northern and western Europe towards a more comprehensive and inclusive fellowship.

The discussions bore fruit in the Porvoo Declaration and the Porvoo Common Statement, which, in effect, meant mutual recognition of the ministries of the participating churches, and established full communion between them. The text of the *Declaration* was published in English in 1994 by the Council for Christian Unity of the General Synod of the Church of England, and this was accompanied by a book entitled *Together in Mission and Ministry,* which described the process which culminated in the Järvenpää meeting, and which also included papers by authors from different national backgrounds on "Episcopacy in our Churches".

Over the next few years, most of the Lutheran churches in the Nordic and Baltic countries joined the Anglican churches in north-western Europe in ratifying the Agreement, and they were joined by the Anglican Churches in Portugal and Spain (2001), and by the Latvian Evangelical Lutheran Church Abroad, and the Lutheran Church in Great Britain (2014). The Church of Denmark joined in 2010, but, possibly because of its increasingly conservative outlook, the Evangelical Lutheran Church in Latvia has been content with observer status.

Unlike the worldwide Anglican Communion, or the Lutheran World Federation, the Porvoo churches have no central executive body, but there is a "contact group", consisting of a representative from each church, and this is moderated jointly by one Anglican and one Lutheran bishop. There is also a research group which has organised seminars and produced reports, including several on the ministry: this was a central theme of the discussions which led to the Agreement, and between 1994 and 1997 four conferences were held which discussed the nature of the ministry of bishops, priests, deacons, and the laity. One of the key features of the Agreement was to encourage the participating churches to explore the ministry of deacons, and this produced two very interesting sets of papers around this topic under the general heading of "The Ministry of the Deacon", and dealing, respectively, with *Anglican-Lutheran Perspectives* and *Ecclesiological Explorations*.

FURTHER READING

Though now dated (it was published in 1963), there is an excellent section on the history of the Nordic churches and their ecumenical relationships in **Church in Fellowship: Pulpit and Altar Fellowship Among Lutherans (ed. Vilmos Vajta: Minneapolis, Augsburg Publishing House, 1963. No ISBN)**. This contains many of the texts relating to inter-communion discussions with the Church of England (see pp.177-221).

The text of the Porvoo Agreement was published in 1994: **(London, the Council for Christian Unity of the General Synod of the Church of England, 1994. No ISBN)** together with an accompanying book **(Together in Mission and Ministry: The Porvoo Common Statement with Essays on Church and Ministry in Northern Europe (London, Council for Christian Unity, 1994. ISBN: 0-7151-5750-7)**. Although there have been changes in circumstance, and this book is, therefore, in some respects out-of-date, it is very useful in giving information about the historical backgrounds to the Baltic and Nordic churches. Other documents related to Porvoo and to the research that has been generated since 1994 include a collection of papers presented at a meeting of the Porvoo Research Network held in Sweden in October 2008 under the title **Together in Mission and**

Ministry (edited by Dr Jaakko Rusama) **(Uppsala, Nordic Ecumenical Council, 2013. No ISBN)**. The most recent publication to emerge is **Towards Closer Unity: Communion of the Porvoo Churches, 20 Years (Helsinki, Porvoo Communion of Churches, 2016. ISBN: 978-9985-879-21-4)**.

The Nordic Churches

The swathe of countries in northern Europe which stretches from Iceland in the west, to Finland in the east, and which also includes Denmark, the Faroe Islands, Norway, and Sweden, is often, erroneously, referred to as "Scandinavia". Strictly speaking, only Norway and Sweden are in "Scandinavia", which is the name of the vast peninsula that they share, and it is more appropriate to refer to them and their neighbours as "the Nordic countries". They share many things in common, notably – but with the exception of Finland – a common linguistic heritage. Denmark, Norway, and Sweden have national languages which descend in different forms from Old Norse, forms of which are still spoken to this day in Iceland and the Faroes. Finland, with its Finno-Ugrian language that is similar to Estonian and distantly related to Hungarian, stands apart in terms of language, as do the native Sami peoples who live in the far north.

In some respects, Nordic history is a kaleidoscope, where the component parts move around from time to time. At the heart of this kaleidoscope is Denmark, which, in the Middle Ages, had an empire that included most of today's Nordic world, including a colony in Greenland. For over a century the Nordic countries were joined in the Union of Kalmar (1397), but this came to an end with a bloody revolution in the 1520s, which resulted in Sweden-Finland becoming a separate kingdom that, at one time, included territories in the Baltic States – Estonia and Livonia – and parts of northern Germany. The kaleidoscope changed as a result of wars at the beginning of the 18th century, when Sweden lost parts of Finland and its territories in the Baltic States to Russia, and after the Napoleonic wars, when Sweden lost the rest of Finland to Russia, and Denmark lost Norway to Sweden, but kept Iceland and the Faroes. A growth in national feeling during the 19th century meant that Norway became an independent kingdom in 1905, Iceland became an independent kingdom (though in a personal union through a common monarch with Denmark) in 1918, and the Faroe Islands gained a degree of autonomy in 1948. So, today, the Nordic countries consist of the sovereign states of Denmark, Finland,

Iceland, Norway, and Sweden, together with the autonomous areas of Åland (the Swedish-speaking islands belonging to Finland, but lying between there and Sweden), and the Faroes, far out in the North Atlantic. Today, these countries (and Greenland, which still has links with Denmark) all co-operate in the Nordic Council, and there are close links between their national churches.

Historically, the Reformations in the Nordic countries were Lutheran, though with significant differences from country to country. Although there was German influence across the area, this was at its strongest in Denmark and its related territories, where the bishops were initially replaced by Superintendents and the so-called "historic succession" was lost, though the title of "bishop" was soon reintroduced. In Sweden and Finland, on the other hand, the succession of bishops was retained. Similarly, although worship in the Nordic countries retained many traditional features, such as Mass vestments, the western churches (Denmark, Iceland, and Norway) had, for centuries, a simpler liturgy than in Sweden and Finland. In the 18th and 19th centuries each of these churches was influenced in one form or another by pietism, and, with some variation in the different churches, by forms of "high" churchmanship.

Each of the Nordic churches has a close relationship to the people of the country they serve: this closeness is expressed most obviously through the parish system, and they still are, or have until recent times been, "state churches", although in the past two decades most of them have re-negotiated their relationship with the governments of their respective countries.

FURTHER READING

A very useful book, but long out of print, is Leslie Stannard **Hunter's Scandinavian Churches: A Picture of the Development of Life in the Churches of Denmark, Finland, Iceland, Norway and Sweden (London, Faber and Faber, 1963. No ISBN)**. Also useful is Lars Österlin's **Churches of Northern Europe in Profile: A Thousand Years of Anglo-Nordic Relations (Norwich, The Canterbury Press, 1995. ISBN: 1-85311-128-7)**. For readers specifically interested in history, two titles are of interest: Ole Peter Grell's (ed.) **The Scandinavian Reformation: From Evangelical Movement to Institutionalisation of Reform (Cambridge, Cambridge University Press, 1995. ISBN: 0-521-44162-5)**, and James L. Larson's **Reforming the North: The Kingdoms and Churches of Scandinavia, 1520-1545, (Cambridge, Cambridge University Press, 2010. ISBN: 978-0-521-76514-5)**.

The Danish Church

The Church of Denmark, which includes a diocese for Greenland, defines itself as the *Folkekirke* – the church of the Danish people – and although regular church attendance is low, a majority of the population of the Kingdom of Denmark still belong to it. The attitude of most people might be described as one of sentimental attachment to the church, which is seen as an important expression of Danish nationality.

The ultimate responsibility for church administration rests with the Ministry of Church Affairs, which acts on behalf of the sovereign and Parliament, but the responsibility for spiritual affairs is in the hands of the eleven diocesan bishops. In common with Norway, Denmark has no archbishop, but the Bishop of Copenhagen is honoured as first among equals. The devolution of church affairs to a diocesan level is reflected in the fact that there is no national church synod, and although the 1849 Constitution envisaged the possibility of such a body, it failed to materialise.

As with the other national churches in the Nordic countries, there are different doctrinal emphases within the church, some of which can be traced back to the 19th century. The *Indre Mission* ("Inner Mission"), which remains strong in some areas, has its roots in a 19th century pietistic movement that stressed personal faith and experience, and which was led by men such as Vilhelm Beck (1829-1901). A towering figure at the same time was the honorary bishop, Nikolaj Severin Grundtvig, who was an historian, hymnwriter, and educationalist who inspired the growth of the archetypically Danish phenomenon of the "Folk High Schools". A thinker of international importance was the philosopher Søren Kierkegaard, who had some severe things to say about the alliance between church and state.

Although the Church of Denmark participated in the discussions which led up to the Porvoo Agreement, the lack of a central ecclesiastical body, and a referendum to all congregational church councils resulting in a clearly negative outcome towards a Danish membership in Porvoo, meant a long delay before it could find the right mechanism to join the communion; but it has now done so.

Relations between Britain and Denmark, though not always peaceful, stretch back more than 1,200 years. In the time of Anglo-Saxon England there was a period when half of England was ruled by the Danes, who established important administrative centres in places like York, and the "Five Boroughs" of Derby, Leicester, Nottingham, Peterborough, and Stamford. England had three Danish kings – Canute, Harald I, and Hardacanute – and the English language – particularly in the North of England – owes a lot of its vocabulary and grammar to the Danes.

Over the succeeding centuries, relations between Britain and Denmark have been good (we leave aside the embarrassment of the British bombardment of Copenhagen in 1807 during the Napoleonic Wars) and three British monarchs have had Danish spouses: James I and VI's wife, Anne, was Danish; a century later Queen Anne's husband was Prince George of Denmark; and Edward VII's wife, Alexandra, was a Danish princess. Today, the close cultural and trading ties remain.

The Danish churches in Britain now come under the jurisdiction of the "Danish Seamen's Church and Church Abroad", which was established in 2004, and which has responsibility for Danish churches throughout the world, including those in South Schleswig, which is in Germany. Over the years there have been churches serving seamen and local Danish communities in several different places in Britain, and in 1951 there were three churches – London, Hull, and Newcastle-upon-Tyne – to which a fourth was added in 1961 when a second church was built in London, primarily to serve seamen. Today, there are only two churches left: in London there is St Katherine's Church beside Regent's Park, and in Hull there is St Nikolaj, right in the heart of the city, close to the railway station. Like all Member Churches of the Council of Lutheran Churches in Great Britain (CLC), the Danish church appoint two members (clergy and lay), one of whom is usually the pastor. The pastor of the Danish Church in London has been elected as a member of the Board of Trustees of CLC in 2017.

FURTHER READING

So far as can be ascertained, no book in English on the Church in Denmark is currently available, but there is a long out-of-print publication by E. H. Dunkley, entitled **The Reformation in Denmark (London, SPCK, 1948. No ISBN)**.

There are two books available about the Danish Church in London. The first, in Danish with an English summary, is by Poul-Erik Fabricius, who was for many years the pastor of the church: **Den danske Kirke i London, 1692-1992 (ISBN: 87-7468-326-8)**. The second book, written by Vilhelm Lauritzen, is only in Danish: **Den danske Kirke i London gennem 60 år: 1912-1972 (Odense, Andelsbogtrykkeriet, 1973. ISBN: 87-1111-111-1)**.

The Faroe Islanders

The Faroe Islands lie to the north of Scotland, roughly midway between Shetland and Iceland, and are home to a population of around 48,000. Legally, the islands are still part of the kingdom of Denmark and send two members to the *Folketinget* in Copenhagen, but since 1948, and as an indirect result of wartime occupation by the British, which gave them experience of managing their own affairs, they have enjoyed an increasing level of autonomy. Today many areas are the responsibility of the local parliament, the *Løgting*. Among the matters recently devolved to the local administration, and taking effect on 29 July 2007 (St Olaf's Day), is that of the church, which until then had been a diocese within the Church of Denmark.

The islands were originally settled in the 10th century as part of the westward migration of men, women and children from Norway, which eventually led to Norse colonies in Greenland, Iceland, Ireland, the Isle of Man, Orkney, and Shetland, and the north of England. To begin with, the Faroes were a commonwealth with a yearly assembly which met in what is now the capital, Tórshavn, but in the 12th century they came under Norwegian rule, and then became part of the Danish kingdom. Christianity was adopted on the eve of the second millennium (in 999) and until the mid-16th century, the islands had their own bishop. With the advent of the Reformation the office of bishop was abolished and local church leadership was in the hands of a Dean, who functioned as a representative of the bishop of a mainland Danish diocese. This remained the situation until 1990, when the Faroes again became a separate diocese of the Church of Denmark, eventually becoming, as we have noted, a separate church, *Folkakirkjan,* in 2007.

For almost four centuries the official language of the church in the Faroes was Danish, even though the people spoke Faroese, a Nordic language closely related to both Icelandic and the dialects of western Norway. Part of the problem was that the language was not a written one, but this situation began to change in the latter part of the 19th century, and today Faroese is the first language of the islands, though everyone is still taught Danish. There are two Bible translations (one official one, and one used by the sizeable Brethren community), and hymnbooks and books of liturgy. In many respects, the church is similar to the Church of Denmark, but one distinctive feature is the use of "deacons" – lay leaders who are authorised to conduct worship on Sundays when an ordained pastor cannot be present. These *deknur* are not lay preachers, but lead an abbreviated service and read from permitted books of sermons. A little over 10% of the population belong to the (Open) Brethren, known locally as "Baptists", who have their own meeting houses scattered across the archipelago, but who are particularly strong in the north-eastern islands.

Today, there may be as many as 300 Faroe Islanders in Britain, some of whom are students or business people, but the longest established group are women who married British servicemen stationed in the Faroes during the Second World War, although inevitably this is a generation which is passing away. There are no regular services in Faroese, although a pastor comes to conduct worship – usually held in the Danish Church in Regent's Park – two or three times a year. Although not yet a formal Member of CLC, the Faroese church has been supported by CLC grants and fellowship.

FURTHER READING

Roy Long has written a series of papers (including an extensive bibliography) on the Church in the Faroe Islands, and these can be obtained by contacting him at roy.long485@btinternet.com or via the Council of Lutheran Churches office. There is a long out-of-print publication by E. H. Dunkley, entitled **The Reformation in Denmark (London, SPCK, 1948. No ISBN)**. Roy Long has written a series of seven papers (including an extensive bibliography) on the Church in the Faroe Islands, and these are available electronically by contacting him at roy.long485@btinternet.com. There are two books available about the Danish Church in London. The first, in Danish with an English summary, is by Poul-Erik Fabricius, who was for many years the pastor of the church: **Den danske Kircke i London, 1692-1992 (ISBN: 87-7468-326-8)**. The second book, written by Vilhelm Lauritzen, is only in Danish: **Den danske Kirke i London gennem 60 år: 1912-1972 (Odense, Andelsbogtrykkeriet, 1973. ISBN: 87-1111-111-1)**.

The Finnish Church

For centuries Finland has been at the interface between the West and the East, which, in Christian terms, means that it is one of the points in Europe where the "Latin" tradition of western Christianity meets the "Greek" tradition of Eastern Orthodoxy. In more recent times, it was also the interface with the Soviet Union, and was one of only two countries in Europe which shared a border with the USSR, but which was not part of the Soviet bloc (the other nation being Norway, which has a short border with Russia in the extreme north-east of the country).

Finland is both an ancient country and a modern nation, because for centuries the country was effectively under the rule of other powers: until 1809 it was part of Sweden, but in that year the country came under Russian control and became a Grand Duchy within the Tsarist Empire. This state of affairs continued until 1917, when Finland became an independent republic, although the birth of the new nation was accompanied by the bloodshed of civil war between forces of the right and the left.

As part of the Kingdom of Sweden, the church in Finland became Lutheran at the time of the Reformation and was subject to the same rules and regulations as those in other parts of the realm, but the Finnish Reformation played a significant part in the development of the Finnish language through Bible translations and catechetical material. With the transfer of power to Russia, new forms of church government had to be developed, and from 1809 the Lutheran Church became, in effect, one of two established churches, sharing that status with the Orthodox Church. For fifty years the church was a "state" church, but in 1869 new legislation led to the development of an episcopal-synodical form of church government, which gave it more independence.

Like the other Nordic Lutheran churches, the Finnish church is episcopal and is organised around eight geographical dioceses, which are Finnish-speaking, and one non-geographical diocese which links together the Swedish-speaking parishes, including those in the semi-autonomous Åland Islands (a little under 5% of mainland Finnish have Swedish as their first language). There is also a military bishop with responsibility for the work of chaplains to the armed forces. Each diocese is organised into parishes. Traditionally, the Church of Finland has been quite conservative, but in more recent times has become increasingly involved in social affairs, although some matters, such as the ordination of women and liberal attitudes towards homosexual issues, have been controversial, and have led some people to leave the church. Today, Finland is sometimes described as "the most Lutheran country in the world", but like all countries there has been a decrease in church attendance, although the different pietistic movements, which are integrated in the church, remain strong.

The Church of Finland has a long tradition of providing sound theological education, and the Faculty of Theology in Helsinki University has a distinguished record in Luther studies. In the 1980s, under the leadership of Dr Tuomo Mannermaa, and as a consequence of increasing ecumenical contact with the Orthodox Churches, the Faculty pioneered research into different ways of thinking about some aspects of Luther's theology. Since his death in 2015, Dr Mannermaa's controversial theses are increasingly questioned.

Finnish church work in Britain began in 1880, when a pastor was sent by the Finnish Seamen's Mission Society to Grimsby to work in the Humberside area, and this work was followed by similar activity in London and Cardiff. Eventually, the work out of Grimsby was transferred to Hull and the work in Cardiff was closed down. Finnish church ministries in Britain were seriously affected by the Second World War, but by 1951 the *Manual* was able to report that work was continuing in both Hull and London. Today, work is focused on the beautiful Finnish Church close to Rotherhithe Underground Station, although pastors from the church take regular services in other places. For decades a very significant feature of the Finnish church in Britain was the role played by the "Finnish Church Guild", which encouraged many social and cultural activities across the country. One interesting suggestion – although it was never translated into anything practical – was a suggestion that was made at a theological conference in Hothorpe Hall in 1961 by the then pastor in London, Jorma Luohivouri, that, as a means of developing closer unity among Lutherans in Britain, they should establish a school.

FURTHER READING

Published in connection with the Assembly of the Lutheran World Federation, which was held in Helsinki in 1963 – and therefore not up-to-date – is Geert Sentzke's **Finland: Its Church and Its People (Helsinki, 1963. No ISBN)**. A more recent, though slender, publication in an English translation by Jaana Shelby, entitled **Lutheran and Ecumenical: The Evangelical Lutheran Church of Finland and Her Connection with Other Churches (Helsinki, Evangelical Lutheran Church of Finland Department for International Relations, 2010. No ISBN)**. Two emeritus professors at the University of Helsinki, Markku

Heikkilä and Simo Heininen, have recently published **A History of the Finnish Church (Helsinki, Suomalaisen Kirjallisuuden Seura, 2016. ISBN: 978-952-222-732-4)**, which provides a good up-to-date treatment of the subject.

There is a bilingual book entitled **100 Vuotta: 100 Years of the Finnish Seamen's Mission in London (London, The Finnish Seamen's Mission in London, 1982. No ISBN)**.

The Icelandic Congregation

With a population of around 330,000, Iceland today is a sovereign republic lying midway between Europe and North America. Actually, in geological terms, it lies in both Europe and America because the tectonic plates which house both continents run right through the centre of the island. After centuries of being ruled, first by Norway and then by Denmark, Iceland voted to become an independent republic in 1944, but co-operates closely with the other Nordic countries and is a part of the North Atlantic Treaty Organisation (NATO). It is not a member of the European Union.

Although there are traces of early settlement by monks and hermits from Ireland and Scotland, the main settlement of the country came in the 9th century, when migrating Norsemen settled and then went on to explore the more westerly countries that we now call Greenland and Canada. These first settlers were pagan, but in 1000 AD the great annual assembly of clan chieftains, the *Alþingi*, adopted Christianity, and from then onwards the country became more integrated, ecclesiastically, into the western Catholic Church. Historically, there were two dioceses – Skálholt in the south, and Hólar in the north – but today there is one diocese which covers the whole country, although there is a *Vígslubiskup* (roughly speaking, a "suffragan") in each of the old episcopal sees. By the time of the 16th century Reformation, Iceland was part of the Danish kingdom and reform was imposed in spite of resistance by one of the bishops, Jón Árason, who was eventually executed in 1551.

In its first centuries as a Lutheran country, the church enjoyed a rich liturgical heritage, but suffered as rationalism and liberalism made significant inroads. A theological and liturgical revival took place from the middle of the 20th century, and new churches were built to accommodate a growing population. The church's official name is *Þjóðkirkja Íslands* ("Church of the Icelandic People"), and it is a member of the LWF and part of the Porvoo process. Students can study theology in the University of Iceland, and many pastors have also taken the opportunity to study abroad.

One very important contribution of the Icelandic Church is to be found in the *Passiusálmar* ("Hymns of the Passion") written by the 17th century priest-poet Hallgrímur Pétursson. Sadly, these meditations on the sufferings of Christ are little known outside Iceland, although they were translated into English at the beginning of the 20th century by a Brethren missionary, Arthur Charles Gook, who worked for many years in the northern town of Akureyri.

There have been Icelanders in Great Britain for decades: there have always been strong ties between the two countries through trade and fishing – although the latter has not always been amicable! – and as a result of the British occupation of Iceland in 1940 dozens of Icelandic women married British soldiers and came to settle here. There was, however, no Icelandic church work in Britain until the early 1980s, when, in 1983, the Rev'd Jón Aðalsteinn Baldvinsson was sent to work in London. He was attached to the Icelandic Embassy in London and much of his work was to help the increasing number of patients coming to London for medical treatment. He began holding monthly services and eventually organised a congregation, but his ministry also included services twice a year on Humberside, twice a year in Luxembourg, and occasionally elsewhere in Europe. His successor was Rev'd Sigurður Árnarson, who served the community for several years, and who developed the life of the congregation – including doubling the number of services each year in Luxembourg. However, the financial difficulties which beset Iceland after 2008 meant that he had to return to Iceland, and, despite the remarkable economic recovery that the country has recently experienced, there are no plans to re-establish the London chaplaincy. However, the congregation continues to exist in London, and pastors from Iceland come four times a year to London, and once a year to Humberside to hold services and exercise pastoral care.

The Icelandic congregation has never had a church building of its own, but has, at various times, held services in the Danish Church, the Swedish Church, and the German-speaking Christus Kirche in Knightsbridge.

FURTHER READING

There are many books about Iceland and its religious history. An excellent book in English is by Michael Fell: **And Some Fell into Good Soil (New York, Peter Lang, 1999. ISBN: 0-**

8204-3881-2). This contains a detailed, but very readable, survey of Christianity in Iceland from the time of the Settlement to the present day. There is no publication available about the Icelandic congregation in London.

The Norwegian Church

Thanks to the development of the North Sea oil industry, Norway is, today, one of the richest (and most expensive) countries in Europe. It is also home to some of the most inhospitable and rugged terrain on the continent, and the combination of fjords and high mountain ranges mean that isolated communities have developed strong traditions of local independence. This has been particularly true for language, and there are now two official Norwegian languages, *Bokmål,* which bears a close affinity with Danish, and *Nynorsk,* which is closer to Faroese and Icelandic.

In the early Middle Ages, Norway was a great power in the North, with colonies and settlements flung wide across the North Atlantic, but it came increasingly under the domination of Denmark, and after the Reformation was reduced to being a Danish province. The situation changed after the Treaty of Kiel (1814) awarded it to Sweden, and the country remained united with Sweden until it gained independence in 1905. Today, Norway is a monarchy, and it is an important part of NATO, but has decided not to enter the European Union.

Like its sister church in Denmark, the Church of Norway is a *Folkekirke* – a term that is difficult to translate exactly into English, but which might be rendered as "national church" or "people's church", but, unlike the Church of Denmark it has a General Synod, which brings together bishops, priests, and laity in a representative body. The country is divided into parishes, which are grouped into eleven dioceses, but there is no archbishop: since 2011 the Norwegian church has a special bishop called the "Preses" presiding in the bishop's conferences and sharing her office between Trondheim and Oslo. As in the other Nordic countries, regular church attendance is low and Norway is largely secular, though the church is respected as a guardian of an important part of the nation's history. Today, the Church of Norway participates in many ecumenical activities, including the LWF and the Porvoo communion.

As in some of the other Nordic countries, pietistic movements grew up in 19th century Norway, and, in particular, the Haugean movement, which originated in the work of the lay preacher, Hans Nielsen Hauge (1771-1824). Hauge's followers were persecuted at the start of the 19th century, although, by and large, they stayed within the church. Over the years there have been considerable tensions between groups that we might term "liberal" and "conservative", and so serious were these that they led to the establishment, in 1907, of *Menighetsfakultetet* (The "Congregational" Faculty), as a place where conservative-orientated students of theology could be educated. Prior to this, all potential pastors had to study in the theological faculty of the University of Christiania (Oslo). Today there is no significant theological difference between *Menighetsfakultetet* and the University.

There have always been close ties between Britain and Norway, and these were particularly evident during the Second World War, when there was a strong Norwegian presence in Britain. After Norway was occupied by the Germans in early 1940, King Haakon and his government managed to reach London, and their armed forces played a significant part in the war effort. The war years saw a proliferation of Norwegian church work in Britain, especially in Scotland, but this came to an end in 1945, when the majority of Norwegians returned to their homeland.

For those who had to stay behind in Norway, the war years were a time of great difficulty. There was strong resistance to the occupying power, and this was reflected in the church, most notably in 1942 when the bishops, led by Eivind Berggrav, Bishop of Oslo, issued a declaration called *Kirkens Grunn* ("The Foundation of the Church") and resigned as civil servants. For these actions Bishop Berggrav was initially imprisoned in the Bredtvet concentration camp (along with four fellow members of the "Christian Council for Joint Deliberation") and then placed in solitary confinement at an isolated location in the forests north of Oslo. The other bishops and clerical supporters were closely monitored for the duration of the occupation.

After 1945, many Norwegians remained in Britain – some, because they had married British women – but they were scattered widely across the country. The resumption of trade across the North Sea meant that the pre-war work among seamen was developed, and the 1951 *Manual* recorded that there were five centres of Norwegian church activity around Great Britain – Cardiff, Edinburgh, Liverpool, London, and North Shields. These centres of church work were, in effect, the heirs to the first Nordic church built in Wellclose Square in the late 17th century. Although it was always known as the "Danish" church, the congregation that worshipped there in London's East End was also home to Norwegians, since, as noted above, Norway was part of the Kingdom of Denmark until 1814.

The first purely Norwegian churches in Britain were all established to serve the spiritual needs of seamen, although inevitably congregations of resident Norwegian often grew up around them as well. The earliest seamen's church was established in Leith – the port of Edinburgh – in 1864, but the number of such missions grew rapidly during the succeeding decades. Changes in practice meant that there were no longer the same opportunities for pastoral ministry to seamen, and now the only church to remain is the church in London, which is situated at the southern end of the Rotherhithe Tunnel. Like the other Lutheran clergy based in London, the Norwegian pastors and student or welfare ministers travel to conduct ministry across the UK, in borrowed premises. They are also responsible for the Norwegian community centre in Aberdeen. The Pastor of the Norwegian Church in London has been elected to serve on the Board of Trustees of the Council of Lutheran Churches.

FURTHER READING

There is a handy book about the Church of Norway, simply entitled **The Church of Norway (Oslo, The Church of Norway Information Service, 1993. ISBN: 82-7545-000-4)**, which gives a brief overview of the history of the church and its activities. There are two books about the Seamen's Church in London. The first, in Norwegian with a summary in English, is **Vår Arv: Streif fra norske kirke- og kulturhistorie in London, (Bergen, Den Norske Sjømannsmisjons Forlag, 1967. No ISBN)**, written by Leif Frivold. The second book, in Norwegian only, was published by the Seamen's Church in London to celebrate its 125th anniversary. It is entitled **Ankerfestet ved Themsen: Den Norske Sjømannskirke I London 1868-1993**, and was written by Helge Pettersson, who was then the pastor of the church.

The Swedish Church

Alone among the Nordic countries, Sweden was able to maintain its neutrality during the Second World War, and this meant that it was able to offer asylum to different groups, such as the Jewish population of Denmark, many of whom were spirited across the Sound in 1943, and refugees from the Baltic States – particularly from Estonia, as well as about 15,345 Jews from concentration camps in Germany at the end of the war in the "white buses" run by the Swedish Red Cross.

Until 1809, the Swedish Church included the diocese of Turku, which covered the whole of Finland, and in the 17th century it had included what is now Estonia and northern Latvia. The Reformation had begun in the 1520s, and, despite some setbacks, the country became progressively Lutheran: in 1593 it adopted the Augsburg Confession, and, almost a century later, in 1686, the Book of Concord.

From the start of the reform process the Swedish church maintained episcopal continuity, which meant that it was ultimately able to develop a close relationship with the Church of England, and eventually establish inter-communion and mutual recognition of the ministries of the two churches. In the 1920s and 1930s interest in the Swedish church on the part of some "high church" Anglicans resulted in the publication of the works of several prominent Swedish theologians, such as Gustaf Aulén, Yngve Brilioth, and Anders Nygren.

The Church of Sweden has been an active participant in different ecumenical and missionary endeavours: the founding assembly of the Lutheran World Federation was held in Lund in 1947, where Anders Nygren – shortly to become Bishop of Lund – was elected as its first President. More recently, the church took an active part in establishing the Porvoo communion.

The Church of Sweden can be characterised as being diocesan, episcopal, and parochial, with 13 dioceses and around 5,000 clergy (bishops, priests, and deacons): the presiding bishop is the Archbishop of Uppsala, and it is indicative of changing attitudes in the church that whilst there was fierce opposition to the ordination of women priests when it was first mooted, the current Archbishop is a woman (2016): Antje Jackelén. From the time of the Reformation until the year 2000, the Church of Sweden was a state church, but in that year it gained more independence and was disestablished, entering into a new relationship with the state.

As we saw in Part Three, it was the Swedish ambassador who took a leading role in helping to establish the first Lutheran congregation in Britain in 1669. That congregation was a very mixed one, and included people from the Nordic countries as well as from Germany, but most of them left when the "Danish" church was established in 1694. That new congregation naturally included Norwegians, since Norway was part of the Kingdom of Denmark, but also included Swedes and possibly Finns. The Swedes withdrew in the first decade of the 18th century, when Denmark and Sweden were at war, and, having founded their own congregation in 1710, eventually built their own church in London. As with the other Nordic communities, the number of Swedish churches grew during the 19th century as mission work among sailors increased. At different times there were no less than twelve churches across the country. In 1951, there were ten places where services were held regularly in Swedish, and these were served by eight pastors. Since then the number of congregations has dropped to one (London), although as late as 2010 there were still seamen's churches in Middlesbrough, Liverpool, and London. The Middlesbrough church closed around that time, but, faced with closure and the possible sale of its listed building, the church in Liverpool joined the Lutheran Church in Great Britain. The seamen's church in the East End of London was sold in 2014.

Although the church in London is largely self-governing, and its senior pastor holds the title of Rector (and sometimes has been given the honorary title of Dean), it comes under the episcopal oversight of the Bishop of Visby, who is responsible for all Swedish churches abroad. Swedish clergy travel to conduct ministry across the UK in various borrowed premises, and the Rector has served on the Board of Trustees of the Council of Lutheran Churches.

FURTHER READING

Published in 1961, Robert Murray's **A Brief History of the Church of Sweden: Origins and Modern Structure (Stockholm, Diakonistyrelsens Bokförlag, 1961. No ISBN)**, provides a snapshot of the Church of Sweden in the early 1960s. Also of historical interest is an earlier work written by H. M. Waddams: **The Swedish Church (London, SPCK, 1946. No ISBN)**. There are several books about the Swedish Church in London, of which two are of particular interest. The first is by Sven Evander, who was pastor of the church for many years: **London Svenskarnas Kyrka genom 250 År (Stockholm, Berlingska Boktrykeriet, 1960. No ISBN)**. Pastor Evander co-operated with his successor, Lennart Sjöström, on **Svenska Kyrkan i London, 1710-2000 (London, The Swedish Church in London, 2001. ISBN: 0-9541708-0-1)**. Although the bulk of the text in both books is in Swedish, they have good summaries in English.

The Baltic Churches

It is very common for people to talk in generalisations about geographical areas, so, we get used to hearing about "The Middle East", or "Central America", or "East Africa", when, in fact, these broad-brush terms cover a vast array of areas with cultural, economic, linguistic, national, and religious differences. What is true of large swathes of territory is often true of smaller areas, and one of the most obvious examples of this is that of the "Baltic States" of Estonia, Latvia, and Lithuania, which are often spoken of as though they are an homogenous entity, whereas they are, in fact, different nations with diverse cultures, albeit that their histories are very much intertwined and share some common features.

Historically, the indigenous populations of Estonia and Latvia were trapped by their geographical location, with Germany to the south-west, Russia to the east, and Sweden to the north-west. Throughout most of their history since the 12th century, German influence was strong, and, whichever nation happened to rule the areas occupied by Estonian and Latvian-speaking peoples, it was the "Baltic Barons" who exercised power locally, and for centuries German was the language of government and culture. The foreign rulers who lorded it over the area were successively German, Swedish, and Russian, and it was not until the years following the end of the First World War that Estonia and Latvia became independent republics. This independence was lost after the Second World War, and it was only after fifty years of brutal oppression within the USSR that they regained their freedom in 1991. Since then, although there have been hard times, the two countries have grown economically and politically, and are now members of both the NATO and the European Union.

The people of the territory now occupied by Estonia and Latvia were mainly Lutheran, although parts of southern and eastern Latvia, which were under Polish and Lithuanian influence, were Roman Catholic. Lutheran influence arrived in what was then Livonia very shortly after Luther had posted the 95 Theses, and the Hanseatic city of Riga became a focus for Lutheran activity: a Lutheran congregation was established in the city in 1524, and Luther himself wrote encouragingly to this community. This was followed by the growth of congregations in other towns, who often saw this as a means of freeing themselves from the financial oppression of the Catholic Church.

In the Lutheran areas, especially in the countryside, the church was a rather remote institution for most people. Much good work was done in the late 18th and early 19th centuries by Moravian missionaries, who established mission houses in many areas and introduced a warm pietism which contrasted with the formal orthodoxy of the official church. In the 19th century, during a period of intense Russification, it was economically advantageous for people to become Orthodox, and many did so, especially in Estonia, and during the fifty years of Soviet occupation severe restrictions on religious activity adversely affected all the churches. Since regaining independence in 1991, there has been some revival in the fortunes of the churches, but this has included the growth in the number of new religious groups that have come into the countries from abroad.

So much for Estonia and Latvia, but what of Lithuania? Its history is different, and Lithuanians today look back to the later Middle Ages, when the country was a mini-empire which at times stretched from the Baltic to the Ukraine. In the 16th century Lithuania entered into a federal commonwealth with Poland, and it subsequently became one of the "great powers" of Europe. These two nations shared a patriotic and staunch Catholicism, which has remained to the present day – which is not to say that Protestantism, in its many different forms, has not played a part in both countries. In the mid-16th century, there were strong Lutheran, Reformed, and Hussite influences and, until the start of the counter-Reformation, spearheaded by the Jesuits towards the end of the century, the Commonwealth was a model of religious tolerance.

There is a rather interesting connection between Lithuania and the Reformation in England. This concerns Katherine, Duchess of Suffolk, who was a member of the English royal family and a convinced evangelical. She came into grave danger after Mary I ascended the throne and left England during the Marian persecution of Protestants. With the help of John à Lasco, the former Superintendent of the "Strangers' Church" in London, Katherine found refuge in Lithuania under the protection of the country's Chancellor, Mikołaj Radziwiłł, who was himself a convinced supporter of reform.

Over the course of the next two centuries, Poland-Lithuania was subject to immense pressure from surrounding nations, and, by the end of the 18th century, Poland had disappeared as a political entity

– partitioned by Austria, Germany, and Russia – and Lithuania had become a Russian province.

Lithuania's history during the 19th and 20th centuries was much like that of Estonia and Latvia, and the country experienced a severe attempt at Russification, including the insistence that the Lithuanian language be written in Cyrillic characters. However, the religious situation was very different from that of its two northern neighbours, because it was predominantly Roman Catholic, though with a significant Jewish population. During the first period of independence (1919-1940) there was a small, but significant, multicultural Lutheran church, with German, Latvian, and Lithuanian linguistic synods. During the Soviet occupation, the Roman Catholic Church, though much persecuted, was able to serve as a focus for national unity and resistance.

One last word needs to be said here about language, because this is one of the biggest differences between Latvia and Lithuania on the one hand, and Estonia on the other. Latvian and Lithuanian are Indo-European languages belonging to a distinct sub-group which includes the now extinct Old Prussian. Indeed, Lithuanian is probably one of the oldest languages in Europe. However, although the two languages are closely related, they are not close enough for Latvians and Lithuanians to understand each other without learning the others' language. Estonian is quite different: it is a Finno-Ugrian language, close enough to Finnish for Finns and Estonians to understand each other, although the history of the two nations means that Finnish has been influenced by Swedish, whereas Estonian has more German influence. A very important Lutheran influence in each of the Baltic States has come through Bible translation and the production of catechetical materials, which helped to standardise the written languages.

The Estonian Church

The Estonian Evangelical Lutheran Church was established at the end of the First World War, when the country became independent for the first time. The foundation of the church was marked by some difficulties because of the tensions which existed between Estonian-speaking pastors and the significant minority of pastors who were German-speaking, but who had exercised considerable influence during the preceding centuries. The church was established with an episcopal polity: the first bishop, Jacob Kukk, was consecrated in June 1921 by the Archbishop of Uppsala, Nathan Söderblom, assisted by Jaakko Gummerus, Bishop of the Finnish diocese of Porvoo/Borgå.

During the next twenty years the Estonian church was able to develop its institutions and initiate ecumenical contacts, not only with its fellow Lutheran churches in the Nordic countries and Germany, but also with the Church of England. Two conferences were held between the Estonians and the Church of England (the Lutheran Church of Latvia was also involved), in London in 1935 and in Tallinn in 1938, as a result of which ultimate fellowship and mutual recognition of ministries was seen as a distinct possibility. Sadly, the outbreak of war in 1939 and the subsequent turmoil in the Baltic States prevented further developments, and it was not until the second period of independence, which began in 1991, that the hopes of the 1930s could be realised.

The Soviet occupation of Estonia in 1940 devastated the church: its buildings were confiscated and many pastors were deported to Siberia. For four years the country was fought over by German and Soviet troops, and the outcome was that the country was once again occupied by the Soviet Union. At this point, the leaders of the Estonian church, headed by Archbishop Johan Kõpp, fled to Sweden, from where he and his colleagues began to organise a "church in exile" among the thousands of Estonian displaced persons scattered across the world.

The church in Estonia was re-established in 1949, but its opportunities for witness were massively curtailed during the nearly fifty years of Soviet occupation. It re-emerged after the collapse of the USSR and now has five bishops, including an Archbishop, whose episcopal residence is in Tallinn, and over 200 pastors, of whom around 30% are women. Although the church is theologically quite conservative, it has had female pastors since 1967, and unlike the church in Latvia has made no move to cease ordaining women.

The church outside Estonia, now known as the Estonian Evangelical Lutheran Church Abroad, continues to exist. The headquarters of this body, which reunited with the church in Estonia in 2010, are currently in Canada, where its bishop, Andres Taul, lives. Bishop Taul studied his theology at Mansfield College and was for several years pastor of the Estonian parish in the north of England. Oversight of Estonian Lutherans in Britain is now the responsibility of Bishop Tiit Salumäe, who is bishop for the diaspora in Europe and Russia.

Not very much is known about Estonians in Britain in the years before the Second World War. After independence in 1918 an Estonian embassy was established in London, and trade between the two countries brought workers, and especially seamen, to these islands. It is certain that some Estonian students came to Britain in the pre-war period in order to learn English, and an Estonian Society developed around the Embassy in London. There was also some church activity among seamen, and, although there was no Estonian pastor, the minister of the Finnish Church in London, Pastor Harjunpää, who spoke fluent Estonian, conducted services both in the Swedish Church in London and the Finnish Seamen's Church in Cardiff. After he was called back to Finland during the war, the Swedish pastor in London, Pastor Söderberg, continued this ministry. Although figures are not known, some Estonians – including the ambassador, Mr August Torma – remained in Britain during the war, and some Estonian merchant seamen served alongside other allied seamen.

We have already alluded to the arrival of large numbers of Baltic displaced persons in the years after 1948, and by 1951 five parishes of the Estonian Lutheran Church in Exile had been established across Britain, served by four pastors (one of whom, Dr Jaak Taul, served as Dean), and a theological candidate. Although the estimated number of Estonians at the time was around 5,000 – a figure which included not only Lutherans but also Orthodox and Baptists – only 2,100 were actually registered as church members of Lutheran congregations, with the main centres of activity being the London area, the East Midlands, the West Riding of Yorkshire, and south Wales.

As the years went by, the number of these post-war Estonian Lutherans in Britain declined significantly, with many emigrating further, to countries such as Canada and Australia. Although a small number of Estonians still remain in Britain, many of them are elderly and there are only intermittent church services. The arrival of Estonians after the country joined the European Union did not result in any significant increase in church membership, and today services are only held three times a year in London (usually in the Swedish church), and elsewhere on an occasional chaplaincy basis. There is one pastor resident in Great Britain, but she is involved in full-time secular employment.

The Latvian Church

Although Estonia and Latvia are different countries with their own distinctive histories and cultures, their church histories up to the resumption of independence in 1991 are very similar. In its present form the church came into existence after the First World War, and, as was the case with Estonia, its first bishop, Kārlis Irbe, was consecrated by Archbishop Nathan Söderblom in 1922. There was, however, one difference: there were similar tensions between native Latvians and Germans as in Estonia, but in Riga Archbishop Söderblom consecrated two bishops – one for Latvian speakers, and one for those who spoke German. The title of "Archbishop" which Nathan Söderblom had wanted for Bishop Irbe, was adopted by his successor, Teodors Grīnbergs in 1933.

The history of the church from 1940 to 1988 parallels that of Estonia – the deportation of pastors under the first Soviet occupation, the flight into exile in Germany of Archbishop Grīnbergs, and the subsequent establishment of a church in exile. In Latvia itself, a new archbishop, Gustavs Tūrs, was elected in 1948, and the church struggled to survive through to the re-establishment of independence. In 1993 the church in Latvia elected as its new archbishop pastor Jānis Vanags, and under his leadership the church has moved to a very conservative theological position, and has established fellowship with the Lutheran Church–Missouri Synod. It no longer ordains women, which it had done since 1975, and takes a strict attitude towards other social issues. The church has three dioceses: the Archbishop's seat is in Rīga, where he is assisted by a suffragan bishop, and there are bishops in Liepāja and Daugavpils.

The Latvian congregations in Britain are part of the Latvian Evangelical-Lutheran Church Abroad, which, although it maintains contact with the church in Latvia, differs from it in a number of ways. The church outside Latvia not only ordains women, but recently (2014) elected a woman, Lauma Zušēvica, to be its archbishop. She was consecrated in 2015. The church has a worldwide membership and, together with the Lutheran Church in Great Britain, subscribed to the Porvoo Agreement in 2014.

Like the Estonian church, the Evangelical-Lutheran Church in Latvia had participated in the pre-Second World War conversations with the Church of England, and although the outbreak of war prevented the tentative agreement being ratified, it did mean that senior Anglican clergy in England were willing to help after 1945. It was largely through the good offices of the then Bishop of Gloucester that a Latvian pastor was able to come to Britain to minister to his fellow exiles. This tradition of ecumenical involvement was continued, for example, by Dean Ringolds Mūziks, who worked tirelessly to develop relations with the Church of England, and by the Latvian Pastor and Bishop of the Lutheran Church in Great Britain, Right Reverend Jana Jeruma-Grīnberga, who served for a while as President of Churches Together in England, representing Lutherans, Germans, Quakers, and New Churches.

According to *The Manual*, there were an estimated 12,000 Latvian Lutherans in Great Britain in 1951, of whom 3,458 were registered members of Lutheran congregations. They were served by nine ordained pastors and were grouped into eight parishes, covering England, Scotland, and Wales. One of the pastors, who was resident in Nottingham, was responsible for Inner Mission work. At that time, the church had no buildings of its own, but in the late 1950s a parish hall was built in Corby, Northamptonshire; otherwise, Latvian Lutherans held their services in churches belonging to other churches – principally those of the Church of England, or other Lutheran churches, such as the Swedish Church in London. Rowfant was a tumbledown house in Sussex which was bought and renovated by an independent Latvian Lutheran congregation. Its pastor Roberts Slokenbergs was the first Latvian pastor to arrive in Britain after the end of World War II in 1945. However, when the former Dean of Riga, Edgars Bergs, arrived a few years later, a fight for power started and Slokenbergs and his congregation left. The congregation joined the Latvian Evangelical Lutheran Church Abroad long after his and Berg's death and Rowfant was used for retreats by various Lutheran churches, as well as serving as a hotel and a care home for the elderly. It took a few more decades for the Latvian Lutheran congregations in London to merge in 1994, forming The United London Latvian Lutheran Church, which eventually sold Rowfant House in 2016.

As can be seen, the origins of the Latvian Lutheran Church in Great Britain are very similar to those of the Estonian Church, and the majority of its members came here in the years after the Second World War. There must have been a small Latvian community in Britain before the Second World War, and we have already referred to the work of Pastor Konstantīns Ūdris in Wales in the early years of the 20th century. As with the Estonians, many of the Latvians who had come to Britain post-1945 moved on to other countries. Those who remained clung tenaciously to their linguistic and cultural heritage, although several pastors served English-language congregations alongside their Latvian parishes.

The Latvian church in Britain is part of the Latvian Evangelical-Lutheran Church Abroad: today, there are six congregations, served by four pastors, one of whom serves as the Dean, and, although services are no longer held in Scotland, there are now occasional services on Guernsey. About 100,000 Latvian citizens have come to Britain since the country's accession to the European Union: many of these Lutheran, and some have joined existing congregations. Among the new arrivals, especially noteworthy are the Latvian Roma, who make up a major part of the congregation in Derby.

Lithuanian Lutherans

The *Manual of Lutheran Activity in Great Britain* of 1951 contains only the briefest of references to Lithuanian Lutherans in Britain. Noting that Lithuania was predominantly Roman Catholic, it gave a figure of 7,000 Lithuanian EVWs in Britain, of whom it estimated that there were probably 300 Lutherans, but no Lithuanian-speaking pastors. Although there were plans that Pastor Keleris, the President of the Lithuanian Lutheran Church in Exile, might come to take occasional services, there is no record as to whether this ever happened. The *Manual* notes that "sacred acts are performed for Lutheran Lithuanians by Latvian pastors", and, at a later stage, this became a more formal arrangement when Rev'd Aldonis Putce began holding regular services in both Bradford and Derby. Pastor Putce, who himself had come to Britain as an EVW, and who had subsequently studied in Mansfield College, was born and brought up in Lithuania, close to the border with Latvia, and spoke fluent Lithuanian. There is no information available as to when these services ceased, but at the time of writing (2016) no Lutheran services in Lithuanian are held in Britain.

FURTHER READING

There is useful information about the Baltic churches in Andrejs Plakans' **A Concise History of the Baltic States (Cambridge, Cambridge University Press, 2011. ISBN: 978-0-**

521-54155-8), with specific information about Estonia in Toivo U. Raun, **Estonia and the Estonians (Stanford, Hoover Institution Press, 1991. ISBN: 0-8179-9132-8)** and about Latvia in Andrejs Plakans' **The Latvians: A Short History (Stanford, Hoover Institution Press, 1995. ISBN: 0-8179-9302-9)**.

Chapter 26 | German-speaking Lutherans in Britain

Germany is the homeland of the Lutheran Reformation, and Martin Luther is a figure of great cultural, national, and religious significance in German history. Of great importance was his translation of the Bible into German, which provided a standard language which helped to overcome the sometimes mutually unintelligible dialects in the German of his day. But his was not the only Reformation in Germany and in the German-speaking areas in neighbouring countries, particularly south-west Germany and Switzerland, significant differences developed between Luther's understanding of Word and Sacraments and that of reformers such as Huldrych Zwingli, Johannes Oecolampadius, Johann Heinrich Bullinger, and John Calvin. Over the years, theologians who stood somewhere in between – men like Martin Bucer – tried to mediate between the different theologies, and there were centuries of misunderstanding and suspicion. These differences can be traced back to the early days of the Reformation: in 1529, at what has become known as the "Colloquy of Marburg", Luther and the other reformers achieved agreement on almost everything, but could not agree about the presence of Christ in the Sacrament of the Altar.

The subsequent history of the Reformation churches in Germany is convoluted and difficult to summarise, and includes not only disagreement between Lutherans and what became known as the "Reformed", but also tensions within the different groups. After Luther's death in 1546 there were disagreements among Lutherans about a range of issues, including, among other things, how far Lutherans should compromise with Roman Catholics; what is the nature of faith; what is the relationship between Law and Gospel – the list seems almost endless. Most of these disputes were settled with the adoption of the *Book of Concord* in 1580. Although that ushered in a period of "Lutheran Orthodoxy", a golden age for Lutheran theology, it nevertheless was also a period when it might be said that preaching emphasised sound doctrine but failed to connect with the lives of ordinary people.

Although the debates among the Reformed, largely over predestination, took place mainly in the early 17th century Netherlands, the Reformed in Germany had to fight for their very existence: the "Religious Peace of Augsburg" of 1555 had recognised the right of Lutherans to exist as a distinctive confession, but it had not extended the same rights to the Reformed. In reality, however, the Reformed had managed to thrive in areas such as the Palatinate, and in East Friesland, and were able to take advantage of the principle of *cuius regio, eius religio,* which we might simply translate as "the religion of the prince shall be the religion of his people". This principle, however, did not always work, as, for instance, in early 17th century Brandenburg, when the Elector converted to Calvinism but found that most of his subjects remained stubbornly Lutheran.

Over the centuries, there were several factors which worked against confessionalism: the Thirty Years War wearied people of religious argument; the growth of Pietism in the late 17th and early 18th centuries tended to stress what united Protestants rather than what divided them; moves by the political authorities throughout the 19th century to bring Lutherans and Reformed together into *unierte Kirchen* (although that actually produced a swing back to confessional theology among some Lutherans who objected to being forced into unions with non-Lutherans) and the tragic confrontation between church and state during the time of the Third Reich. To all of this must be added, of course, the increasingly prevalent secularism which seems to challenge the very existence of Christianity, and which makes, in the eyes of many people, emphasis on confessional differences seem irrelevant.

To Christians in Britain, the present situation of the *evangelische* ("Protestant") churches in Germany is confusing. There are twenty *Landeskirchen* ("territorial" or "regional" churches") some of which are Lutheran, some *Unierte,* and some Reformed, and they all belong to the *Evangelische Kirche in Deutschland* ("Protestant Church in Germany"); at the same time, seven of the Lutheran territorial churches also belong to the *Vereinigte Evangelisch-Lutherische Kirche Deutschlands* ("United Evangelical-Lutheran Church in

Germany"), which has recently changed its status and become an administrative part of the EKD. These churches also belong to the LWF. One German-speaking pastor in Great Britain has recently said that, were he to stand at the church door and ask his parishioners which confession they subscribed to, they would not know: they would simply say that they were *evangelisch*. This is not, of course, the whole story: historically, some of the Lutheran *Landeskirchen* have been more aware of their confessional identity than others, and there is a small confessional Lutheran church, *Die selbständige evangelisch-lutherische Kirche* (The Independent Evangelical-Lutheran Church) which very firmly emphasises its Lutheran identity.

All but one of the first German-speaking congregations in Britain were Lutheran – the exception was St Paul's Reformed Church (1697) – but the new wave of congregations that were established in the 19th century reflected the growing confessional diversity in Germany: the majority would have seen themselves as Lutheran, but some defined themselves simply as *evangelisch.* In effect, these were independent congregations, although by the beginning of the 20th century most of the congregations and pastors had banded together in the "Association of German Evangelical Congregations in Great Britain and Ireland", which was, essentially, an organisation founded to provide its members with mutual support. Of course, this body did not survive the First World War and nothing similar was created in the inter-war years. In fact no over-arching ecclesiastical body came into existence until 1956, when the congregations which considered themselves Lutheran organised themselves as the *Evangelisch-Lutherische Synode Deutscher Sprache in Groß Britannien* ("German-speaking Evangelical Lutheran Synod in Great Britain"). Congregations such as Sydenham, Christus Kirche, Bradford, and the churches in Scotland, remained outside this Synod until the early 1970s when the *unierte* congregations joined – at which point the word "Lutheran" was dropped from the synod's title.

Today, the German-speaking Synod is known in English as the "Synod of German-speaking Lutheran, Reformed and United Congregations in Great Britain", and it has 19 congregations spread out among six parochial districts, served by nine pastors. This contrasts with 1951, when there were nine pastors and five church workers, serving 38 congregations or preaching stations. At the time when the congregations which had remained outside the

Synod joined it in 1970, there were 28 pastors and church workers serving 34 congregations. The reasons for these changes include the dwindling numbers of members in some congregations, leading to the congregations being closed, and to the reduction in what had, at one time, been very generous funding of the Synod by the church in Germany.

There is a hidden message in the titles that have been adopted by the Synod since 1956, because the phrase "German-speaking" has always been included, and this reflects the fact that not everyone in its constituent congregations is from what we now call "Germany". The congregations certainly do have many members whose roots lie there, but there have also been many members from the German-speaking diaspora across Europe, for example from East Prussia and the Baltic States, from parts of Poland, from the Transylvania district of Romania, and the Banat in Serbia. None of these groups have ever formed their own congregations, but occasionally attempts have been made to bring some of them together, as was the case with the people of *Siebenbürgisch* ("Transylvanian Saxon") heritage, in whom Pastor Martin Krapf – pastor first in Newcastle-upon-Tyne and subsequently in Cambridge in the late 1950s and early 1960s – took a great interest. One congregation, that in Leicester, had a strong core of Transylvanian people, many of whom had reached Britain by very circuitous routes after the Second World War.

Although the German-speaking Lutheran congregations had been involved in the Lutheran Council of Great Britain from the time of its establishment, the Synod suspended its membership in 2002, although since then it has co-operated with some aspects of the Council's work.

An important ecumenical understanding linking Germany and England was created when the *Evangelische Kirche in Deutschland* in the German Federal Republic, the Federation of Evangelical Churches in the German Democratic Republic, and the Church of England concluded the "Meissen Agreement", which provided for limited inter-communion and mutual recognition of pastoral ministries and pledged the participating churches to work towards closer unity.

One of the things which had helped to facilitate this was the European-wide "Leuenberg Agreement" of 1973 which gave mutual recognition between most of the mainstream Protestant churches of Europe who now come together in the Community of Protestant

Churches in Europe. However, the main impetus for the process which led to "Meissen" were the celebrations which took place to celebrate the 500th anniversary of the birth of Martin Luther in 1983. Robert Runcie, the then Archbishop of Canterbury, took part in the celebrations in both parts of Germany, and took the opportunity of suggesting that it might be a good idea for the Church of England and the German Evangelical Churches to pursue the goal of developing closer relations. During the Second World War, there had been a strong interest in the German churches (see Part Three for the role played by Bishop George Bell), and this had increased in the years after the war. A good example of the sort of relationships that had developed was that between the cathedrals in Coventry and Dresden, but other, similar, twinnings has also grown up.

The discussions proposed by Dr Runcie began in 1985. From the start, they avoided re-inventing the wheel and made use of the results of wider ecumenical theological discussions, not only those involving Anglicans and Lutherans, but, in particular, the "Lima" document that had been produced by the Faith and Order Commission of the World Council of Churches, with the title *Baptism, Eucharist, and Ministry*. In all, three conferences took place, culminating with one in Meissen in 1988 that produced a unanimous statement, which was subsequently submitted for acceptance to all three participating bodies. This document was entitled *On the Way to Visible Unity: A Common Statement*, and had six sections, five of which built on previous discussions. The sixth section, "Mutual Acknowledgement and Next Steps", recognised that what was being proposed was a process which might lead to visible unity, rather than an acknowledgement that visible unity already existed. The document was approved by the participating bodies and was formally instituted by services in Westminster Abbey (29 January 1991) and the Kaiser Wilhelm Memorial Church in Berlin (2 February 1991).

Unlike the Porvoo Agreement, which established full communion from the outset, Meissen recognised that there were significant theological differences which still had to be discussed – most notably, the question of episcopacy: it is appropriate, therefore, to describe it as an on-going process. A continuation body, known as the Meissen Commission, was set up in order to oversee how the agreement was being implemented and to stimulate further discussion. Although the German-speaking

Evangelical Synod in Great Britain was not a formal signatory to the Agreement, its observers have been involved from the outset.

Much remains to be done to draw the participating churches together, but a lot of good work has been done, not least through the arrangements that have been made whereby ministers from both England and Germany have worked in parishes in both countries.

FURTHER READING

We have already mentioned Vilmos Vajta's **Church in Fellowship: Pulpit and Altar Fellowship Among Lutherans**, and its section on developments between the Nordic and Baltic Churches and the Church of England. The book's section on Germany – pages 73-148 – (*Church and Altar Fellowship in the Evangelical Churches of Germany*) is very helpful in disentangling the complexities of German evangelical church history.

The Church of England's Council for Christian Unity has published several papers which relate to the Meissen Agreement, the most interesting of which are Occasional Paper No.2, **The Meissen Agreement: Texts (London, CCU, 1992. No ISBN)**, and Occasional Paper No.1, **The German Evangelical Churches: An Introduction Following the Meissen Agreement (London, CCU, 1992. No ISBN)** by Dr Colin Podmore. Like the section in Dr Vajta's book, Dr Podmore's contribution is particularly interesting because he helps readers to understand German Protestant history and theology. The text of the Leuenberg Agreement was published by the United Reformed Church in 1973.

Chapter 27 | Lutherans from Central Europe

The Hungarian Lutheran Church

Hungary today is a small central European nation of around 9 million people with a long and fascinating history. It owes its present size largely to the 1920 Trianon Treaty which sliced away large parts of the former kingdom of Hungary, which up to that time had, in theory, been an equal partner in the Austro-Hungarian Empire. The territories that were lost as a result of the treaty were incorporated into the surrounding countries, some of which, such as Czechoslovakia or Yugoslavia, were new creations, but the eastern area of Hungary, known in English as Transylvania, was incorporated into Romania.

Historically, Hungary has largely been a Roman Catholic country, but it also had a sizeable Reformed Church, and a small, but culturally important, Lutheran Church. Although the Lutheran Church never exceeded half-a-million members in post-First World War Hungary, it had, throughout its history, provided the nation with political and cultural leaders, such as Lajos Kossuth. After the Second World War, the country slowly slid into subjugation by the Soviet Union, and it found itself struggling to survive under a brutal totalitarian regime which persecuted all the churches in Hungary. One of the leaders who was particularly targeted was Bishop Lajos Ordass, a vice-president of the LWF, who was put in prison for several years on fabricated charges.

Although there may have been individual Lutherans from Hungary in Great Britain before the Second World War, it was only after 1945 that they arrived in any significant numbers, and even then, the number was very small compared to other Lutheran groups, and many of them actually moved on after a short time to other countries. Those who remained in Britain were scattered across the country, so it was very difficult to provide them with any spiritual support. Things became a little easier when a Hungarian pastor, Bela Karolyfalvi, arrived in the country in 1948, and although not able to do very much for the scattered diaspora, he was able to conduct services on a regular basis in London. The first service was held in the Swedish Church in Harcourt Street, but from then onwards the services were held each Sunday evening in Luther-Tyndale Memorial Church. Although Pastor Karolyfalvi did conduct occasional services elsewhere, his main contact with Hungarian Lutherans outside London was through a monthly newsletter called *Jojjetek Enhozzen* ("Come to Me").

Pastor Karolyfalvi remained in England for just over three years, but then emigrated to Canada in 1951. Services in Hungarian ceased at that point, and the members of the congregation either joined Luther-Tyndale Church in Kentish Town (ELCE), or the fledgling English-speaking congregation that was growing up in St Mary's German-speaking Church. This situation prevailed until the winter of 1956-57, when much larger numbers of Hungarian Lutherans found themselves in Britain.

The cause of this new wave of immigration was the abortive Hungarian revolution of October-November 1956, when hundreds of thousands of people rose up spontaneously against the regime, and it looked, for a time, as though Hungary would emerge from behind the Iron Curtain. The revolution was brutally put down by the Soviet army, and thousands of Hungarians fled westwards into Austria, and from there to other destinations across the world.

Among the Hungarians who came to Britain was Pastor Robert Pátkai, who arrived in London early in 1957, and who almost immediately began to minister to his fellow refugees. In this he was greatly helped by the tiny Hungarian Lutheran community that survived after Pastor Karolyfalvi's departure, and soon regular services were being held in London in the Lutheran Church House on three Sundays in the month, and in Bradford on the fourth Sunday, and the "Hungarian Lutheran Church in Great Britain" was formally constituted on 22 January 1961. Back in Hungary, Lutherans had always enjoyed a working relationship with the Reformed Church, and this continued in Britain, so that the Hungarian Reformed minister in London provided services for Hungarian Protestants in Manchester.

This situation continued for several years, but in 1964 another Hungarian Lutheran pastor, Jenő Weisz, who had studied in

Mansfield College, Oxford, and had been ordained in 1963, was sent to Leeds to establish an English-speaking congregation, and also took on the responsibility for the Hungarian services in Bradford. Pastor Weisz emigrated to the United States in 1967.

Pastor Pátkai continued to work assiduously in serving Hungarian Lutherans across the country, and also played a significant role in the United Lutheran Synod (now the LCiGB) before his eventual retirement. Eventually, a combination of factors, including further emigration, meant that the London congregation shrank to the point that it was no longer feasible to conduct regular services, and they were discontinued, although Pastor Pátkai continues a less formal ministry among those people who remain.

The Polish Lutheran Congregations

From the end of the Middle Ages, and until the early 18th century, Poland was one of the great nations of Europe, but by the end of the 18th century it had disappeared as a political unit, swallowed up by its neighbours – Austria, Prussia, and Russia. Millions of Poles remained in what had been Poland, struggling to keep their language and culture alive, but many went into exile in other parts of Europe and the new world. Finally, in the aftermath of the First World War, Poland was re-born, only to be torn apart again by the Second World War, at the end of which the whole country seemed to move westwards: pre-war eastern Poland remained occupied by the USSR, but, almost as recompense, large tracts of former eastern Germany were incorporated into the country. Although nominally independent again after 1945, Poland was absorbed into the Soviet orbit until the downfall of the USSR at the end of the 1980s. The country is now an active member of both the European Union and NATO.

Poland is famously a predominantly Roman Catholic country, and today over 95% of the population are nominally part of the church, but this has not always been the case. In the early stages of the Reformation, Poland was a haven for different religious groups – including Lutherans – but the situation changed with the onset of the counter-Reformation at the end of the 16th century, and the nation became increasingly intolerant of non-Catholic groups. However, there were Lutheran congregations in the country, and after the partitions of the late 18th century Lutherans in territories taken over by Prussia were increasingly absorbed into the *Unierte*

Kirche, whereas those under Austrian suzerainty remained confessionally Lutheran. After the country was finally reunited in 1918-19, it became crucial to bring together these different confessional groups into one church, a process which was achieved only very slowly. Persecution during and after the Second World War reduced the numbers of pastors and people, but the "Evangelical Church of the Augsburg Confession", as the Lutheran Church is known, remains the largest Protestant church in the country. The frequent border changes have also meant that there is a Polish-speaking Lutheran Church in the Czech Republic.

During the Second World War – and, indeed, right down to the restoration of a free and independent Poland in 1991 – there was a "Government in Exile" in London, which saw itself as the continuation of the pre-war administration, and was recognised as such by the British government. During the war there was a strong Polish presence in the United Kingdom, which started when Polish army and air force units arrived after the fall of France in the early summer of 1940, to be augmented in 1942 when the army units formed from former prisoners-of-war released from Siberia arrived. Although Lutherans were in a minority among these military personnel, by 1945 they were being served by four chaplains, among whom Dr Andrzej Wantuła served as Senior Chaplain. A third wave of Polish Lutherans arrived when the Polish Second Army Corps came to Britain from Italy in 1946, among whom was Chief Chaplain Władysław Fierla. After 1948, when Dr Wantuła returned to Poland, Pastor Fierla was elected as Senior Pastor, and with the establishment of the Polish Evangelical–Lutheran Church in Exile in 1953, he was given the title of Bishop. One of the provisions that went along with the establishment of the church was that it would cease to exist when democracy was re-established in Poland.

The subsequent history of the Polish Lutheran Church in Exile, which had drawn closer to the ELCE during the 1950s, is convoluted and reflects tensions within the community, and in 1991 it ceased to exist when democracy returned to Poland. By this time, some of the Polish parishes had joined the LCiGB, indeed, it was a Polish pastor, Walter Jagucki – jointly serving Polish and English-speaking parishes – who became the first bishop of the LCiGB. Today, most Polish Lutheran parishes in Britain are part of the LCiGB, and only the Midlands parish is outside it. In spite of these divisions, however, Polish Lutherans worked together in the Association of

Polish Protestants, which was founded in 1943 and continued to exist as a forum for discussion until 1996. In the following year the Association of Polish Lutheran Congregations in Great Britain was established, and among its main tasks today is seeking ways to minister to new Polish immigrants who are Lutheran. In order to do this, the Association receives some financial help from the Lutheran Church in Poland, a body which now also arranges for regular services in Dublin.

The 1951 *Manual of Lutheran Activity in Britain* calculated that there were 2,200 Polish Lutherans in Britain, of whom 805 were registered members in 42 congregations grouped in four organised parishes. Today, the number of congregations has diminished significantly, although in one or two of them numbers have been augmented by new Polish immigrants.

Although, as we have seen, there was no organised Polish Lutheran presence in Britain before the Second World War, there is an interesting by-way of Lutheran history concerning an exiled Polish Lutheran of the 19th century, Count Krasinski. He had played a leading role in an abortive Polish uprising against Russia in 1864 and, as a result came into exile in Britain, where he settled in Scotland. Krasinski was a scholar, and he had written a *History of the Reformation in Poland*, but we know very little of his time in Edinburgh, except that he is buried in one of the city's graveyards. In 1989 the Polish Lutheran community in Scotland held a service at his graveside to commemorate the 125th anniversary of the uprising that exiled him from Poland.

Slovak Lutherans in Britain

For centuries Slovakia was a part of the Habsburg Empire, and after the establishment of the Dual Monarchy in 1867, it was administratively part of the Kingdom of Hungary. The free movement of people across the empire means that there are now significant minority groups of Slovak speakers in both Hungary and the Vojvodina region of Serbia. The present day Slovak Lutheran Church was organised in 1922, and now accounts for around 7% of the country's population: it has 326 congregations, and a bishop whose office is in Bratislava.

There has never been an organised Slovak Lutheran congregation in Britain, although *The Manual* of 1951 envisaged that such a congregation might develop. While he was alive, Bishop

Fierla of the Polish Lutheran Church in Exile, who was a Slovak speaker, conducted occasional services in Luther-Tyndale Memorial Church (ELCE), and since Slovakia gained its independence after the "velvet revolution" in the early 1990s, a number of Slovak Lutherans have come to Britain. Because of similarities in language, where possible these short-term visitors have worshipped in Polish Lutheran congregations.

FURTHER READING

There is very little that is available in English about Lutherans in either Poland or Slovakia, although useful information can be found by trawling through the internet. Although it is now out-of-date, there is a brief booklet entitled **A Short History of Lutheranism in Hungary (Budapest, Press Department of the Lutheran Church in Hungary, 1997. ISBN: 963-7470-41-7)**, by the late Dr Tibor Fabiny (Sr.), sometime Professor of Church History.

Chapter 28 | Lutherans from Africa and Asia

One of the things that is very obvious from the 1951 *Manual* is how Eurocentric it was: all of the Lutheran groups mentioned in its pages were European, although, in passing, there were also references to North American Lutherans. To a lesser extent this was also true of the book produced by the Lutheran Council of Great Britain in 1974, but today no book would be complete without mentioning the many Lutherans who have come to Britain from many other parts of the world. In fact, there were such Lutherans around in 1951 – one of the reasons that St Mary's German-speaking congregation established its English language ministry was to serve the increasing numbers of overseas students who did not speak any of the "traditional" Lutheran languages – but no individual congregations developed until the last two decades of the 20th century.

Chinese-speaking Lutherans

It is estimated that mainland China contains one-fifth of the world's population and the People's Republic is one of the fastest growing economic powers. The Chinese have always been noted as traders and businessmen, and for centuries there have been Chinese communities across south-east Asia in places such as Taiwan, Malaysia, and Singapore. There are Lutheran Churches in each of these territories – as well as in Hong Kong – established originally through the work of missionaries from Germany, the Nordic countries, and the United States – at one time there were no less than 25 different missionary bodies doing work among Chinese-speaking people.

There has been emigration from Chinese-speaking countries for more than a century-and-a-half, and several of the major cities of

Britain, such as Birmingham, Liverpool, London, and Manchester, have their distinctive Chinatowns. Today, there are thousands of students from mainland China, Hong Kong, and other places studying at British universities, and a cursory glance at lists of Chinese-speaking Christian congregations reveals that they are a growing phenomenon.

So far as is known, the first Chinese Lutheran pastor to work in England was Rev'd James Ma, who conducted a ministry on Merseyside in the late 1950s and early 1960s, working, primarily, among Chinese seamen. He was as equally fluent in English as in Chinese, wrote a book about ministry among the Chinese seamen in Liverpool entitled "Look Back in Hope", and he actually preached at a service during a youth rally at the German-speaking church in Liverpool on 5 February 1961, but no amount of research has been able to discover much about his ministry, and at some stage after that he simply disappeared. Readers might be interested to read "Look Back in Hope" (published by Light and Salt Publishers, with no ISBN, though there are copies in Liverpool City Library) and note the links with the chaotic post-war years in East Asia when many Chinese Christians and missionaries in China fled to other parts of Asia and to Europe.

Two Chinese-speaking Lutheran congregations eventually emerged in London, although one of them, the Chinese Rhenish Church, was actually the offspring of missionary work by the Rhenish Mission in the 1970s to the 1980s, which was a mixed Reformed and Lutheran mission society. For several years the Rhenish Church in Orange Street behind the National Gallery in London was a member of the Lutheran Council of Great Britain, but for some unknown reason it terminated its membership in the early 1990s.

The London Chinese Lutheran Church was first gathered in St Mary's German Church in Sandwich Street on 17 June 1990, by some families from the Chinese Rhenish Church in Orange Street. Part of the Lutheran Church in Great Britain, it now holds weekly services in the early afternoon each Sunday in the American Church on Tottenham Court Road.

The services are held in both Cantonese and Mandarin, and, although it has usually been possible to have a permanent Chinese-speaking pastor, there have been occasional periods when services have had to be partially in English with the sermons interpreted consecutively in Cantonese and Mandarin.

Swahili-speaking Lutherans

In the present offices of the Council of Lutheran Churches there are two paintings by a Tanzanian artist named Sam Ntiro. Originally painted in the 1950s and hanging in the dining room at Hothorpe Hall until it was sold, these pictures demonstrate early links between Lutherans in Britain and East Africa. From 1955 to 1963 Hothorpe Hall operated a language school for overseas missionaries, many of whom were from Finland and Germany and who were destined to work in Tanzania, but who needed to be fluent in English. The initiative for this venture came from Marja-Lisa Swantz, the wife of Hothorpe's first director, Lloyd Swantz: Mrs Swantz had herself been a missionary in Tanganyika, so she was able to add instruction in Swahili to that of English. She and her husband subsequently returned to the mission field, but in her later years at the University of Helsinki, she wrote an authoritative work on the Swedish missionary bishop, Bengt Sundkler, who had also worked at one time in Tanganyika. Incidentally, at the back of Hothorpe Hall there was a summer house with a thatched roof that was always known as "the Tanganyika Hut", and which served as accommodation for volunteer workers during the summer months.

Tanzania is the successor to two separate countries – Tanganyika and Zanzibar – which, in post-colonial times, decided to unite together as one nation. Tanganyika had been a German colony until the end of the First World War, when its governance was taken over by Great Britain, but German missionaries from the Bethel and Leipzig Missionary Societies remained active throughout the period. They were joined by American missionaries from the Swedish-background Augustana Synod in the United States, and as a result of all this activity there were no less than seven different Lutheran bodies in the colony. In 1938, they came together in the "Federation of Lutheran Churches in Tanganyika", which, after independence, united in 1963 into the Evangelical Lutheran Church in Tanzania, and which today has over 6 million members. A high point in the history of Lutherans in Tanganyika occurred in 1977 when the LWF held its Sixth Assembly in Dar-es-Salam.

The first congregational work in Swahili in England started in the Lutheran Church House at 8 Collingham Gardens in South Kensington, as a result of work by an American pastor of Swedish background, Ronald Englund, who had been a missionary in East Africa. This work was an ecumenical venture involving Anglicans and well as Lutherans, and served Swahili-speaking people from across East Africa. The first service, which only a handful of people attended, was held in July 1974, but this ministry still continues today under the pastoral care of an indigenous Swahili-speaking pastor, and as part of the ministry of St Anne's Lutheran congregation of the LCiGB. This community, with its vibrant and ecumenical outreach, makes a distinctive contribution both to the life of St Anne's and the wider church. It has greatly benefited from the contributions of its lay members, and it was they who ensured that the community continued to worship after Pastor Englund left. There is also an independent Swahili-speaking Lutheran congregation in Reading.

Lutherans from the Horn of Africa

Two of the countries of the Horn of Africa, Ethiopia and Eritrea, have Lutheran Churches which have their origins in the work of north European missionaries – especially from Sweden – from the end of the 19th century onwards.

Today, with an estimated membership of over 7.5 million, the *Mekane Yesus* Church can claim to be one of the largest members of the LWF. One of its leaders in the latter part of the 20th century was Immanuel Abraham, who in the early 1960s was Ethiopian ambassador to Britain, and a member of what was then St John's Lutheran Church (his daughter Ruth later returned to England to study, and was a member of St Luke's Lutheran Church in Leeds). The small Ethiopian Lutheran community began holding services in St Anne and St Agnes' Church in the City of London, which was then the home of St Anne's Lutheran Church, and a theological student, Barnabas Daniel, was ordained by the LCiGB to minister to the Amharic-speaking Lutherans. These services were eventually transferred to the nearby St Vedast parish church. It is known that there was also a community of Oromo-speaking Lutherans in London, but no information is currently available about its activities.

The Lutheran Church in Eritrea is much smaller (around 20,000 members) than the church in Ethiopia, and has recently, along with other Christian churches, suffered considerable persecution at the hands of the government. Eritrean emigration to the United Kingdom began in the 1990s, and among those who came were considerable numbers of Lutherans. They began to hold lay-led services in 1999 in St Anne and St Agnes Church in the City of London, which was then the home of St Anne's congregation, and were eventually able to establish a congregation, which became part of the LCiGB. The LCiGB appointed Rev'd Roy Long to assist this congregation by holding a monthly bi-lingual service in addition to the services on other Sundays. This post was later taken over by the bishop, Jana Jeruma-Grīnberga.

Both the Amharic-speaking congregation and the Eritrean congregation felt ill-at-ease with what they perceived as "liberal" views – especially over homosexuality – in the LCiGB, and eventually they left the church and became independent congregations. The Eritrean congregation formally left the LCiGB in 2013. It is not known whether or not these congregations are continuing to hold services.

Chapter 29 | Lutheran Ministries in English

We have already made reference to Lutheran ministries in the English language in Part Three and we have seen that attitudes towards the use of the language in non-English-speaking congregations have varied considerably. Towards the end of the 18th century, for instance, we saw that the pastor of St George's German congregation was reprimanded for attempting to use English, whereas in the latter part of the 20th century several German-speaking congregations were happy to have regular English services. Congregations using other languages have also held occasional "Family Services" in English, so that families with an English-speaking spouse and children could worship together.

At present there are two Lutheran bodies which make use of English as their official language, the Evangelical Lutheran Church of England (ELCE) and the Lutheran Church in Great Britain (LCiGB). Since details of the histories of these two churches have already been interwoven into the general history of Lutherans in Great Britain in the preceding Part, only brief descriptions are provided here.

The Lutheran Church in Great Britain

The LCiGB, which now has twelve congregations and places of worship, was originally known as the United Lutheran Synod in Great Britain and was established in April 1961 when four previously independent congregations joined together to form a new church body. Although its first congregations were originally English-speaking, each of them had members who came from many different parts of the world, and multi-ethnicity has been a feature of the life of the church from the outset. Today, it has several congregations who do not use English as their first language of worship: respectively, these congregations or worshipping communities may use Chinese, Polish, Swahili, or, in the case of the congregation in Liverpool, several of the Nordic languages. The LCiGB has always had close ties with the Lutheran Council of Great Britain, and three of its congregations, Birmingham, Leeds, and Leicester, were started as a direct result of the Council's "Development Plan" of the mid-1960s.

Over the decades since it was founded, the LCiGB has had to face some difficult times, and its work has been seriously affected by financial problems, but it has flourished, even in the face of these adversities. The end of the LWF's involvement in theological education in Mansfield College in the 1990s meant that potential ordinands had to find other ways of studying, and several pastors in the LCiGB have been theologically educated through part-time ecumenical study programmes. Of necessity, the church has had to experiment with what it called "tent-making" ministries, ie part-time ministries conducted alongside full-time secular employment. Like the ELCE, several of its pastors have come from other countries, and their different backgrounds and experiences contribute towards a vibrant and challenging approach to theological and social issues.

A factor which should not be overlooked is the contribution made to the LCiGB by English-speaking Lutherans from other countries, in particular Australia, Canada, Guyana, and the United States. Many pastors, particularly from the United States, have served in its congregations, and alongside them countless lay people from these countries have supported the work of the church. For several years, the LCiGB has had a fruitful relationship with the Evangelical Lutheran Church of America's Arkansas-Oklahoma Synod which continues today, and also with the Lutheran Church in Schaumburg-Lippe in Germany. Lacking the resources to produce things like hymn books or catechetical materials, the LCiGB has always had to make use of publications originating in larger English-speaking churches, although this has meant that there has been little incentive to develop home-grown materials.

The LCiGB's presiding minister, known first as Chairman, then as Dean, has, since 2000, carried the title of Bishop, and since then three pastors have occupied that position. They reflect the diversity to be found within the church: Walter Jagucki, Jāna Jēruma-Grīnberga, and Martin Lind, are respectively of Polish, Latvian, and Swedish background, and each has brought his or her own distinctive gifts to the office. Previous presiding ministers have been of American background (William B. Schaeffer and Wayne C. Stumme) or Hungarian (Robert J. Pátkai). The church's main decision making body is the Annual Synod, and its office is in the International Lutheran Student Centre in Bloomsbury.

The LCiGB has, from its foundation, been an active participant in both inter-Lutheran and inter-denominational activities. It has always had close ties with the Lutheran Council and from time to time pastors from member churches of that body have served LCiGB congregations. Since the late 1980s it has been a member of the LWF. It has also participated actively in the work of such ecumenical organisations as Churches Together in England, and for several years Jāna Jēruma-Grīnberga was one of its presidents and helped to maintain contact with the European scene.

In 2014, the LCiGB became a signatory to the Porvoo Agreement, but although it is too soon to say how this will affect the future life of the church, it opens up all sorts of interesting possibilities.

The Evangelical Lutheran Church of England

The ELCE is a confessional Lutheran church which, as we have seen in Part Three, had its origins in the establishment of two German-speaking congregations in Kentish town (1896) and Tottenham (1903). From their very beginning these congregations had pastoral and financial support from the Lutheran Church–Missouri Synod (LCMS) and good fraternal relations have continued between the two churches right down to the present day. The ELCE also maintains close contact with other confessional Lutheran churches through the International Lutheran Council (ILC) and the European Lutheran Conference (ELC).

For several decades after the two north London congregations were founded, German continued to be the main language of worship and church life, but English was gradually introduced and, after a period of bi-lingualism, became the main language. Their first pastor after the Second World War was a former Canadian army chaplain, E. George Pearce, and he had a clear vision for the future of Lutheranism in Great Britain. With support from the LCMS it took steps to translate that vision into reality: the ELCE was officially organised in 1954 and it adopted a "Master Plan" whereby it would extend its ministry to other places. It proceeded to organise congregations across Great Britain, especially in the "new towns" that were springing up at the time, and it absorbed the independent mission in Cornwall and thereby took over responsibility for its work in the west of England. Particularly important was the decision to begin a programme of theological education in Cambridge. The central office of the ELCE is located next door to Westfield. The central body of the church is its annual Synod, and its presiding minister has the title of Chairman.

Inevitably, not all of the congregations that originated in the ELCE Master Plan flourished and some had to be closed because of dwindling numbers, but others have developed and new congregations have grown up. Today the ELCE has 14 organised congregations and six missions, and although its congregations worship in English, it also has services in some places in Portuguese. Like the LCiGB, the ELCE has benefited from the ministry of pastors from Lutheran churches in other countries.

The ELCE has played a distinctive role in both inter-Lutheran and inter-denominational relations. It was a founding member of the Lutheran Council and E. George Pearce was its first chairman. Part of his vision was to bring Lutherans of different national backgrounds into closer fellowship on the basis of the Lutheran Confessions, and in an effort to achieve this he actively promoted a series of regular "Lutheran Free Conferences". For various reasons – partly to do with confessional identity – the ELCE left the Lutheran Council in 1957. Recently the ELCE broke new ground by joining Churches Together in England.

Since the LCiGB was established in 1961 there have been conversations between the two bodies from time to time, but no theological agreement has been reached. Significant differences remain, including such matters as the ordination of women.

Appendices

Appendix 1 | Relations with the Roman Catholic Church

Martin Luther was seldom mealy-mouthed or diplomatic in what he wrote about those whom he considered to be his opponents, and we can easily see this in what he had to say about the Roman Catholic Church of his day. A sample of a few of the titles of his anti-Catholic writings will suffice to demonstrate this: they included *Against the Spiritual Estate of the Pope and the Bishops Falsely So-called* (1522), and *Against the Roman Papacy, and Institution of the Devil* (1545). One document along these lines, the *Treatise on the Power and Primacy of the Pope* (1537), actually made it into the *Book of Concord* (1580), so is one of the Lutheran confessions. Of course, Luther was writing in the context of his own time, and few modern Roman Catholic scholars would defend the worldliness and immorality of the early 16th century papacy – and, it has to be said, Roman Catholic scholars of the day gave as good as they got when it came to rough language.

Luther's reforming theology, though radical in the eyes of his Roman Catholic opponents, was actually very conservative, and his thinking about worship and the sacraments was criticised by many of the other reformers – especially those from Switzerland – who saw the Lutheran reformation as a sort of halfway house on the road to a purer church.

Sadly, as is so often the case, relations between Lutherans and Roman Catholics hardened, positions became set in stone, and the war of words eventually degenerated into physical warfare. Shortly after Luther's death in 1546, the Emperor Charles V took up arms against the Schmalkaldic League, defeated it at the battle of Mühlberg (24 April 1547), and imposed the so-called "Augsburg Interim", which sought to undo many of the institutional changes in

Lutheran territories. Seventy years later, what became known as the "Thirty Years War" broke out: this devastated large parts of what we now call Germany, and left behind a legacy of mistrust and suspicion between Lutherans and Roman Catholics. Even the use of the word *Catholic* in the creeds was avoided, and Lutherans frequently abandoned it in favour of the word *Christian*. For centuries, Lutherans and Roman Catholics were like two trains running parallel to each other on separate railway tracks – usually with the blinds down so that they did not have to see one another!

Although there were some tentative steps to break down the barriers, as for example when Archbishop Nathan Söderblom invited official Roman Catholic participation in the Stockholm Conference of 1925, a big change came with the Second Vatican Council, called by Pope John XXIII in the early 1960s. This eventually brought about immense changes within the Roman Catholic Church itself, but also had the important effect of improving relations with other churches and faith groups. Representatives of other church bodies, including Orthodox and Protestant churches – who were increasingly referred to as "separated brethren" – were invited to be observers at the Council, and contacts and friendships were formed which led to significant improvements in relations.

Where Lutherans were concerned, a Lutheran-Roman Catholic Working Group held meetings in 1965 and 1966, and out of its discussions came the proposal to establish an official body to engage in comprehensive dialogue about matters of debate between the two church bodies. Starting in 1967, the Joint Lutheran-Roman Catholic Study Commission, consisting of representatives of the LWF and the Pontifical Council for Promoting Christian Unity, has produced a number of study documents dealing with important issues between the two churches, the most recent of which have been *The Apostolicity of the Church* (2006), and *From Conflict to Communion: Common Commemoration of the Reformation in 2017* (2012).

Parallel to these international discussion there have been more local dialogues, especially in Germany, Sweden, and the United States, and these have contributed towards the discussions between the LWF and the Pontifical Council. Of particular importance was the *Joint Declaration on the Doctrine of Justification* (1999), which dealt positively with the question that had been at the heart of the Reformation itself. In Britain, discussions have, of necessity, been on a smaller scale than elsewhere, and have often come about as a result of personal contacts and friendships. In 2002 a mixed group of Lutherans and Roman Catholics participated in an ecumenical pilgrimage to Vadstena, in Sweden, sponsored by the Lutheran Council and the Catholic Bishops' Conference of England and Wales. In 2008 the same two bodies sponsored a seminar on *The Apostolicity of the Church,* which was held at the International Lutheran Student Centre in London, where participants heard papers from Lutheran, Roman Catholic, and Methodist speakers.

FURTHER READING

The document on justification, issued jointly by the LWF and the Catholic Church, is available from the Catholic Truth Society: **Joint Declaration on the Doctrine of Justification (London, the Incorporated Catholic Truth Society, 2001. ISBN: 1-86082-120-0)**. Also available is the study document of the Lutheran-Roman Catholic Commission on Unity: **The Apostolicity of the Church (Minneapolis, Lutheran University Press, 2006. ISBN: 978-1-932688-22-1)**. The document issued in connection with the 2017 commemoration of the Reformation, **From Conflict to Communion**, can be downloaded at http://www.vatican.va/roman_curia/pontifical_councils/chrstuni/lutheran-fed-docs/rc_pc_chrstuni_doc_2013_dal-conflitto-alla-comunione_en.html.

Several books about Luther by Roman Catholic writers are now available. A straightforward and easily readable book is Peter Stanford's **Martin Luther: Catholic Dissident (London, Hodder and Stoughton, 2017. ISBN: 978-1-473-62166-4)**. Philip D. W. Krey and Peter D. S. Krey have drawn together a number of (mostly) early writings by Luther, in **The Catholic Luther: His Early Writings (New York, The Paulist Press, 2016. ISBN: 978-0-8091-4988-9)**.

There are two more general books that readers might find interesting. The first is by Eamon Duffy, Emeritus Professor of Christian History in the University of Cambridge, **Reformation Divided: Catholics, Protestants, and the Conversion of England (London, Bloomsbury, 2017. ISBN: 978-1-4729-3436-9)**. The second is by the former politician and Cabinet Minister, Roy Hattersley, and is simply entitled **The Catholics (London, Chatto and Windus, 2017. ISBN: 978-1-7847-4158-7)**. Mr Hattersley's book has a particularly good account of the Reformation period in Britain.

Appendix 2 | The Anglican-Lutheran Society

Ecumenical work is not always conducted at the level of theological committees or commissions of highly academic intellectuals. Indeed, though they may discuss doctrinal matters at great length and forge ecumenical friendships, it is equally important that ordinary parishioners should have the opportunity to get to know about their partner churches. Increasingly, this is happening: there are inter-church partnerships and twinned parishes and dioceses, so, for instance, a member of an Anglican parish may find that the minister preaching at the service is from Germany or one of the Nordic countries. Groups from one country may visit their ecumenical partners and get to know something of the similarities and differences that exist.

The Anglican-Lutheran Society, which was founded in the early 1980s after informal conversations between an Anglican and a Lutheran who discovered how little they knew of each other's churches, is "a 'grassrooots' organisation that aims to help members of congregations to make links with another church tradition and to make good use of the opportunities opened up by recent ecumenical developments." Its quarterly magazine, *The Window*, regularly contains reports of Anglican-Lutheran activities, including reports from ministers who have had experience of working in the other tradition, along with book reviews and informative articles from around the globe.

One of the Society's major achievements is its international conferences, which take place every second year, and which in recent years have taken place in Sweden (2016), Hungary (2014), and Salisbury (2011). These conferences bring together the Society's international members and help to strengthen inter-church fellowship. The Society's executive committee benefits greatly from the presence of an official Roman Catholic observer, and from having close links with the Lutheran Council of Great Britain.

Appendix 3 | Useful Addresses

Further information about Lutheran churches in Great Britain associated with the **Council of Lutheran Churches** can be obtained by contacting the Council at: 30 Thanet Street, London WC1H 9QH; tel: 020 7388 4044; www.lutheran.org.uk.

The **Lutheran Church in Great Britain** has its main administrative office at: 30 Thanet Street, London WC1H 9QH; tel: +44 (0)20 7383 0301; www.lutheranchurch.co.uk.

Similarly, information about the **Evangelical Lutheran Church of England** can be obtained from its central office at Westfield House in Cambridge: ELCE Central Office, 28 Huntingdon Road, Cambridge CB3 0HH; tel: 01223 355625; www.lutheran.co.uk.

The address for obtaining information about German-speaking church activity in Great Britain is: **The Council for German Church Work**, c/o The German YMCA, 35 Craven Terrace, London W2 3EL; tel: 0207 7706 8589; www.ev-synode.org.uk.

The Nordic churches can be contacted at their London churches, as follow.

The Danish Church, 4 St Katherine's Precinct, London NW1 4HH; tel: 0207-935-1723; www.danskekirke.org/.

The Finnish Church, 33 Albion Street, London SE16 7HZ tel: 0207-237-1261; https://lontoo.merimieskirkko.fi/.

The Norwegian Church, 1 St Olav's Square, Albion Street, London SE16 1JB; tel: 0207-740-3900; www.sjomannskirken.no/london/.

The Swedish Church, 6 Harcourt Street, London W1H 4AG; tel: 0207-616-0271; www.swedishchurch.com or www.svenskakyrkan.se/london.

The **Lutheran Church in Ireland** (An Eaglais Liútarach in Éirinn) is an independent Lutheran church body. Information about its activities in both Éire and Northern Ireland can be obtained from The Lutheran Church in Ireland, c/o St Finian's Lutheran Church, 24 Adelaide Road, Dublin 2, Republic of Ireland; tel: 01-6766548; www.lutheran-ireland.org.

Appendix 4 | Maps

The maps on the following pages indicate historical and present day Lutheran Communities in London and Great Britain.

Lutheran Churches in London, 17th-18th Centuries

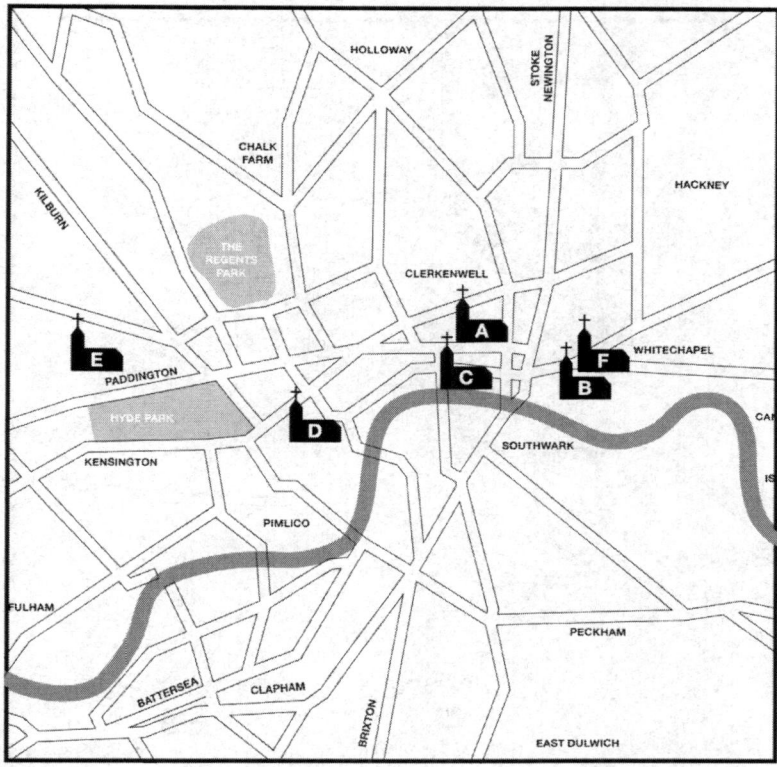

- A   Holy Trinity in Trinity Lane
- B   Danish Church in Wellclose Square
- C   St Mary le Savoy in the Strand
- D   St James's Palace
- E   Swedish Church in Prince's Square
- F   St George's in Alie Street

CLC Member Churches in London, Present Day

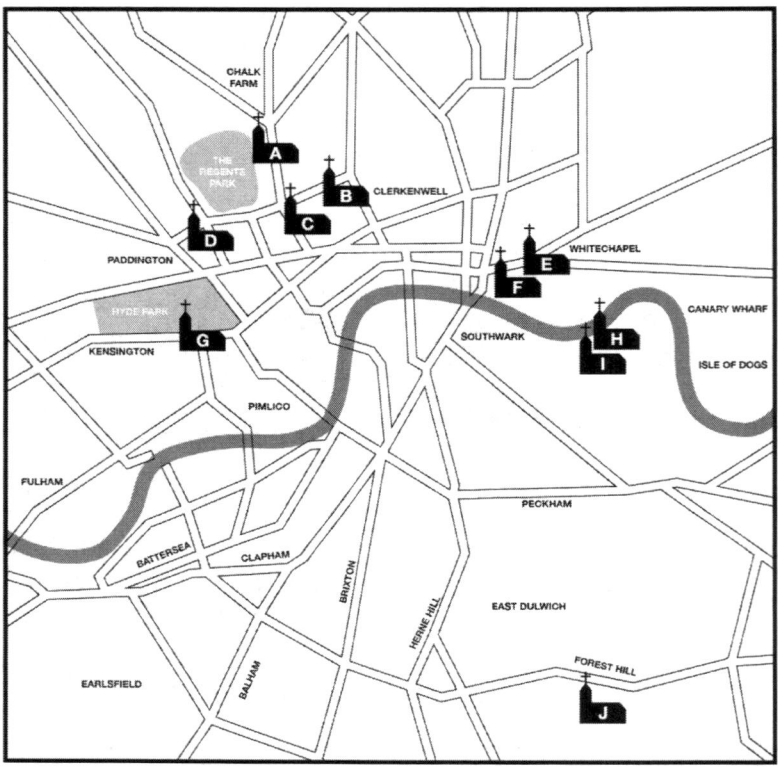

- A St Katharine's Danish Church, NW1 4HH, inc. Faroe Islands congregation
- B St Mary's with St George's German Lutheran Church, WC1H 9PL
- C London Chinese Lutheran Church, W1T 4TD
- D The Swedish Church, W1H 4AG, inc Latvian, Icelandic and Estonian congregations
- E St George's German Lutheran Church, E1 8EB (no active congregation)
- F St Anne's Lutheran Church, EC3R 8EE
- G German Protestant Christ Church SW7 1HJ, inc Polish congregation
- H The Finnish Church in London, SE16 7JG
- I St Olav's Norwegian Church, SE16 7JB
- J Dietrich Bonhoeffer Church, SE23 2NR

Lutheran Communities in the British Isles Today

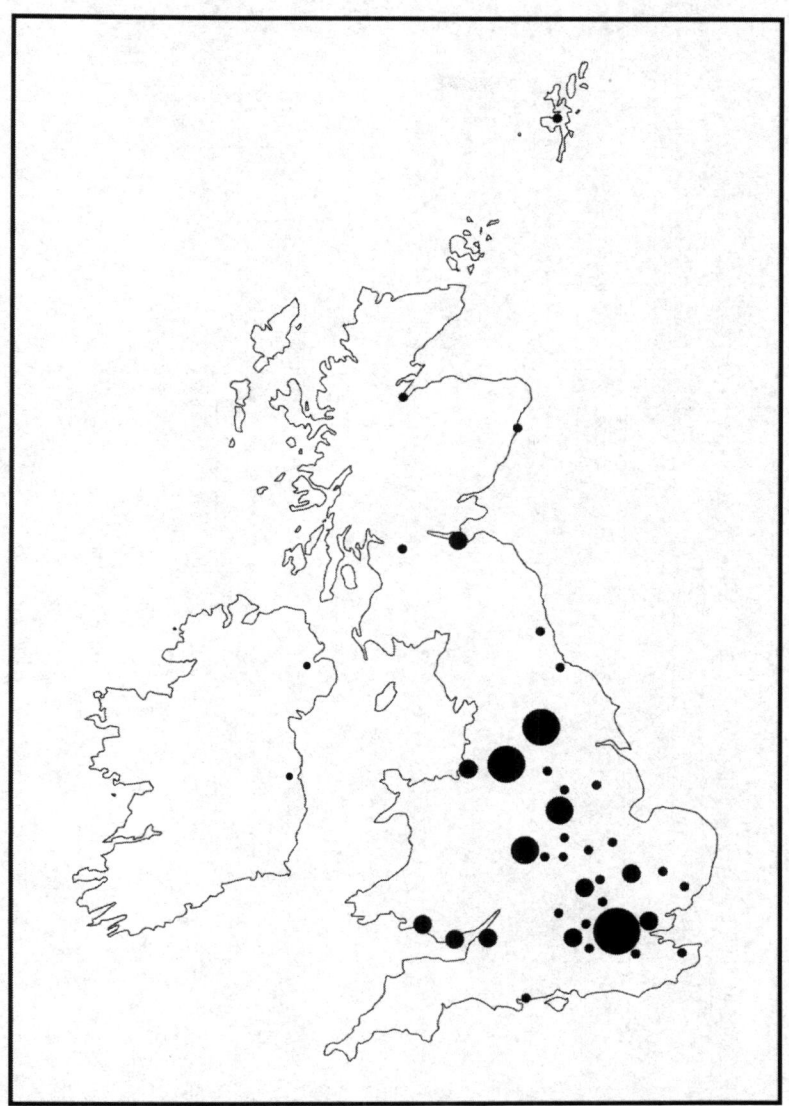

Acknowledgements

As mentioned in the Introduction, this book was commissioned by the Council of Lutheran Churches as a small contribution from Lutherans in Britain to the commemoration of the 500th anniversary of the Reformation. Originally planned as three separate booklets, a rather late decision was made to combine the content of these into one book. If there are any resulting repetitions it is hoped that readers will forgive them; if there are any contradictions, then the author hopes that someone will (kindly) point them out. The author can be contacted at roy.long485@btinternet.com.

Particular thanks go to Rev'd Susanne Freddin Skovhus, who has co-ordinated many of the 2017 Reformation commemorative events on behalf of the Council of Lutheran Churches, and to Mr James Laing, its General Secretary. Thanks are also due to Bishop Walter Jagucki, and to Pastors Georg Amann, Tom Bruch, Lagle Heinla and Eliza Zikmane, as well as to Mrs Sally Barnes, all of whom read and commented on different parts of the book during its progress to publication. Thanks to everyone else who answered the many questions I have had. Thanks also go to Robin and Sarah Farrow for their work in preparing the typescript and gathering together the illustrations.

Finally, the author would also like to thank his friend Tom Moriarty – at whose baptism he preached nearly three decades ago – and whose skills as a proof reader develop with everything that he writes!

About the Author

Roy Long is a retired pastor in the Lutheran Church in Great Britain. He was born in Nottingham in 1942. He trained as a teacher at Nottingham College of Education (now part of Nottingham Trent University) and subsequently taught in primary and secondary schools. He studied theology at Mansfield College, Oxford, and was ordained on Reformation Day (31 October) 1970. He served as pastor of St Paul's Lutheran Church in Corby, where he was also head of Religious Education at Corby Grammar School (1971-1976) and then head of Religious Studies at Lodge Park Comprehensive School (1976-1984). He later served as assisting pastor in Trinity Lutheran Congregation, Leicester/Nottingham, and in the Eritrean Lutheran Congregation in London. From 1984 to 2002 he worked full time as one of Her Majesty's Inspectors of Schools, specialising in the inspection of independent faith schools. After retirement in 2002, he continued to inspect schools for the Office for Standards in Education. Between 2005 and 2008 he was Co-ordinating Inspector of the (then) thirty-two schools affiliated to the Focus Learning Trust, the umbrella organisation for [Exclusive] Brethren education. He holds a Master of Philosophy degree from the University of Nottingham for research into the ecclesiology of Dietrich Bonhoeffer, and a Doctor of Philosophy degree from the same university for a thesis on the historical and theological background of faith schools in England. He has close personal ties with both Iceland and the Faroe Islands, and in 2006 the Church of Iceland published his translation into English of the Icelandic Baptism, Communion, and Wedding Services. His other publications include *The Lutheran Church* in the series *Christian Denominations* (Religious and Moral Education Press, 1984) and the article *Educational Work of Martin Luther* in *A Dictionary of Religious Education* (SCM Press, 1984). He has written extensively on the history of Lutherans in Britain and Ireland and on the church in the Faroe Islands, and has privately published a number of papers in both areas. At the time of writing *Luther and his Legacy* he was beginning research into Luther's attitude towards Jews and Muslims. From 2008 Dr Long was Secretary of the Anglican-Lutheran Society, and is now a co-opted member of its Executive Committee. His hobbies are philately, swimming, and fell-walking. He lives in Northamptonshire.